The Betrayal

The Betrayal

How Mitch McConnell and the Senate Republicans Abandoned America

Ira Shapiro

ROWMAN & LITTLEFIELD
Lanham • Boulder • New York • London

Published by Rowman & Littlefield
An imprint of The Rowman & Littlefield Publishing Group, Inc.
4501 Forbes Boulevard, Suite 200, Lanham, Maryland 20706
www.rowman.com

86-90 Paul Street, London EC2A 4NE, United Kingdom

Distributed by NATIONAL BOOK NETWORK

British Library Cataloguing in Publication Information Available

Library of Congress Cataloging-in-Publication Data

Names: Shapiro, Ira S., 1947– author.
Title: The betrayal : how Mitch McConnell and the Senate Republicans abandoned
   America / Ira Shapiro.
Other titles: How Mitch McConnell and the Senate Republicans abandoned America
Description: Lanham : Rowman & Littlefield, [2022] | Includes bibliographical references
   and index. | Summary: "Shapiro documents the challenges facing the Senate during the
   Trump administration, arguing that the body's failure to provide leadership represents
   the most catastrophic failure of government in American history. He also evaluates the
   Senate during President Biden's first year in office and looks forward to the 2022 Senate
   elections and beyond"— Provided by publisher.
Identifiers: LCCN 2021048556 (print) | LCCN 2021048557 (ebook) | ISBN
   9781538163979 (cloth) | ISBN 9781538163986 (epub)
Subjects: LCSH: McConnell, Mitch. | United States. Congress. Senate. | Republican
   Party (U.S. : 1854–) | Government accountability—United States. | United
   States—Politics and government—2017–2021. | United States—Politics and
   government—2021–
Classification: LCC E912 .S525 2022 (print) | LCC E912 (ebook) | DDC
   973.933—dc23/eng/20211206
LC record available at https://lccn.loc.gov/2021048556
LC ebook record available at https://lccn.loc.gov/2021048557

∞™ The paper used in this publication meets the minimum requirements of
American National Standard for Information Sciences—Permanence of Paper
for Printed Library Materials, ANSI/NISO Z39.48-1992.

To Nancy

With love and gratitude

Now and forever

Under our Constitution, there are simply not that many people who are in a position to do something about an executive branch in chaos. Too often we observe the unfolding drama along with the rest of the country, passively, all but saying: *"Somebody should do something"* without seeming to realize that that someone is us.

—Senator Jeff Flake, "My Party Is in Denial about Donald Trump," *Politico*, July 31, 2017

I don't think they [the founders] suspected we could have a rogue president and a rogue leader in the Senate at the same time.

—House Speaker Nancy Pelosi, December 19, 2019

He who rides the tiger cannot choose where he dismounts.

—Undersecretary of State George Ball, dissenting from the escalation of America's engagement in Vietnam, 1964

Contents

Preface

$\mathcal{T}$his is the story of the most catastrophic failure of government in American history.

This failure undermined the rule of law and threatened our constitutional rights. It deepened our divisions, pitting red states against blue states, whites against blacks. It endangered our national security, weakening our alliances and strengthening our adversaries. It produced unprecedented economic hardship, throwing millions of hard-working Americans into poverty and despair. It caused many thousands of Americans to die needlessly before their time. It led directly to the insurrection at the Capitol.

It was the failure of the United States Senate, from January 2017 to February 2021.

Most American history is written about the presidents—Washington, Jefferson, Lincoln, the Roosevelts, Kennedy, Johnson, Nixon, Reagan—or great events like the American Revolution, the Civil War, the Great Depression, World War II, and Vietnam. Donald Trump's aberrational presidency has already been the subject of more than twelve hundred books; at least twelve hundred more will emerge in the years to come. People here, and around the world, will ask how America, the greatest power in the world, elevated to the presidency a celebrity reality TV star with no experience in government, whose tumultuous business record, deeply flawed personality, abuse of women, and hatred of minorities were all plainly visible.

I am quite certain that Trump will be judged harshly. His mishandling of the COVID-19 pandemic, his refusal to acknowledge the 2020 election results, and his incitement of the Capitol insurrection on January 6, 2021, are likely to make him the most reviled person in our country's history—even more so than other failed or discredited presidents, criminals, assassins, or traitors. There was never any basis for believing that he would govern competently or that he cared about doing so. Still, Trump accomplished what appears to be his life's goal: he became the most famous person in the world.

But in the American constitutional system, no one person—not even the president—is supposed to be able to undermine our institutions and jeopardize our democracy. The framers of the Constitution wanted a strong central government because the weakness of the Articles of Confederation showed the limits of what the states could accomplish on their own. But having fought the American Revolution to free the colonies from Great Britain and its monarch, our founders feared the possibility of an overreaching executive who would seek to become a king or an autocrat. They also feared that a president might be corrupt, pursuing personal gain instead of the national interest, and that he could be susceptible to powerful foreign influences.

Consequently, the founders designed a system of checks and balances, the most distinctive feature of which was the Senate. They made it the strongest upper house in the world, with the power to "advise and consent" on executive and judicial nominations, to ratify treaties, and to hold impeachment trials. Robert C. Byrd, the longest-serving senator and its most dedicated historian, who understood the Senate's potential and hated when it failed to reach that mark, wrote that "the American Senate was the premier spark of brilliance that emerged from the collective intellect of the Constitution's framers."[1]

James Madison, characteristically, cut to the heart of things in a letter to Thomas Jefferson in 1787. He called the Senate "the great anchor of the government. . . . Such an institution may be sometimes necessary as a defense to the people against their own temporary errors and delusions."

The Senate would be assigned many functions, but it had one fundamental responsibility: to be a bulwark against any leader who would abuse the great powers of the presidency in ways that threatened our democracy. Some 230 years later, when just such a president finally reached the White House, the Senate should have been democracy's strongest line of defense. Instead, a nightmare scenario followed: the Senate, weakened from a long period of accelerating decline, proved utterly incapable of checking Trump's authoritarian desires. Sometimes the Senate aided and abetted Trump; often it simply stood by and allowed him to rampage unchecked. America had no defense against the novel threat presented by the unholy alliance between Trump and the Senate majority leader, Mitch McConnell. Speaker of the House Nancy Pelosi, in a moment of anger, correctly observed that the founders had not contemplated the combination of "a rogue president and a rogue majority leader."

The magnitude of the Senate's failure should be clearly understood. The Senate did not fail because of its arcane rules or because of the abuse of the filibuster. It did not fail because its members lacked the ability to do their jobs. It did not fail because the senators missed the danger signs. The overwhelming majority of the Senate knew that Trump was incompetent, corrupt, and dangerous; indeed, many saw him as a witting or unwitting agent of Vladimir Putin.

No, the Senate failed because its Republican members, led by McConnell, abandoned the late senator John McCain's guiding principle: "Country first." When it mattered most, the Republican senators put their personal political interests first, the Republican Party's interests second, and the country's interests nowhere. As America faced unprecedented, cascading, intersecting crises, the Republican senators chose to stand with Trump, either actively supporting him or silently acquiescing. Some undoubtedly convinced themselves that Trump would wither away or that they would find an exit ramp. But as George Ball, the State Department official who famously dissented from the escalation of the Vietnam War, observed, "He who rides the tiger cannot choose where he dismounts."[2]

The litany of failures on the part of Mitch McConnell's Senate is striking:

- In July 2018, in Helsinki, when Trump accepted Vladimir Putin's denial that Russia had interfered in the 2016 presidential election, dismissing the consensus of the US intelligence community, the Senate Republicans collectively shrugged.
- In April 2019, when Attorney General William Barr blatantly mischaracterized the report of Special Counsel Robert Mueller as having exonerated Trump from the charge of obstructing justice, key senators, led by McConnell, quickly claimed "case closed," rather than questioning what Barr had done.
- In January 2020, the Senate's first impeachment trial of Trump—a solemn responsibility, only the third impeachment trial of a president in history—proved to be an utter farce. The Senate Republicans refused to subpoena relevant documents and key witnesses. Led by the respected senator Lamar Alexander, they justified their Potemkin Village trial by saying it was an election year, so the voters should pass judgment on Trump's presidency. They exonerated Trump without even censuring him.
- But when Justice Ruth Bader Ginsburg died in September 2020, the Senate Republicans quickly forgot about the voters, moving with unseemly speed to ram through the confirmation of Amy Coney Barrett eight days before election day, even after millions of votes in the presidential election had already been cast.
- In November 2020, after every media organization had confirmed that Joe Biden had secured more than the 270 electoral votes needed to win the presidency, the Senate Republicans refused to acknowledge Biden's victory until all the votes were counted (ignoring the fact that enough votes had been counted to guarantee the outcome) and all legal appeals, no matter how frivolous, were ruled on.

- When Trump and his lawyers had lost sixty-one cases—every case they brought—the Republican senators decided that Biden could not be president-elect until the Electoral College met on December 14.
- When the electors met, did their duty, and confirmed Biden's 306–232 electoral vote victory, most of the Senate Republicans finally acknowledged that Biden was the president-elect, but some continued to fight on. Even on January 6, when the Congress met for the ceremonial purpose of accepting the Electoral College vote, Senator Josh Hawley and eleven other Republican senators forced both houses of Congress to debate the issue of whether Biden had won.

In all these ways, they created the occasion for Trump to invite his supporters to attack the Capitol.

With several notable exceptions, these Senate failures implicate virtually all the Republican senators during the Trump presidency. But in the words of the Sicilian proverb, "A fish rots from the head." The story of the Senate's rot is first and foremost the story of Mitch McConnell. He was an unyielding obstructionist during the Obama presidency, culminating in his refusal to hold a vote on Obama's Supreme Court nominee Merrick Garland following the death of Justice Antonin Scalia in February 2016. In contrast, McConnell became a relentless battering ram with Trump in the White House. He rode roughshod over one Senate custom, norm, and tradition after another. After Trump shocked the world by winning the presidency, America urgently needed a strong Senate, with a leader in the mold of Democrat Mike Mansfield or Republican Howard Baker, politicians who are rightly remembered as great statesmen and patriots. Instead, America got McConnell, a superb political strategist and tactician who was extraordinarily effective in achieving his partisan objectives, at great cost to the Senate and the country that depended on it.

Of course, even McConnell, the most powerful Senate leader in history, could not have done what he did without his troops. Throughout the Trump presidency, McConnell had only a very narrow majority with which to work. At any moment, three or four Republicans could have stopped him in his tracks. This happened exactly once, in July 2017, when John McCain, dying of brain cancer, memorably joined Susan Collins and Lisa Murkowski in defeating McConnell's brazen attempt to repeal the Affordable Care Act without hearings, committee action, or floor debate. But McConnell was never thwarted again.

Just as McConnell enabled Trump, the other Senate Republicans enabled McConnell. With the exception of Mitt Romney, who cast the only Republican vote to remove Trump from office in the first impeachment trial, all the Republican senators were complicit. The shameless Lindsey Graham, who had been John McCain's best friend and Donald Trump's most scathing critic, spun 180 degrees to become Trump's favorite golf partner and McConnell's wingman. Less obvious, and simply shameful, Lamar Alexander and Rob Portman, two superb public servants, became virtually invisible at every moment when their voices and their stature would have been useful to call attention to Trump's abuses of the presidential office.

The reality of this breakdown was widely acknowledged. On February 25, 2020, in the tiny window between the end of Trump's first impeachment trial and the onset of the pandemic, seventy retired senators, including seventeen Republicans and four independents, joined in a letter published in the *Washington Post* that stated, "The Senate is failing to perform its Constitutional duties." One sentence in the letter leaped out: "We have been told by sitting senators that the diminished state of the Senate has left them doubting whether there is any point in continuing to serve." Others, like New Mexico senator Tom Udall, concurred that "the Senate is broken" but attributed the brokenness to hyperpartisanship, the shrill cable news cycle, the "permanent campaign" in which there is never any time to govern, and the harsh politics of personal destruction, usually credited to the rise of Newt Gingrich in the 1980s and 1990s and intensified by the advent of Twitter and Facebook as major outlets for political discourse. All these factors are real, but they do not add up to the right explanation.

The Senate failed because Mitch McConnell and his Republican caucus repeatedly and deliberately took actions they knew to be wrong and failed to take actions they knew to be right. They averted their eyes as Trump lied about COVID-19, hawked fake cures for the virus, and mocked masks and social distancing—a deluge of misinformation that caused thousands of needless deaths. They opted for silence when Trump invited his supporters to indoor rallies in the midst of the pandemic. They refused to act when Trump attempted to bribe foreign governments with military aid in exchange for campaign assistance. They stood by silently as Trump cast aspersions on the military, the FBI, the State Department, and anyone else who for even the briefest moment pushed back against his authority and omniscience. They allowed Trump's "big lie" that the election was stolen to poison the thinking of 70 percent of his voters—roughly fifty million Americans. The Senate's Republican members did not just fail; they betrayed their oaths of office, sacrificing American lives and American democracy.

On January 20, 2021, Joseph R. Biden Jr. became president of the United States. Could Biden, a man of unmatched government experience and unquestioned decency, bring our country back together? Would the Senate work with a president who was one of the most experienced former senators in the history of the chamber? McConnell, who had known Biden for more than thirty-five years, waited five weeks after the election to offer his congratulations. Lindsey Graham, who has an over-the-top opinion about every subject, said in 2019, "If you can't admire Joe Biden as a person, you've got a problem and need to do some self-education, because God never created a better human being than Joe Biden." His immediate response to Biden's election was to resume the pursuit of the president-elect's son, Hunter Biden, for alleged misdeeds in business dealings in Ukraine and China.

I have spent much of my career working in and writing about the Senate. It often seems to me that I have spent too much time thinking about the Senate; it took me months to decide whether to write this book. Ultimately, two things convinced me to do it. The Senate—and the one hundred men and women who serve in it—has the potential to do great good or great harm to our country; it is crucial to understand how things went terribly wrong in recent years and how the institution might move on to a better course. And in an era of alternative facts, it is vital to get the history right. Future students of history and politics need to understand how Mitch McConnell and his Senate betrayed America.

Many political observers, ranging from casual to experienced, believe that the partisan division in the Senate and the behavior of the senators are inevitable, given the deep divisions in our country. I categorically reject that formulation. These people who have the extraordinary privilege of being US senators have the responsibility to work to overcome those divisions, not simply to reflect or exacerbate them. Senators have agency; they can shape the times, not simply be buffeted by them. To take the most obvious example, McConnell's unrelenting partisanship has shaped our era because he passed up every opportunity to work constructively in good faith, to turn down the heat, and to bring people together. Years before Donald Trump became president, we were living in Mitch McConnell's America, and, to a greater extent than might have been anticipated, we still are.

America has paid a terrible price for the experiment with Trump, a narcissistic outsider and disrupter, with authoritarian impulses and contempt for our democratic institutions. But it is McConnell, the political stalwart and faux institutionalist, who poisoned and undermined our political system from within, transforming the Senate into a hyperpartisan battle zone, draining it of the trust and pride that made it work in its great days, while using it for his own purposes. The scope of the damage that McConnell has done to our government, our politics, and our country is still not understood. This book is intended to cast light on that damage and to chart a better path forward for the Senate and for America.

The End of the Last Great Senate

$\mathscr{I}$n 2015, former Senate leaders Tom Daschle and Trent Lott published a book called *Crisis Point: Why We Must—and How We Can—Overcome Our Broken Politics in Washington and across America.*[1] Daschle and Lott represented the epitome of Washington's political establishment. After a combined fifty-nine years in Congress, they continued to work in the nation's capital as strategic advisers, lobbyists, board members, and leading participants in the Bipartisan Policy Center.

Lott, the Senate majority leader from 1996 to 2001, came from a sharecropper family in Mississippi, and one of his earliest political activities was lobbying in favor of maintaining the racial segregation of his fraternity at Ole Miss; he was one of the first of the generation of Southern Republicans who capitalized on popular opposition to civil rights to turn the South red. Daschle, a Democrat who succeeded Lott as Senate majority leader, serving from 2001 to 2004, was a former Air Force intelligence officer who won his seat in Congress in a prairie-populist state that had previously elected George McGovern, the 1972 Democratic presidential nominee.

It is impossible today to imagine Senate leaders from opposite sides of the aisle—say, Mitch McConnell and Charles Schumer—writing a book together. But Daschle and Lott were from a different generation. They had worked together amicably and were aghast at the vicious partisan divide that had come to characterize the Senate in the years since they had left office. They had many reasons, as active lobbyists, not to be critical of Capitol Hill, and they had a natural reluctance to criticize their successors as Senate leaders. Consequently, their unflinching indictment carried an extra force:

> America's strength has always come from its unique diversity—its willingness to not just permit but to encourage competing viewpoints in order to strengthen the whole. The adversarial system, embedded by the Founding Fathers into our system of government, was meant to spur debate, challenge complacency, and drive progress. It has sustained our Republic for over 225 years, but we have to face a sad truth: *it has stopped working.*[2]

Daschle and Lott's anguished assessment was widely shared by journalists, historians, the senators themselves, and the American public. Despite their different vantage points, they all saw the federal government failing the American people. Congress lurched from crisis to crisis, unable to pass a budget and appropriations laws to run the country, forced instead to resort to last-minute, omnibus continuing resolutions. In each Congress, the number of laws passed declined; the number of filibusters increased. Increasingly ineffectual Congresses ceded more and more power to the president and ultimately to the Supreme Court. Talented legislative dealmakers from both parties quit in frustration. Public approval of Congress, declining since the 1960s, spiraled downward, as more and more Americans concluded that Washington worked only to protect and further the interests of the wealthiest.

Daschle and Lott recognized that the Senate had become ground zero for America's political dysfunction, the political institution that had failed America the longest and the worst. The Senate's failure was particularly crippling because it is supposed to be the balance wheel and moderating force in the American constitutional system, the place where the two parties come together to find common ground through vigorous debate and principled compromise to advance the national interest. The House of Representatives was designed to be the people's chamber, subject to short, two-year terms that are apt to reflect changing passions and priorities. It had 65 members in 1790, a number that continued to grow with the population until 1929, when the House established its current size of 435 members. The Senate, with its six-year terms and limit of two senators per state, was the elite chamber, what Walter Mondale once described as "the nation's mediator" and Howard Baker called the nation's "board of directors." But to perform that role, the Senate required a bipartisan comity that disappeared long ago. Without that bipartisan comity, the Senate not only reflects the polarization in the country but also exacerbates that polarization by demonstrating it constantly at the highest and most visible level of government.

The Senate's long decline has been acutely painful to a generation that grew up with a special attachment to it. The Senate first gained the attention of many Americans in 1939 with Frank Capra's film *Mr. Smith Goes to Washington*, starring Jimmy Stewart as an idealistic young senator who battles political corruption. The film, widely regarded as a classic, catapulted Stewart to stardom and captured eleven Academy Award nominations. It created in the minds of Americans an indelible image of what a filibuster should be, and more recent, real-life filibusters by Rand Paul or Ted Cruz would always draw unfavorable comparison to Stewart's valiant effort.

But the Senate truly seized the attention of the American public in 1950 when Estes Kefauver, a little-known Democratic senator from Tennessee, launched an extraordinary series of investigative hearings into organized crime in America.[3] The "Kefauver hearings," as they became universally known, took place in fourteen cities around the country. They illuminated the workings of the Mafia and forced J. Edgar Hoover, the FBI director, to admit that organized crime was a national problem. Television was still very new in America, and the Kefauver hearings became the first nationally shared television experience, viewed by more than thirty million Americans in their homes, bars, restaurants, and movie theaters. At one time, an astonishing 72 percent of Americans expressed familiarity with the committee's work.

During eight days of hearings in New York in March 1951, more than fifty witnesses described the highest-ranking crime syndicate in America, an organization allegedly led by Frank Costello, who had taken over from Lucky Luciano. "The week of March 12, 1951 will occupy a special place in history," *Life* reported. "People had suddenly gone indoors into living room[s], taverns, and clubrooms, auditoriums, and back-offices. There, in eerie half-light, looking at millions of small frosty screens, people sat as if charmed. Never had the attention of the nation been riveted so completely on a single matter." *Time* wrote, "From Manhattan as far west as the coaxial cable ran, the U.S. adjusted itself to Kefauver's schedule. Dishes stood in sinks, babies went unfed, business sagged, and department stores emptied while the hearings went on."

The Senate continued to be a source of fascination through the 1950s. In 1954, the country again became enthralled, by the "Army-McCarthy hearings," conducted by the Permanent Subcommittee on Investigations, into Senator Joseph McCarthy's demagogic charges that the US Army was infiltrated by communists. The hearings produced one of the most famous moments in American political history when Joseph Welch, the army's chief counsel, challenged the junior senator from Wisconsin: "At long last, have you left no sense of decency?" That dramatic exchange highlighted a hearing that sent McCarthy's popularity into a tailspin and opened the door to his censure by the Senate, ending the "Red Scare" that he had done so much to precipitate.

In 1956, John F. Kennedy, a little-known Massachusetts senator, published the book *Profiles in Courage*, eloquently describing inordinate acts of political courage and sacrifice by eight of his senatorial predecessors.[4] *Profiles in Courage* would become one of the most indelible phrases in American life and one of the best-known political books ever written, winning the Pulitzer Prize and springboarding Kennedy to national prominence.

In 1959, Allen Drury, a *New York Times* reporter covering the Senate, wrote *Advise and Consent*, a novel about a brutal Senate confirmation fight over Robert Leffingwell, a liberal nominated to be secretary of state. *Advise and Consent* became the most famous political novel ever written. It spent 112 weeks on the best-seller list, and the movie version, with memorable scenes of Senate floor debate and off-the-floor intrigue, captivated many Americans. In 2009, Thomas Mallon, writing for the *New York Times Book Review*, observed, "Fifty years later, most of the subject matter remains recognizable. Drury's 99 men and one lone woman wrestle with the issue of pre-emptive war, the degree of severity with which lying under oath must be viewed, and the way that the coverup is invariably worse than the crime."[5] Scott Simon of National Public Radio, writing in the *Wall Street Journal*, put it succinctly: "Fifty years after publication and astounding success, Allen Drury's novel remains the definitive Washington tale."[6]

By the end of the 1950s, many Americans found the Senate familiar and thought they understood it: the high-profile investigations, the all-night filibusters, the occasional acts of conscience, the behind-the-scenes intrigue. John Kennedy's glamour and rise to the presidency further bolstered the Senate's standing in America. In the 1960 election, Kennedy narrowly prevailed over Vice President Richard Nixon (himself a former senator), and both presidential candidates chose as their running mates other familiar figures from the Senate: Lyndon Johnson, the incumbent Senate majority leader, and Henry Cabot Lodge, a former senator from Massachusetts.

The Senate's visibility and glamour masked a darker reality. In his 2005 book *The Most Exclusive Club: A History of the Modern United States Senate*, the political historian Lewis L. Gould reached a depressing conclusion: "For protracted periods—at the start of the twentieth century, in the era of Theodore Roosevelt, during the 1920s, and again for domestic issues in the post-World War II era—the Senate functioned not merely as a source of conservative reflections on the direction of society but as a force to genuinely impede the nation's vitality and evolution."[7]

Throughout the 1950s, as the Senate became recognizable and fascinating to many Americans, it remained dominated by Southern senators who used their seniority, committee chairmanships, and the filibuster to bottle up civil rights and other progressive legislation. The Senate was, in the words of the Pulitzer Prize–winning author and journalist William White, "The South's permanent revenge for Gettysburg . . . the only place in the country where the South did not lose the Civil War."[8] In the late 1950s, Majority Leader Lyndon Johnson would use his extraordinary energy and force of personality to drag the Senate, kicking and screaming, into the twentieth century. Johnson spearheaded the passage of the 1957 Civil Rights Act, a modest measure but the first ever to prevail over the fierce opposition of Southern senators.[9]

It was in the 1960s and 1970s that the Senate finally reached its potential, playing a central role in facing the challenges and seizing the opportunities presented during crisis years in America.[10] The Senate of that era was an extraordinary collection of individuals whose character had been forged in the fires of the Great Depression and World War II. Their ranks included many veterans, some of whom—Daniel Inouye, Robert Dole, Philip Hart, and Paul Douglas—still lived with the pain of grievous war wounds. Having been involved in the invasions of Normandy, Italy, and Iwo Jima, they did not believe that casting a hard vote was the most difficult thing they would ever do.

The senators of this era were disproportionately progressives, and while they were mostly Democrats, even the Republican ranks included some liberals and many moderates. They had a shared sense of America's destiny and recognized the existential challenge posed by the Soviet Union in the Cold War. They were members of what the journalist Tom Brokaw would later call "the Greatest Generation," those who had been part of America's triumph but were aware of our country's shortcomings, particularly where the treatment of black Americans was concerned.

They also benefited from an extraordinary leader. Although Lyndon Johnson would always be remembered as "the master of the Senate," immortalized in Robert Caro's magisterial biography, it was his successor, Montana's Mike Mansfield, the laconic, pipe-smoking professor of Asian history turned politician, who would lead the Senate for sixteen years through its period of greatest accomplishment.[11]

Mansfield was an improbable leader in all respects. He had no interest in the position and accepted it reluctantly only after President-elect John Kennedy, a close friend, asked him to do so. Lyndon Johnson had convinced most political observers that the Senate required a very strong leader, but Johnson's tactics—which included intimidation, learning senators' weaknesses and exploiting them, and depriving those he disliked of major committee positions, staff, and budgets—repelled Mansfield. As Tom Daschle and Trent Lott would later write in *Crisis Point*, "It's unlikely that [Mansfield] twisted one arm in his sixteen years in charge."

Even more fundamentally, Mansfield did not believe in a Senate dominated by its leaders and a few senior senators. He believed in a democratic Senate, in which all senators were adults and all senators were equal, having been elected by their constituents. He even treated senators in the minority as equals. To a degree that stunned his colleagues, Mansfield believed in the "golden rule" and acted accordingly. He treated each senator the way he wanted to be treated himself, and he expected reciprocity.

Most senators, starting with Everett McKinley Dirksen, the legendary Republican minority leader, doubted that Mansfield could possibly run the Senate in that way. And initially events seemed to prove the skeptics correct: Mansfield's democratized Senate, operating without a leader's whip, quickly became paralyzed. By the fall of 1963, Mansfield's leadership was subject to such fierce criticism that he prepared a floor speech explaining his approach to leadership and offering to resign if the senators did not like it. It included an eloquent explanation of how he viewed the Senate: "The Constitutional authority does not lie with the leadership. It lies with all of us individually, collectively, and equally. . . . In the end it is not the senators as individuals who are of fundamental importance. In the end, it is the institution of the Senate itself, as one of the foundations of the Constitution. It is the Senate as one of the rocks of the Republic."

Mansfield never delivered the speech. It had to be inserted in the *Congressional Record* because several hours after he informed the Senate of his intent to speak, the country received word that President Kennedy had been assassinated in Dallas.

Mansfield's leadership would never be questioned again. Galvanized by the tragedy of Kennedy's assassination, the leadership of President Lyndon Johnson, and the moral imperative to take action on civil rights, Mansfield's democratized Senate met the challenge of history. In the summer of 1964, with the country and the world watching, the Senate broke the filibuster of the Southern bloc to enact what is generally regarded as one of the most important pieces of legislation in American history: the Civil Rights Act of 1964. The Senate would go from there to an extraordinary period of activism and productivity. Under Mansfield's leadership, the Senate would no longer be the gridlocked graveyard of progressive dreams. It became the place where those hopes and dreams were translated into the legislation, moved forward with presidents where possible or, where necessary, despite them.

After tragically acquiescing in the Gulf of Tonkin Resolution, which President Johnson would use as a "blank check" to escalate the Vietnam War, the Senate became the forum in which the war was debated and that ultimately forced Richard Nixon, Johnson's successor, to negotiate its end. And after the abuses of Nixon's 1972 reelection campaign came to light, the Senate unanimously created a select committee to investigate the allegations. What became known as the Senate Watergate Committee paved the way for the exposure of Nixon's crimes and his resignation. Reacting to the lessons learned from the "imperial presidency" of Johnson and Nixon, the Senate then investigated the abuses committed by America's intelligence agencies, limited the president's ability to wage war, and established a budget process to regain Congress's power over the purse.

Mansfield and his Republican counterparts—first Dirksen and then Hugh Scott—built a Senate based on trust and mutual respect.[12] Mansfield's Senate was bipartisan to the core. Everyone—senators and staff—knew it was impossible to get anything done on a partisan basis. The majority leader himself ate breakfast every morning with his best friend, Vermont's Republican senator George Aiken. When a Democratic staff member would suggest a new initiative to his boss, the first response would always be "Get a Republican co-sponsor."

During most of the 1960s and 1970s, the Senate, although a political institution, was surprisingly free from partisanship. The herculean effort to secure civil rights for black Americans, the tragedy of Vietnam, the crisis of Watergate, checking the "imperial presidency" of

Johnson and Nixon—these were not partisan issues, and the Senate responded in a bipartisan way. Thanks to Dirksen's leadership, the Civil Rights Act of 1964 passed with the votes of twenty-five out of thirty-three Republican senators, even though Arizona's Barry Goldwater, about to accept the Republican presidential nomination, opposed it. Democratic senators like Eugene McCarthy, Robert Kennedy, George McGovern, J. William Fulbright, and Frank Church were joined by Republicans like George Aiken, John Sherman Cooper, Mark Hatfield, and Charles Goodell in opposing the Vietnam War. Watergate had the potential to divide on partisan lines, but Sam Ervin and Howard Baker, the Senate Watergate Committee's Democratic chairman and Republican vice chairman, understood that a partisan split would destroy the committee, and they worked closely together to avoid it. The great issues that threatened the country's stability were too important; the senators understood the stakes.

US senators take an oath to "support and defend the Constitution," but there was also an unspoken oath in Mansfield's Senate, a shared concept of what it meant to be a senator. The people of their states had given them the incredible privilege and honor of being US senators, the most venerable title that the Republic can bestow, along with a six-year term, usually leading to multiple terms. These senators would have the opportunity to deal with the full spectrum of issues, domestic and foreign, and they would develop unique expertise, valuable to the Senate and the country. In return, when they sorted out the competing, cascading pressures on them, they would serve their states and would not forget their party allegiance, but the national interest was overriding. Every state had many officials at the local and state levels working to protect that state's interests. But each state had only two US senators.

The second part of the unspoken oath was an obligation to help make the Senate work. As Mansfield noted, "In the end, it is not the individual senators who are important. It is the institution of the Senate." The senators understood that the nation relied on the Senate to take collective action. Understanding that brought a commitment to passionate, but not unlimited, debate, tolerance of opposing views, principled compromise, and a willingness to vote bills up or down, even if it sometimes meant losing.

Those qualities characterized Mansfield's Senate and its members. A liberal like Hubert Humphrey and a conservative like Barry Goldwater may have been ideological polar opposites, but they were also great friends, and no one doubted their commitment to the national interest and to the institution of the Senate. Because of those overriding commitments, the members of Mansfield's Senate competed and cooperated, clashed and compromised, and then went out to dinner together.

Mansfield was a great leader for the Senate in crisis times. On March 4, 1976, with the Vietnam War ended and Nixon gone, as the United States prepared for its bicentennial, Mansfield stunned his colleagues and the country by announcing his intention to retire. "There is a time to stay, and a time to go," Mansfield told the Senate. "Thirty-four years in the House and Senate is not a long time"—to a scholar of Asian history—"but it is long enough."

Mansfield would have been the first to say that no leader is indispensable, and his successors proved him right. In November 1976, America, reacting to Watergate, turned to an outsider president, Jimmy Carter, the former governor of Georgia. Mansfield's successor as majority leader was Robert C. Byrd of West Virginia, one of the most conservative Democrats, a former Ku Klux Klan member and opponent of the Civil Rights Act of 1964, who had won the confidence of his caucus through hard work as Mansfield's deputy, as well as constant personal growth. With the retirement of Hugh Scott, the Senate Republicans also had to choose a new leader, and they selected Howard Baker, who had become a national celebrity through his memorable work with Sam Ervin on the Watergate committee.

Byrd and Baker were an odd couple—"the grind and natural," one Senate historian called them.[13] Despite having served together for a decade, they were not particularly close friends. In their first meeting after they were chosen, Baker asked Byrd for one thing: "Don't ever surprise me." Byrd asked whether he could consider the request overnight; he agreed to it the next day.

Yet they became a superb leadership team. President Carter was an unusual politician, who disliked political small talk, politicians, and the give-and-take of politics. He had hated the Georgia legislature and saw members of Congress as captives of special interests or at least too willing to bend to their views. Carter's training as an engineer, combined with a powerful intellect and inordinate self-confidence, convinced him that if he studied a problem closely enough, he could find the right answer, decide what was in the national interest, and pursue it irrespective of political fallout. Carter saw the presidency as a stewardship, and as the only person elected by the whole country, he was the nation's steward.

Compromise, however, is the lifeblood of politics, and Jimmy Carter did not believe in compromise. Plainly, the Senate and Carter were not natural bedfellows, and their initial dealings were rocky. Yet for four years, with the leadership of Byrd and Baker, the Senate worked with Carter and helped him to singular achievements in domestic and foreign policy. While Carter is often recalled as a failed president, recent historians have credited him with a stunning record of accomplishments in domestic and foreign policy.[14] During the Carter presidency, the United States adopted a national energy policy, deregulated the airlines and much of the economy, provided financial rescues for New York City and the Chrysler Corporation, preserved much of the pristine wilderness of Alaska, and approved the fiercely controversial Panama Canal treaties. Decades later, Carter would write, "Barack Obama faced many of the same problems that I did. But I had one advantage: a Congress that I could work with." By that he meant the Senate, led by Byrd and Baker.

Carter could not ultimately overcome double-digit inflation or the crisis of American hostages held for more than a year in the US embassy in Tehran. In the 1980 election, Ronald Reagan won in a landslide that also swept in thirteen new Republican senators. The progressive Democratic Senate of the 1960s and 1970s became the conservative Republican Senate of the 1980s. Byrd and Baker exchanged jobs, and the Senate regrouped and picked up its work. During Reagan's first term, the Senate enacted a historic tax cut and increased defense spending; it also went on to save the Social Security system with an extraordinary bipartisan deal.

When Baker, whose leadership inspired affection and respect, chose to retire in 1984 after three terms in the Senate, Bob Dole, who had compiled a powerful record of accomplishment as chairman of the Senate Finance Committee, became the majority leader. The Senate worked with the Reagan administration to enact a sweeping revision of the tax code, comprehensive immigration reform, and a reform of the Joint Chiefs of Staff. When Reagan's presidency was shaken by revelations that his administration had sold arms to Iran and used the proceeds to illegally fund the right-wing "contras" in Nicaragua, the Senate unanimously created a special committee that investigated, and defused, the most serious threat to the presidency since Watergate. The Senate managed to function as an independent institution throughout the Reagan presidency, never simply rubber-stamping the White House's agenda or failing to investigate wrongdoing on partisan grounds.

But things were changing in the House of Representatives, with an increasingly ideological Republican membership.[15] Newt Gingrich, a congressman from Georgia who rose to prominence in the late 1980s, was the leader of a growing caucus of Republican representatives who did not subscribe to the go-along-to-get-along posture of more establishment House Republicans. They had been in the minority since 1954, and Gingrich believed they were much too comfortable accepting that status. He initiated a series of novel psychological tactics, like training fellow Republicans on how to use language to degrade their opponents unfairly and to pursue ethics violations on the part of Democrats that were left alone when committed by Republicans. Led by Gingrich's crusading spirit, year by year the once-conservative Republican party became ever more radical. When the Republicans gained control of the House in 1994, Gingrich became speaker, and his aggressive, no-holds-barred vision of partisan warfare became institutionalized on the House side of the Capitol.

Gingrich's rise was the culmination of a political evolution that had begun with the passage of the Civil Rights Act of 1964, which had led to an exodus of conservative white Southerners from the

Democratic Party. Lyndon Johnson had said after signing the legislation, "We [the Democrats] just lost the South for a generation." In time, Republicans would begin winning Senate and House seats in the South that had long been held by Democrats. As the Republican Party "Southernized," it became more conservative, and the number of liberal and moderate Republicans from the Northeast and Midwest began to decline as well. In June 1996, when Bob Dole was succeeded by Trent Lott as Senate majority leader, Lott noted proudly that for the first time the Senate and House had Republican leaders from the South, the culmination of the party's transformation that had begun with Barry Goldwater's opposition to the 1964 Civil Rights Act. As David Broder, the preeminent political columnist of the era, observed, "The transfer of the Republican party from the Midwest and Northeast to the South is the single most important transformation in the GOP's 20th century history."[16]

By the 1990s, these forces had taken their toll on the Senate and its operation. Few Republican moderates remained in the Senate, and those who did found it to be a more partisan, less congenial place. New Republican senators who had served in the House of Representatives brought with them hard-edged, right-wing credentials earned in the service of the "Gingrich revolution." The political scientist Sean Theriault has identified "Gingrich senators" such as Rick Santorum of Pennsylvania, Jim DeMint of South Carolina, and Phil Gramm of Texas, former representatives who had been part of Newt Gingrich's takeover of the House, as a principal cause of partisan warfare.[17] His allies and his adversaries would agree that Gingrich changed American politics dramatically; he saw politics as war and conducted it accordingly.

Ironically, Lott, whose anguish about the current condition of the Senate is deep and genuine, contributed significantly to accelerating its decline. Most newly elected senators came to the Senate with a sense of deep respect, if not awe. Lott was an exception. As he described in his candid memoir *Herding Cats*, he hated the Senate from the time he arrived in 1989. "After giving up real power in the House and winning a score of victories for Ronald Reagan," Lott wrote, "I expected

a warm welcome in the Senate." Instead, Lott and the other fresh-
men "found themselves in 'storage' as the Senate machinery creaked
to life." Lott viewed many of his fellow senators as "distant, impossible to befriend." The Senate itself was "a confused and disorganized
institution" with chaotic and unpredictable hours. Along with "a tight
clique of conservative young senators," Lott set out to change the
institution to be more structured and more partisan as he rose in the
Republican leadership. When he became Republican leader in 1996,
Lott showed his preference for working closely with Gingrich and the
House Republicans, rather than looking to collaborate across the aisle
with the Senate Democrats or with the moderates in his own party.[18]

The reaction to Lott's ascendancy was strong and immediate. In
1996, at a time of peace and prosperity in America, a record number
of senators—fourteen—chose to retire. The departing group included
some of the Senate's most respected members, who were known for
their ability to make deals on a bipartisan basis, such as the Democrats Sam Nunn, Bill Bradley, and Howell Heflin, and the Republicans
Alan Simpson, Nancy Kassebaum, and William Cohen. The Senate
had been involved in bruising fights over NAFTA and health care, but
those were par for the course. This time, a common thread in their
farewell speeches was a deep dismay about the Senate and the condition and direction of American politics.[19]

Jim Exon, a Democrat who had served more than a quarter century as Nebraska's governor and senator, put it plainly in terms that the
other senators could identify with:

> Our political process must be "re-civilized." What I have called
> the ever-increasing, vicious polarization of the electorate, the "us
> against them" mentality, has all but swept away the former pre-
> ponderance of reasonable discussion of the pros and cons of many
> legitimate issues. Unfortunately, the traditional art of workable
> compromise for the ultimate good of the nation, heretofore the es-
> sence of democracy, is demonstrably eroded.

Exon focused on a phenomenon increasingly described as "the permanent campaign": "Much to the detriment of our nation, the political

season no longer ends on Election Day. In fact, lately, it never ends. The late level of each campaign not only feeds the next campaign; it distorts the once respected legislative procedures that get trapped in the brief intervals between campaigns."

William Cohen expressed puzzlement about the national mood in 1996, especially when compared to the era when he had begun his service in Congress, two decades earlier:

> Regrettably, contempt for government seems even more dangerous today. . . . Unlike the mid-70's, the cause of today's anger and resentment is less apparent. The country is at peace, employment is high, and inflation is low. We have preserved our original constitutional freedoms and, indeed, even enlarged them, particularly in the field of civil rights. We are a nation more prosperous, better educated, and have at our fingertips and disposal more information than at any time in the history of humankind. Yet there is a wave of unease and negativity surging through the society, a debasement of both language and conduct that threatens to shred the fabric that binds us together as a nation. . . . Congress is an institution designed to permit ideas and interests to compete passionately for public approbation and support. It was never intended to be a rose garden where intellectual felicities could be exchanged with polite gentility. . . . But enmity in recent times has become so intense that some members of Congress have resorted to shoving matches in hallways. . . . [If] we permit the art of compromise to be viewed as abject surrender, then we should not lament that our system has become sclerotic or dysfunctional.

Still, even as late as 1999, the Senate could sometimes function as intended. When the House of Representatives impeached President Bill Clinton for lying under oath about his sexual relationship with White House intern Monica Lewinsky, it fell to the Senate to conduct the second impeachment trial of a president in American history, and the first since 1868. The Senate was in uncharted waters, writing the rules for a trial in the television age. There were many fraught moments, but Senate leaders Trent Lott and Tom Daschle, who had forged a close relationship, succeeded in keeping the hundred senators involved, on track, and committed to a fair process. When the three-week trial concluded with Clinton's acquittal, there was a widely shared view that the Senate could take pride in how it had handled its historic responsibility.[20]

Two years later, the horrific terrorist attacks on the World Trade Center and the Pentagon once again brought America, and the Senate, to a moment of national unity and shared purpose. It proved to be, literally, a moment. The 2002 elections were contested on a fiercely partisan basis, as the Republicans improved their position in Congress by smearing Democrats as lacking in patriotism. The Republicans defeated Senator Max Cleland of Georgia, who had lost an arm and both legs to a grenade in Vietnam, with television ads linking him to Osama bin Laden and Saddam Hussein, questioning his commitment to the nation's security. By 2004, relations were further poisoned when the new Republican majority leader, Bill Frist, took the unprecedented step of traveling to South Dakota to campaign against Daschle's reelection. Daschle lost narrowly, and one more Senate tradition that had contributed to comity was a thing of the past.[21]

In 2005, after the reelection of President George W. Bush, the Senate descended further into partisan conflict. A bitter clash arose when the Democrats filibustered ten of Bush's judicial nominees. Frist threatened to initiate a process to change the Senate rules to abolish the filibuster for judicial nominations, which had become known, in a phrase coined by Lott, as the "nuclear option." A bipartisan "Gang of Fourteen" defused the issue by agreeing that judicial nominations would not be filibustered, except in "extraordinary circumstances," which were left undefined. Cooler heads had prevailed, but the Senate's continued deterioration was painfully obvious. "A profound sense of crisis now surrounds the Senate and its members," wrote the historian Lewis Gould.[22]

In retrospect, the Senate had a clear chance to chart a more bipartisan course around this time. In 2005, Nevada senator Harry Reid became minority leader; after the Democrats regained the majority in the 2006 midterm elections, Reid became majority leader, and Mitch McConnell stepped up to be minority leader after the retirement of Bill

Frist. Together, Reid and McConnell would lead the Senate for the next decade—longer than any other pair of Senate leaders in history.

There were reasons for cautious optimism. Reid and McConnell were both twenty-year veteran senators who had risen through the ranks to be leaders and presumably loved the Senate. Each man had overcome personal adversity: Reid had grown up in terrible poverty, and McConnell had beaten childhood polio. They were both hard workers, tough fighters, dedicated politicians fiercely protective of their state's special interests, and good tacticians. Neither man would ever demonstrate the substantive knowledge, broad-ranging intellect, and constant personal growth that characterized Mansfield, Byrd, and Baker, but they should have been well suited to a serious discussion of what was needed to put the struggling Senate on a better course.

In their first Congress working together, Reid and McConnell did come through for America in one moment of absolute crisis. In September 2008, the Bush administration confronted the sudden, devastating financial shock triggered by the subprime mortgage crisis and the collapse of Lehman Brothers. Treasury Secretary Henry Paulson and Federal Reserve Chairman Ben Bernanke went to the Capitol on a Friday evening to meet with the congressional leadership. "Let me say this again," Bernanke said grimly. "If we don't act now, we won't have an economy on Monday."[23]

McConnell and Reid grasped the urgency of the situation and rolled up their sleeves to provide immediate, strong support for the Troubled Asset Relief Program (TARP). When the feckless House Republicans shockingly rejected the legislation, causing the stock market to plunge 770 points, McConnell went to the Senate floor and reassured the nation that the Senate would meet its responsibilities. The Senate voted overwhelmingly for the TARP legislation, and the chastened House soon followed suit. McConnell rightfully expressed pride in what the Senate had done and in his own role. It was a reminder of what the Senate could do for the country.[24]

Optimists might have believed that this cooperation augured well for the future, but things did not work out that way.

McConnell's Bitter Harvest

$\mathcal{O}$n November 4, 2008, Barack Obama, the junior senator from Illinois, won a decisive victory over his fellow senator John McCain to become the forty-fourth president of the United States. Obama's nomination by the Democrats had excited the country and captivated the world, and his victory—the election of the first African American president—was an extraordinary moment where hope seemed justified and change seemed a very real possibility.

The election result did not surprise Mitch McConnell. A political realist to his core, McConnell recognized Obama's superb political talent. During the crucial meeting on TARP in Speaker Nancy Pelosi's conference room in late September, Senator Obama had spoken for the Democrats. "Obama had masterfully shown how well he understood the issue—delivering what sounded like third draft prose without any notes," McConnell recalled. "Everyone in the room was spellbound." He left the room with no doubt that Obama would be elected.[1]

Every year as Republican leader, McConnell brought his caucus together to plan strategy. On January 9, 2009, the Senate Republicans met in the Library of Congress. "The weather was perfect for the occasion: cold, dreary and rainy," McConnell recalled. "Nobody was in a good mood."[2]

McConnell knew that his caucus was shell-shocked by the election results. The Democrats had won the White House and both houses of Congress; Obama would become president in eleven days with an approval rating close to 80 percent. McConnell knew that the new president would press for a strong progressive agenda and feared the combination of a troubled economy and one-party control would lead to an "explosion of legislative and government control, just like we saw in the New Deal and the Great Society." He felt the need to rally his troops, and he saw a strategy for doing it.

McConnell told his colleagues, first and foremost, to have patience; no majority was permanent. The American people, exhausted by eight years of the Bush presidency and two wars, had voted for change, he said, but America was still a right-of-center country. Using one of his favorite lines, McConnell told his colleagues, "We hadn't suddenly become France." There were, he pointed out, still one hundred million Republicans looking to them for leadership.

He intended to provide it. A few days after the election, McConnell had told the columnist George Will, "Governing is hazardous business for presidential parties."[3] Now, he sketched a strategy of opposition. The Republicans would pick fights they could win to show that Obama was not invulnerable. They would obstruct and oppose him on virtually everything, to undercut his basic promise of ushering in a new era of postpartisan cooperation.[4] The Republican senators left the meeting feeling energized, with a new sense of purpose and unity.[5]

Missing from the Republican senators' retreat was any discussion of the economic crisis that was devastating the nation. In October, the TARP legislation rescued the banking system when it could have collapsed. By January, the economic crisis that began on Wall Street had spread to every Main Street across the country; Americans had lost 16 percent of their net worth in the past twelve months, far more than in any year of the Great Depression. With the value of their houses and stocks sharply reduced, American workers and families were cutting back on demand. Banks, traumatized by the Lehman shock and the rapidly sinking economy, hoarded their assets, and credit dried up. Major companies like Boeing, Caterpillar, Pfizer, and Corning had responded to the deteriorating climate with major layoffs.[6] As Obama prepared to start his presidency, America lost 750,000 jobs in one month. As Tim Geithner, about to become Obama's treasury secretary, recalled, "This vicious cycle of financial and economic contraction was gaining momentum, and no one was sure how it would end."[7] When the president-elect held a conference call with his transition team to discuss what he should seek to accomplish in his first term, Geithner spoke first: "Your accomplishment will be to prevent the second Great Depression."[8]

Democratic and Republican economists agreed that a massive economic stimulus by the federal government was the only thing that could combat the drastic loss of private demand. McConnell had rightfully taken pride in his calm, strong leadership on TARP and regarded the Senate's action as one of its finest moments. He had spoken forcefully about the need for national unity in response to an economic emergency. But that was ninety days earlier, before the election and when the president was a Republican. Now, as the crisis continued to rage, McConnell condemned the proposed spending. Even after Obama agreed to make tax cuts part of the stimulus, McConnell pressed his caucus to be united in opposition. If three Republican senators— Olympia Snowe and Susan Collins of Maine, along with Arlen Specter of Pennsylvania—had not resisted McConnell's pressure, the economic recovery that began in 2009 would have been delayed for years. A second Great Depression would have been quite likely.[9]

This was a singular moment in Senate history. Mitch McConnell was starting his third year as minority leader, but now, for the first time, he was the *opposition* leader. He began immediately to transform a Senate struggling unsuccessfully to rise above the polarization of American politics into a bitterly partisan, paralyzed Senate where no effort would be made to overcome the divisions. The Senate always had its share of obstructionists, but the institution's leaders saw it as their responsibility to overcome them so that the business of the country could get done. A Senate leader was not supposed to function as a party chairman but rather to temper his partisanship because of his obligation to the Senate and the country. A Senate leader was supposed to work across the aisle and work respectfully with the president, regardless of whether the president was a Democrat or a Republican.

It is impossible to imagine Howard Baker or Bob Dole opposing an economic stimulus as America teetered on the edge of a second
Great Depression. Baker or Dole would have told his caucus, "We'll
have plenty of issues on which to differ with the president, but right
now, we have to work together to save the country." McConnell had
a different agenda; any show of bipartisanship could serve as evidence
that Obama was succeeding in his promise to heal the divide in the
country and producing results. Therefore, bipartisanship was unacceptable. His goal, which he stated clearly, was for Obama to fail, and
he had no concern about the impact that his obstruction would have
on actual Americans, including those who lived in his home state of
Kentucky.[10]

For McConnell, the fight over the economic stimulus in 2009 was
a minor skirmish compared to the titanic political battle he would wage
over health care. Every Democratic president since Harry Truman had
been committed to extending health-care coverage to all Americans, but
none had succeeded in getting legislation through Congress. Obama,
and virtually all Democrats, were appalled that the United States spent
twice as much per capita on health care as any other country, while
more than forty million Americans had no health insurance. Unjust and
inefficient, the "health-care system" exacerbated the growing inequality that afflicted America. Obama believed that the economic crisis had
provided the moment for action; his chief of staff, Rahm Emanuel,
would famously say, "It would be a shame to waste a crisis."

To McConnell, Obama's ideas about health care represented the
classic illustration of an attempt to "Europeanize" America. Because
it was "the worst bill that had crossed his desk in his Senate career,"
he did not want a single Republican to vote for it. "It had to be very
obvious to the voters which party was responsible for this terrible policy," McConnell contended. "The best thing we could do was ensure
that there was no confusion in the public's mind come the next election that this was in any way a bipartisan proposal. So, the strategy simply stated was to keep everybody together in opposition."[11]

Over the next ten months, McConnell repeatedly blasted Obama
and the Senate majority leader, Harry Reid, for trying to ram through

health care on a strictly partisan basis. But in his memoir, recounting the challenges he faced in maintaining a unified opposition, McConnell noted that "early on, the administration reached out to members of our conference who were deeply involved in health care issues."[12] Clearly, it was not Obama who was standing in the way of addressing health care on a bipartisan basis; it was McConnell who was committed to keeping the process partisan.

Even more fundamentally, Obama had embraced what was essentially a Republican template for health care. He did not seriously consider a single-payer model championed by Senator Bernie Sanders of Vermont and many other progressives, nor did he endorse having a "public option": a government-run health plan as an alternative to private insurance. He turned instead to a model endorsed by the conservative Heritage Foundation that had been proposed in 1993 and 1994 by several Republican senators, including Orrin Hatch of Utah and Charles Grassley of Iowa, who were still key players in the Senate in 2009. In fact, Obamacare most resembled the state insurance framework in Massachusetts, which had been championed by its Republican governor, Mitt Romney.[13]

None of these facts mattered to McConnell; in this war, as in others, truth was an early casualty. He allowed Grassley and two other Republican senators, Mike Enzi and Olympia Snowe, to engage in months of highly visible "Gang of Six" negotiations with three Senate Democrats, Max Baucus, Jeff Bingaman, and Kent Conrad. Many observers expressed frustration that the fate of health-care reform was being negotiated by six senators representing small states that were mostly rural and white.[14] (Grassley was from Iowa, and his two fellow Republicans were from Wyoming and Maine; the three Democrats represented Montana, New Mexico, and North Dakota.) In practice, though, the "Gang of Six" were senators who came to the table with a good deal of knowledge about health-care issues. They plunged into talks, meeting more than thirty times over the next four months, often twice a day for several hours. "It was a compatible group composed of senators who were all committed to upholding the integrity of the legislative process," Snowe observed.[15]

McConnell allowed these talks to progress, but his basic position remained unchanged. As he described in his memoir, he had one-on-one meetings with Grassley, Enzi, and Snowe "to encourage them to stay with the party" and not to sign on to any compromise that might be acceptable to the Democratic majority. He also met every Wednesday with the entire Republican caucus, "trying to build on the vision that we were all in this together." Every morning, he was on the Senate floor "pounding away at the bill." He gave 105 daily speeches in all. If the Republican members of the "Gang of Six" were going to reach agreement with the Democrats, they would be taking a position completely contrary to what their leader was preaching.[16]

It was hard to envision that happening, and of course it did not. When Congress recessed for August, the senators encountered angry and fearful reactions from many of their constituents. Whipped up by the right-wing media and the blogosphere, many people believed "Obamacare" (as the Republicans jeeringly called the proposed legislation) was "socialized medicine" that would prevent them from seeing their doctors. Talk grew that the legislation contained provisions establishing "death panels" to determine the fate of grandparents and parents. Obama's optimistic message of hope and change virtually disappeared as the Tea Party came of age as a political force vehemently opposed to any guarantee or new provision of health care to the American people.[17]

On August 25, Senator Edward Kennedy died after a valiant fight against incurable brain cancer, having served nearly forty-seven years in the US Senate. The loss of a national icon, a beloved senator, the last of the Kennedy brothers, and a tireless champion of health care for all Americans momentarily quieted the partisan rancor. But within days, the health-care wars resumed.

By early September, the "Gang of Six" talks were on life support. "They all want to do health care," Baucus asserted, "but they've been told by the Republican party not to participate." Grassley, a principal target of the Tea Party during the August recess, returned to the conference room saying he could only support an agreement that would attract seventy-five senators—an impossibility. Enzi assured the press in his home state of Wyoming that his efforts were simply to change the bill; he would never support it. Snowe, independent and gutsy, hung in long enough to allow the Finance Committee to report legislation, but ultimately backed away as well.[18]

It later became known that McConnell had told Senator Chris Dodd of Connecticut, the chairman of the Banking Committee, that the two of them might be able to negotiate something on financial reform, but never health care.[19] Norman Ornstein, probably the most respected observer of Congress, would write, "What became clear before September when the talks fell apart is that [McConnell] warned Grassley and Enzi their futures in the Senate would be much dimmer if they moved toward a deal with the Democrats that would produce legislation that Barack Obama would sign. They both listened to their leader."[20]

Legislating on complex issues for a diverse, contentious country will always be bone-crushingly difficult. If extending health insurance to all Americans were easy, it would have been done long ago. But the essence of successful legislating is good-faith engagement designed to build understanding needed to find common ground and reach compromises that can win broad support. In health care, as with the economic stimulus, McConnell had already decided that a result that could command such support would not be tolerated. Even if the senators in the room were serious, they were participating in what Ornstein termed "a faux negotiation," the failure of which was foreordained months before.

For Obama, and the overwhelming number of congressional Democrats, passing health-care legislation had become an almost existential priority. If this could not be done on a bipartisan basis, then the Democrats would have to do it alone. Speaker Pelosi had a clear majority in favor of whatever health-care legislation Obama would sign and the benefit of House rules that ensured limited debate. Majority Leader Harry Reid faced a different challenge in the Senate. If the Republicans stayed united in opposition, Reid would have to hold all sixty Democrats together to break any Republican filibuster. The Senate rules and traditions provided for extended debate and numerous opportunities for obstruction that McConnell was skilled in exploiting.

Moreover, the Senate Democrats might not hold together as the public anger toward "Obamacare" was not lost on them, particularly those who were up for reelection in conservative states in 2010.[21]

Reid worked tirelessly to hold together his caucus. Ornstein would observe later, "When Republicans like Hatch and Grassley began to write op-eds and trash the individual mandate, which they had earlier championed, as unconstitutional and abominable, it convinced conservative Democrats in the Senate that every effort to engage Republicans in the reform legislation had been tried and cynically rebuffed."[22]

McConnell spearheaded a fierce counterattack. His policy team watched carefully for provisions that were added to the bill to keep conservative Democrats on board. When they found such provisions, they alerted the majority leader's communications shop, which quickly flooded the media and the blogosphere with unforgettable names. A provision addressing Louisiana senator Mary Landrieu's concerns became "the Louisiana Purchase"; one for Bill Nelson of Florida became "Gator Aid." Special treatment was reserved for the last wavering senator, Nebraska's Ben Nelson, when he agreed to sign on to the legislation only if it contained increased Medicaid reimbursements for Nebraska. Josh Holmes, McConnell's communications director, dubbed it "the Cornhusker Kickback" and said, "We're going to make this bill as popular as an internment camp."[23]

In fact, it is likely that every major piece of legislation ever enacted has contained within it provisions designed to win over key votes. Mitch McConnell had excelled at inserting such provisions throughout his career, particularly during his long decades on the Appropriations Committee. But this was political war. As McConnell would later recall, "Within hours, the Cornhusker Kickback took on a life of its own and became emblematic of an entire process that had made the American people absolutely disgusted."[24]

Even so, on December 24, 2009, the Senate, on a straight party vote of 60–39, passed the Affordable Care Act. Ted Kennedy's seat had been filled on an interim basis by Paul Kirk, a longtime Kennedy aide, pending the outcome of a special election, which in January returned Scott Brown, the first Republican senator from Massachusetts in more than thirty years. Brown's election shook American politics; the Massachusetts seat had been regarded as absolutely safe for the Democrats, and now things were much harder for Harry Reid. He needed sixty votes to overcome a Republican filibuster, and he no longer had them. Without sixty votes, Reid would have to resort to the little-understood "reconciliation process," which would allow the Senate to pass the conference report (the bill reflecting the agreement between the House and Senate versions) with just fifty-one votes, further amplifying the Republican message that budget-busting "socialist" legislation was being rammed through using shady procedures.

Even so, the measure passed both houses, and President Obama signed the Affordable Care Act into law on March 25, 2010. Mitch McConnell had lost the legislative fight, but he won the political war. "The narrative of Obama steamrolling over Republicans and enacting an unconstitutional bill that brought America much closer to socialism worked like a charm to stimulate conservative and Republican anger," Ornstein wrote later.[25] That anger would fuel a sweeping Republican victory in the 2010 midterm elections, enabling the party to reclaim the House majority and narrowing the Democrats' edge in the Senate. While McConnell was still minority leader, he was plainly the most powerful and effective Republican in the country. In early 2011, an *Atlantic* profile by Joshua Green, titled "Strict Obstructionist," described McConnell as "the master manipulator and strategist—the unheralded architect of the Republican resurgence."[26]

By the end of 2010, the Senate had reached an extraordinary juncture. Against the odds, it had passed three momentous pieces of legislation—the economic stimulus, the Affordable Care Act, and the Dodd-Frank reform of financial regulation—yet it was universally regarded as dysfunctional. Carl Levin of Michigan, a thirty-two-year Senate veteran, was struck by the paradox. "It's been the most productive Senate since I've been here in terms of major accomplishments," Levin said, "and by far the most frustrating. It's almost impossible day to day to get almost anything done. Routine bills and nominations get bottled up indefinitely. Everything is stopped by the threat of filibusters—not real filibusters, just the threat of filibusters."[27]

In a widely read *New Yorker* article titled "The Empty Chamber," George Packer noted "the two lasting achievements of the Senate, financial regulation and health care, required a year and a half of legislative warfare that nearly destroyed the body."[28] Olympia Snowe, the respected Republican moderate from Maine, retired in disgust, saying, "We have been miniaturized." Indiana's Evan Bayh, a moderate Democrat, also called it quits.[29] Democrats and Republicans called for "regular order," a return to real legislating,[30] but the continued threat of Republican filibusters, and the requirement of sixty votes to get anything done, made that impossible.

McConnell felt no such frustration. As the 2012 elections approached, he was virtually measuring the drapes in the majority leader's office. The *Huffington Post* called it "McConnell's moment," and he described himself as "prepared, and more than a little eager."[31] As early as October 2010, McConnell had told the *National Journal* that "the single most important thing we want to achieve is for President Obama to be a one-term president."[32] Thus, McConnell was stunned by Obama's reelection and a sweeping victory for the Senate Democrats, who retained every contested seat that they had held and added two more. Bitterly disappointed, McConnell recognized the real possibility that he might never reach his goal of being majority leader. Moreover, polls indicated that he was so unpopular in Kentucky that he might be defeated in his race for a sixth term in 2014. He was facing a tough primary challenge from a Tea Party Republican named Matt Bevin, and then there was the prospect of a fierce contest in the general election. Chagrined that he was apparently the most endangered Republican incumbent, McConnell momentarily gave serious thought to not running again.[33]

Characteristically, he persevered. McConnell ran a relentless campaign against Bevin and defeated him comfortably. There was not that much room to the right of Mitch McConnell even in a Republican Party increasingly influenced by its Tea Party wing. At the same time, McConnell took the lead in ensuring that Republicans chosen for Senate seats in the other 2014 contests would be strong general election candidates. He helped identify appealing candidates like Thom Tillis, the speaker of the North Carolina house; David Perdue, the CEO of Reebok, to run in Georgia; and Joni Ernst and Tom Cotton, Iraq War veterans, to run in Iowa and Arkansas, respectively. He orchestrated a concerted effort to defeat every Tea Party challenger so that there would be no repeat of what had happened in 2012, when extreme Republican nominees lost Senate seats that could have easily been won in Missouri and Indiana.[34]

With that accomplished, McConnell turned his focus to his own race and decisively defeated Alison Lundergan Grimes, a promising but inexperienced challenger. He made sure to remind Kentucky's voters what it meant to have a senator who was a Senate leader, and the argument for staying with McConnell proved compelling. And throughout 2013–2014, McConnell still found time for his day job: being President Obama's principal nemesis. He thwarted virtually every Obama initiative, blocking consideration of Obama's judicial and executive nominations and driving Harry Reid to distraction. On election night, Mitch McConnell not only won his own race but also gained a Senate majority. It was a political tour de force.[35]

McConnell had been a fixture for so long, having completed thirty years in the Senate, that it was sometimes hard to recognize the unlikelihood of his rise.[36] Born in Alabama and raised in a middle-class home in Louisville, Kentucky, he overcame childhood polio to grow up and develop a passion for politics, starting in high school. He got early experience on Capitol Hill as an intern for Kentucky's Republican senator Marlow Cook in the memorable summer of 1964, when the Senate broke the Southern filibuster to pass the historic Civil Rights Act. Like many young men and women, McConnell found Capitol Hill intoxicating. He became a great admirer of John Sherman Cooper, Kentucky's other senator, also a Republican, who was a leading champion of civil rights and an opponent of the Vietnam War. Also inspired by Henry Clay, the most famous Kentuckian who ever served in the Senate, McConnell set his sights on becoming a US senator.

After law school, McConnell joined a Louisville law firm but was quickly bored with traditional legal work. In the aftermath of Watergate, with many experienced Republicans fleeing Washington,

McConnell parlayed his political connections and Capitol Hill experience to become the deputy assistant attorney general for legislative affairs in the Ford administration. That job bored him as well, and he left after fifteen months, returning to Louisville to launch his political career.

The first political consultants McConnell hired were astonished by his absolute lack of personal appeal, but he impressed them with his drive: he would do anything needed to win. He waged an unlikely but successful campaign to become judge-executive of Jefferson County—essentially the mayor of the county—and held that position for two terms, until he sought and won the Republican nomination for the US Senate in 1984. The incumbent senator, Walter "Dee" Huddleston, was a well-liked and capable, if uninspiring, two-term Democrat who had received significant attention for having served on the select committee chaired by Frank Church that had investigated abuses by the intelligence agencies in the 1970s.

Lefty Gomez, the eccentric Hall of Fame pitcher for the New York Yankees, once said, "I'd rather be lucky than good." McConnell proved to be both. Kentucky, a border state, was closely balanced politically, but Ronald Reagan, coasting to reelection against Walter Mondale, won the state handily, by nearly twenty points. Reagan's coattails pulled McConnell within striking range, and then McConnell's political consultant, Roger Ailes, concocted one of the most brilliant political ads in history. Huddleston had missed some Senate votes while doing speaking engagements, and the ad showed bloodhounds sniffing around hotel pools looking for Dee Huddleston. On election night, Mitch McConnell was elected by fifty-one hundred votes statewide. On such a slim margin, a remarkable career was started.

McConnell was a mainstream conservative Republican with conventional views; he eased into the Senate with no particular distinction. But midway through his first term, Democratic senators Robert Byrd and David Boren introduced legislation to impose contribution and spending limits on political campaigns. Although McConnell had originally endorsed limits on campaign spending, he realized that he would not be able to win reelection without unlimited access to campaign funds. He became, overnight, the leading opponent to campaign finance restrictions.

McConnell had found his calling. He relished being vilified by liberals and by good-government editorial pages, and he became a regular presence on the Sunday morning talk shows. When his critics labeled him "Darth Vader," he appeared at a news conference with a toy light saber. His staff identified new parliamentary maneuvers to expand his ability to block legislation, and in September 1994 he successfully filibustered a major campaign finance reform bill sponsored by the Democratic majority leader George Mitchell. "I've rarely seen a more determined and skilled tactician," said Russ Feingold,[37] the Wisconsin senator who would later cosponsor the sweeping McCain-Feingold legislation limiting the role of "soft money" in politics, another bill vehemently opposed by Mitch McConnell.

In the process, McConnell earned the gratitude of his Republican colleagues, who shared his views but were not prepared to take the criticism for opposing campaign finance reform. "Few members wanted to risk appearing corrupt, so they were grateful to McConnell for fighting one reform after the next—while claiming it was purely about defending the First Amendment," the *New Yorker's* Jane Mayer noted.[38] Armed with money from billionaire conservatives like David and Charles Koch and the DeVos family, McConnell helped take the effort to kill restraints on campaign spending all the way to the Supreme Court. His side won the big prize in 2010, when the Supreme Court, in a 5–4 decision in the *Citizens United* case, opened the door for corporations, wealthy individuals, and secretive nonprofits to pour unlimited and often untraceable cash into elections.[39]

The long war for unlimited campaign contributions fueled McConnell's rise. "McConnell loves money, and abhors any controls on it," said Fred Wertheimer, the president of the advocacy organization Democracy 21, who has devoted forty years to fighting for campaign finance reform. "Money is the central theme of his career. And if you want to control Congress, the best way is to control the money."[40] Money brought McConnell into the Senate Republican leadership. Money established his powerful network of donors. Money gave him influence in choosing political candidates and channeling campaign funds to them.

McConnell joined the Senate Republican leadership as part of Trent Lott's team in the late 1990s, and when Lott was forced to resign as majority leader following racially insensitive remarks at Strom Thurmond's one hundredth birthday celebration, McConnell thought it was his moment to seek the post. But his fellow Senate Republicans, having been embarrassed by Lott, wanted an attractive new face and opted for Bill Frist, who had come to the Senate a decade after McConnell but was an admired heart surgeon who still went to Africa to perform heart and lung surgeries. McConnell swallowed his disappointment, became Frist's deputy, and bided his time.[41] When Frist honored his pledge to serve only two terms in the Senate, McConnell became minority leader in January 2007, having already served twenty-two years in the body. It took eight more years, but after the 2014 election Mitch McConnell realized his long-held dream of becoming Senate majority leader.

For six years as minority leader during Barack Obama's presidency, McConnell's relentless obstruction had paralyzed and demoralized the Senate, driving Harry Reid to distraction and constant rage. As relations deteriorated between the two men, McConnell heaped contempt on Reid and pledged to restore the Senate to being the great deliberative body that the framers of the Constitution had, in their wisdom, intended it to be. He promised to rejuvenate the committee process, so that legislation could be developed thoughtfully and taken to the Senate floor where it would be subject to an open amendment process and freewheeling debate. He proclaimed that under his leadership the Senate would not be "the hollow shell of an institution" that he blamed Reid for creating,[42] omitting the fact that it had been his obstructionism that had hollowed it out.

The promised turnabout started almost immediately. McConnell, notoriously guarded and controlled in his comments, was unusually expansive, even happy, as he reviewed the accomplishments of the Senate in his first year as leader at the end of 2015. A more open amendment process allowed more vigorous debate, and a series of bipartisan legislative accomplishments had followed, including a new formula to pay doctors treating Medicare patients based on the quality of care they provided, rather than the amount of care; a transportation bill that shored up the highway trust fund and allowed the continued repair of America's roads; a massive spending bill that funded the government through October 2016; an education reform bill that gave states a larger say on how to improve schools and evaluate teachers; and a security visa waiver that allowed citizens from thirty-eight "friendly" countries easy access to the United States, while requiring stricter visa reviews for residents of or recent visitors to Iran, Iraq, Sudan, and Syria. Bob Corker and Ben Cardin, the chairman and ranking member of the Foreign Relations Committee, also engineered an ingenious bipartisan compromise to carve out a limited role for Congress in reviewing the nuclear pact with Iran.[43]

"They've really nailed down some festering issues that have been on the agenda for quite a while," noted Sarah Binder, a leading expert on Congress at the Brookings Institution. "And they've done it in this sort of a remarkably bipartisan way."[44]

McConnell generously praised the Democrats for their contributions to the legislation, noting that they had been good collaborators.[45] He even showed a previously undetected wry sense of humor, describing working constructively with the White House to win Trade Promotion Authority for President Obama as "something of an out of body experience."[46] McConnell was in his element, successfully pursuing his political objectives while doing a more than respectable job of leading a Senate comeback.

There was no magic to the turnabout. For the first six years of the Obama presidency, McConnell had "come to embody a kind of oppositional politics that critics say has left voters cynical about Washington, the Senate all but dysfunctional, and the Republican Party without a positive agenda or message," Joshua Green had written in his *Atlantic* profile of McConnell, a description that had held true through 2014.[47] Because McConnell was the cause of the gridlock, once he decided to become a constructive player, the Senate could change overnight. Senate Democrats could gnash their teeth, but McConnell knew he could count on them. By their nature, they wanted government to work and loved to legislate. As Charles Schumer of New York, soon to be the Democratic leader, would say plaintively, "We're Democrats. We cannot just block everything. We believe in government."[48]

At the same time, McConnell remained Obama's nemesis, an insurmountable adversary on the issues that mattered most to him. He systematically blocked Obama's federal court nominations, creating a record number of judicial vacancies.[49] Having already helped to block Obama's effort to legislate a cap-and-trade system to fight climate change, McConnell now waged an imaginative and devastatingly effective attack on Obama's Clean Power Plan, which sought to control emissions through regulatory action. McConnell undoubtedly took great pleasure in working with Republican state attorneys general and with the Harvard Law School professor Laurence Tribe, who had taught Obama constitutional law but was now opposing the Clean Power Plan as "quite literally a power grab" while representing Peabody Energy.[50] "As the iconic left-leaning law professor Laurence Tribe put it," McConnell wrote, "the administration's effort goes 'far beyond its lawful authority.'"[51]

In late November 2015, when 195 nations came to Paris to finalize a global climate change agreement, McConnell issued a stern warning in an op-ed published in the *Washington Post*. "It would obviously be irresponsible," he wrote, "for an outgoing president to purport to sign the American people to international commitments based on a domestic energy plan that is likely illegal, that half the states have sued to halt, that Congress has voted to reject, and that his successor could do away with in a few months."[52]

Clearly proud of what he had accomplished, McConnell published a memoir in early 2016, aptly titled *The Long Game*. Every author hopes to get admiring blurbs for his or her book's dust jacket, but very few could match the endorsements McConnell gathered: George Will, Charles Krauthammer, Walter Isaacson, Jon Meacham, and Doris Kearns Goodwin. Will is a longtime friend of McConnell's, but the praise from the other great biographers and historians was surprising, given the lightweight nature of the memoir. But McConnell was the most powerful Senate majority leader in memory. His wife, Elaine Chao, was one of America's most accomplished women: a former secretary of labor, deputy secretary of transportation, director of the Peace Corps, and president of the United Way. Chao was the daughter of Taiwan's leading shipping magnate, making her and McConnell extremely wealthy. They were one of Washington's leading power couples. Even liberal historians could find a reason to praise the memoir's positive features and ignore its deficiencies.

The memoir was indeed refreshingly candid, engaging, and revealing—the best source of what McConnell was in fact thinking at key moments, and what mattered most to him: winning in politics. But there is not a page in it that shows concern about the people of Kentucky. There is no mention about the fate of coal miners as Kentucky's industry lost ground to western coal and natural gas. Strikingly, McConnell's memoir dripped contempt for President Obama and mocked Nancy Pelosi and Harry Reid, even though all of them were still in office, and he presumably had to work with them on countless vital issues.[53] The book was often disingenuous, replete with half-truths and outright lies; the most partisan Senate leader in memory would berate Obama for his partisanship, even while acknowledging the president's efforts to reach out to Republicans.[54] Having obstructed the Senate for the first six years of Obama's presidency, McConnell praised the first year of his own leadership: "Compared to the legislative graveyard of the prior several years, the new Republican-led Senate looked like an Amazon fulfillment center."[55]

And then, on February 13, 2016, Justice Antonin Scalia, the leading conservative voice on the Supreme Court, died unexpectedly. His death gave President Obama the opportunity to nominate a justice at a time when the court was evenly divided between liberals and conservatives. No issue mattered more to the right wing of the Republican Party than the Supreme Court. The Senate, which had handled many controversial Supreme Court nominations, expected to face one more.

McConnell had shared an office at the Justice Department with Scalia when they were both young lawyers in the Ford administration. Now he responded with extraordinary, even unseemly, speed. About an hour after the announcement of Justice Scalia's death, when other political leaders were expressing condolences, McConnell announced that the Senate would not confirm a replacement for Justice Scalia until after the 2016 presidential election. "The American people should have a voice in the selection of their next Supreme Court justice," McConnell intoned. "Therefore, this vacancy should not be filled until we have a new president."[56]

McConnell did not need time to consult with his caucus because he knew that his Senate Republican colleagues would either agree with him or reluctantly swallow their concerns and go along. He could make the decision alone because only he could balance what he might gain—the Supreme Court seat if a Republican president were elected—against what he might lose: the promising Senate comeback that he had hoped to lead.

"The swiftness of McConnell's statement . . . stunned White House officials who had expected the Kentucky Republican to block their nominee with every tool at his disposal, but didn't imagine the combative GOP leader would issue an instant, categorical rejection of anyone Obama chose to nominate," *Politico* reported.[57] Despite McConnell's statement, there was no precedent for the Senate to refuse to consider a Supreme Court nominee in an election year; it had considered justices nominated by Lyndon Johnson in 1968 and by Ronald Reagan in 1988.

Senator Patrick Leahy of Vermont, the longest-serving senator, blasted McConnell for a blatantly political move when the Senate's calendar appeared to be open most of the summer: "Cancel one of the vacations, one of the recesses," Leahy said. "If this was November, then I could see . . . at least making the argument. But it's February." Charles Grassley, who chaired the Judiciary Committee, brushed Leahy's argument aside. "This president, above all others, has made no bones about his goal to use the courts to circumvent Congress and push through his own agenda," Grassley said. "It only makes sense that we defer to the American people who will elect a new president to select the next Supreme Court Justice."[58]

Legal scholars expressed outrage, pointing out that McConnell's action was unprecedented in American history.[59] The debate became more heated when President Obama nominated Merrick Garland, the universally admired chief judge of the US Court of Appeals for the District of Columbia Circuit, to fill Scalia's seat. Surely, many observers thought, McConnell would not be able to hold his troops together to stonewall an extraordinarily qualified nominee who was known to be moderate in his views.

"The Senate Republicans will sacrifice their majority and their best shot at the White House . . . if they block this nomination," said one Democratic strategist. Many Democrats predicted that McConnell's power play would backfire, by energizing the Democratic base, particularly in key Senate races.[60] Grassley, eighty-two years old, seeking his seventh term in Iowa, seemed uniquely vulnerable. The Democrats found a seemingly formidable candidate, former lieutenant governor Patty Judge, and turned up the heat in their campaign ads.[61]

But McConnell saw things through a different lens. Though he did not expect Donald Trump to win the 2016 presidential election, he saw no reason to give Obama the chance to nominate a justice who would create a liberal majority on the court. With his keen focus on the judiciary, McConnell knew that the issue would galvanize more Republican voters than Democrats, helping Trump and Republican candidates for the Senate. While other establishment Republicans, like Speaker of the House Paul Ryan, might agonize publicly about Trump's bad behavior—particularly his admission that he had groped women—McConnell saw nothing to be gained in criticizing his party's presidential nominee.

McConnell would deliver one more gift to Trump during the election campaign. Trump's inexplicable affection for Vladimir Putin as a private citizen could be rationalized as part of his effort to build a major hotel in Moscow. But as Trump moved inexorably toward the Republican presidential nomination, his defense of Putin and his attacks on America's European allies became more disturbing. Trump also surrounded himself with advisers like Paul Manafort, his campaign chairman, and General Michael Flynn, his senior foreign policy adviser, who had troubling ties with officials close to Putin. The *New York Times* and *Washington Post* carried major stories about a meeting at Trump Tower between senior Trump campaign advisers and representatives of Putin's government.[62] By August, the US intelligence community had found clear evidence of a concerted effort by Russia to interfere in the presidential election, supporting Trump and opposing Hillary Clinton, whom Putin despised.

McConnell, as a member of the congressional leadership, received one of the earliest briefings from the intelligence community about these concerns. In September, Obama requested a meeting with the four congressional leaders, outlined his concerns about the intelligence community's findings, and requested a bipartisan statement expressing anger at the Russian interference in the US presidential election.

Speaker Ryan seemed inclined to join such a statement, but McConnell turned the request down cold and accused Obama of trying to politicize the issue, to benefit Hillary Clinton. He would not provide bipartisan cover for a statement suggesting that Russia was trying to help Trump. McConnell also used the opportunity to attack Obama publicly for his weak policy toward Russia. Two weeks later, he agreed to join a tepid letter to state election officials alerting them to the possibility of foreign interference in the election but not mentioning Russia.[63]

In the end, McConnell triumphed across the board in 2016. It would be hard to identify many votes that were cast or voters who were mobilized for Hillary Clinton or for Democratic Senate candidates because Mitch McConnell had prevented President Obama from nominating a Supreme Court justice. By contrast, McConnell's move galvanized many conservative voters to put aside their misgivings about Donald Trump because of the overriding importance of who would nominate the next Supreme Court justice.[64] Virtually all the close Senate races swung to the Republicans in the end. Grassley won reelection in a landslide.

McConnell's unprecedented action was an exercise of raw political power unmatched in American history. It was a moment that crystallized just how polarized our politics had become and how the institutions and guardrails in our system had eroded. Outrageous acts of partisan obstruction had become normal, and the principal architect of obstruction almost always won.

McConnell had been Republican leader for ten years, and he now stood tall in the wreckage of a broken Senate. He had served as minority leader under a Republican president and a Democratic president, and he had served as majority leader under a Democratic president. In January 2017, he would be majority leader under a Republican president, with his party in control of the White House and both houses of Congress. "You have to remember, it was a pretty grim situation at the beginning of this ten-year period," McConnell recalled. "When I woke up the morning after Election Night 2016, I thought to myself these opportunities don't come along very often. Let's see how we can maximize them."[65]

• *3* •

Handling Trump

$\mathcal{S}$enate majority leaders can be priceless allies to presidents of their own party, particularly those who come to the White House without Washington experience. Virtually every legislative achievement of Jimmy Carter's presidency came about because of the fearsome intelligence, experience, and determination of Robert Byrd. Howard Baker and Bob Dole contributed enormously to Ronald Reagan's successes, although Reagan was blessed with a much stronger White House staff than Carter had. Bill Clinton benefited from George Mitchell's intellect and cunning, and Harry Reid helped carry Obamacare across the finish line against almost insurmountable odds.

From the outset of Trump's presidency, it was likely that Mitch McConnell would play a more powerful role than any of his predecessors. Donald Trump had no Washington experience and no governing experience at all. He had expressed strong views in the presidential campaign but had not defined policies to carry them out. In business, Trump was masterful at branding, but he had proved to be an impulsive, inconsistent decision maker, bludgeoning, bullying, litigating, and lying his way to success, flirting with bankruptcy and disaster. His White House quickly proved to be a chaotic rat's nest of rivals competing for his attention.[1] Trump's daughter Ivanka and his son-in-law Jared Kushner played influential, if undefined, roles in the West Wing, operating outside the supervision of White House chief of staff Reince Priebus, further sowing confusion.

In contrast, McConnell had the breadth and depth of thirty-two years in the US Senate. He had repeatedly proved his remarkable political skill, and he benefited from exercising great control over the fifty-two members of the Republican caucus. No one was more sensitive to the party's donor base, and no one was more influential with it. While many senators put the interests of their states above the national interest, McConnell almost never let the interests of Kentuckians get in the way of his overriding goal: maintaining power for himself and for the Republican Party. Indeed, McConnell was a unique, vertically integrated political force. He played the political long game superbly, not least because he had written the rules. And he would rewrite them whenever necessary to further his objectives.

McConnell would have a new Senate counterpart to deal with. Harry Reid had decided not to seek reelection to the Senate in 2016, and the new Democratic minority leader would be New York senator Chuck Schumer, who had just won his fourth term. Schumer had risen to the position thanks to a superb intellect, prodigious energy, a skill at political messaging, and a zest for schmoozing. Earlier in his career, political observers joked that the most dangerous place to stand in Washington was between Schumer and a television camera. But that image faded over time as Schumer repeatedly proved his seriousness as a legislator, winning $20 billion for New York City after 9/11 and spearheading immigration reform legislation in 2013. Schumer had anticipated working with a president who was his close friend—Hillary Clinton, herself a former senator from New York—and he had expected to be majority leader. Now he would have to deal with a much different New Yorker as president, at a time when the enraged grassroots Democratic resistance to Trump would start from day one.

Schumer also faced the challenge of forging a decent working relationship with McConnell. Schumer had been chairman of the Democratic Senate Campaign Committee in 2008, when the organization ran television ads against McConnell claiming that he had caused the economic meltdown with lax regulation and then bailed out Wall Street.

McConnell, angered by the accusations, held the campaign against Schumer for several years. Now, with no justification, Schumer created new bad blood when he opposed Trump's nomination of Elaine Chao to be secretary of transportation. With her extensive record of accomplishments, Chao faced no serious opposition, and she was confirmed by an overwhelming vote of 93–6, with Schumer casting one of the votes against her. "That was totally uncalled for," said Senator John Thune of South Dakota, a workout buddy of Schumer's and a member of McConnell's leadership team. "I've heard him explain it to me and I still don't understand."[2] Progressive Democratic groups enraged about Trump's election had pressured Schumer to oppose all of the president's cabinet nominees, but he could have brushed that aside in this case. The Senate was counting on the new leadership team to improve on the poisonous dynamic between McConnell and Reid, and Schumer's vote against Chao was not a promising way to start.

McConnell wasted no time in establishing the central governing dynamic of the Trump presidency. Unaccompanied by staff, McConnell visited the president-elect shortly after the election with one item on his agenda: the overriding importance of filling federal judgeships, even at the expense of other priorities, such as confirming Trump's cabinet nominees. McConnell explained to Trump that over the past two years the Republican-controlled Senate had blocked the confirmation of nearly all of Obama's nominees to the federal district and circuit courts, along with blocking Merrick Garland's nomination to the Supreme Court. As a result, Trump would have 105 judicial vacancies to fill, compared to the 54 that Obama had found waiting when he took office in 2009.[3] The long-term consequences were profound. "The thing that would last the longest," McConnell would note later, "is the courts."[4]

Trump needed no convincing. During the 2016 Republican primaries, the evangelical movement and other right-wing conservatives had remained skeptical about Trump's personal behavior and his past politics, which ranged from independent to quite liberal. Don McGahn, a prominent Republican lawyer and a staunchly conservative former member of the Federal Election Commission, had persuaded

Trump that he could win over the doubters by issuing a list of right-wing judges from whom he would choose his Supreme Court nominees if elected. Trump and his advisers saw the benefits of McGahn's idea and readily accepted it. McGahn drew up the list with the advice of the Federalist Society and the Heritage Foundation, two organizations that had long provided the intellectual and financial firepower for the decades-old effort to secure a conservative majority on the Supreme Court.

This seemingly clear plan took months to execute. Assembling the list, McGahn told a friend, "was like juggling chain saws," and Trump wanted to please everyone. McConnell had to intervene, suggesting that the candidate finally "put pen to paper," because "there would be great satisfaction in the conservative community if he made his list public."[5] Ultimately, McGahn's idea had the desired effect, galvanizing the evangelical vote for Trump and guaranteeing the support of the Republican "constitutional" wing. It may have even determined the outcome of the election.

Given that history, Trump welcomed McConnell's postelection initiative to extend conservative control over the lower courts. He also rewarded McGahn with the powerful position of White House counsel, where McGahn, at the urging of McConnell, consolidated the power over the process of nominating federal judges and collaborated with McConnell in confirming them.[6]

Besides the judiciary, McConnell had one other burning priority: the repeal of the Affordable Care Act, which he detested with a passion that he rarely showed for other issues. Nevertheless, he chose not to raise this issue with the president-elect at their initial meeting. During the campaign, when Trump spoke about health care, he called the ACA a "big lie" and a "disaster," but he often sounded disturbingly liberal on the stump. Trump vowed to protect not only Social Security and Medicare but also Medicaid, which had become an increasingly vital safety net for Trump's white working-class base.[7] Trump also had a long history of statements supporting universal coverage. "I'm very liberal when it comes to health care. I believe in universal health care," he had said in a 1999 interview with Larry King.[8]

Trump would need to be educated about the importance of gutting the Affordable Care Act, and for this task McConnell was likely to find a strong ally in Priebus. Having just finished a successful tenure as chairman of the Republican National Committee, Priebus understood the importance of this issue to the Koch brothers and other key Republican donors. Coming out of Wisconsin Republican politics, Priebus was also a close friend and political ally of Speaker of the House Paul Ryan, ensuring constant communication and likely coordination between the Republican White House and Congress.

Before long, McConnell was either satisfied that Trump had abandoned his campaign position or confident that he would do so.[9] On January 11, nine days before Trump took office, McConnell led the Senate to approve a budget resolution, by a vote of 51–48, that would become the vehicle for considering the repeal of the Affordable Care Act.[10] In an emotional end to the debate, the Democrats kept speaking, one after the other, during the roll call. "Ripping apart our health care system—with no plan to replace it—will create chaos," declared Washington's Patty Murray, the ranking Democrat on health issues. "If Republicans repeal the Affordable Care Act, it's women, kids, seniors, patients with serious illnesses, and patients with disabilities who will bear the burden."[11]

McConnell would have to deal with Trump's priorities as well. There was a diamond-hard, substantive core to Trump's message: economic nationalism. He had been sounding this theme since 1987; "the image of the rest of the world laughing at U.S. leaders would become an enduring theme of Trump's political rhetoric," wrote his biographers Michael Kranish and Marc Fisher.[12] During the campaign, Trump pledged to withdraw the United States from the Trans-Pacific Partnership Agreement (TPP), and he did so on his third day in office. McConnell, a strong TPP supporter, knew that this was a disastrous policy choice, devastating America's position in the Asia-Pacific region at a time when China's rise was putting pressure on America's allies. But most progressive Democrats had fiercely opposed TPP; the anti-trade sentiment was strong enough to force Hillary Clinton, who once called it the "gold standard" of trade agreements, to reverse her position during the 2016 presidential campaign. If Trump had bipartisan support for anything, it was for abandoning TPP.

The other major pillar of Trump's agenda was border security. No campaign pledge resonated with his base as much as his promise to "build a beautiful wall on the southern border and have Mexico pay for it."[13] He excoriated immigrants from Mexico as "criminals, rapists, and drug dealers."[14] He also capitalized on fears about attacks on the US homeland to support a ban on immigrants and refugees from predominantly Muslim countries.[15] Trump went beyond incendiary rhetoric by nominating Senator Jeff Sessions of Alabama, the fiercest opponent to immigration in the Senate, to serve as attorney general. No one doubted that a harsh policy would follow, and on January 27 Trump signed an executive order to block entry and to restrict travel from seven majority-Muslim nations and restrict travel by US permanent residents and citizens with dual nationalities.[16]

The Senate Republicans now faced their first test of loyalty to their new president, and, to their credit, they pushed back strongly against what quickly became known as "the Muslim ban." Arizona's John McCain and South Carolina's Lindsey Graham, working together as they often did, issued a statement calling the travel ban "a self-inflicted wound." "Our government has a responsibility to defend our borders, but we must do it in a way that makes us safer and upholds all that is decent and exceptional about our nation," they stated.[17]

Ben Sasse of Nebraska thought the overly broad executive order would help terrorist recruiters,[18] and Rob Portman of Ohio criticized the travel ban as well. (Cincinnati, his hometown and traditionally moderately Republican, quickly declared itself a sanctuary city.)[19] Lamar Alexander of Tennessee stated that "while it is not explicitly a religious test, it comes close to one, which is inconsistent with our national character."[20] For his part, McConnell said that he considered a Muslim ban "completely and totally inconsistent with American values. . . . We don't have religious tests in this country."[21]

In the coming weeks, in the face of political opposition and adverse federal court rulings, Trump would pull back and modify the executive order, but McConnell knew that border security would be a festering issue throughout Trump's presidency. In 2013, the Senate, working with the Obama administration, had passed a comprehensive immigration reform bill, strengthening border security and creating a path to citizenship for eleven million immigrants living in the shadows. This was a monumental achievement, negotiated by a bipartisan "Gang of Eight" senators (with McConnell nowhere in sight), but the House Republicans had refused to take up the bill, and the moment of opportunity had passed. Since then, populist resistance to immigrants and migrants had become the most bitterly divisive issue for many wealthy countries around the world. With Trump in the White House and public attitudes changing, legislation on the 2013 model was beyond imagination.

As McConnell surveyed the political landscape, he saw real danger only in one area: Trump's relationship with Russia. Throughout 2016, the evidence had mounted that Russia had conducted a massive campaign of "active measures" to influence the presidential election in favor of Trump, and now that Trump was in office, the issue would not go away. McCain and Graham, who detested Putin's Russia, had joined the Democrats in demanding a Senate investigation.

From McConnell's standpoint, the quickest way for Trump to recover from the travel ban debacle and to divert attention away from his relationship with Russia was to act like a president and do something historic, which would have the added value of angering and demoralizing the Democrats. It was time to nominate a Supreme Court justice to fill the vacancy that McConnell had kept open for nearly a year.

On January 31, Donald Trump had his first presidential moment on prime-time television, introducing the nation to Judge Neil Gorsuch, his nominee for the Supreme Court.[22] Only forty-nine years old, Gorsuch had already served ten years on the Tenth Circuit Court of Appeals, based in Denver. Educated at Columbia and Harvard Law School (where he was a classmate of Barack Obama) and then Oxford, Gorsuch had clerked for Supreme Court Justice Anthony Kennedy. He was respected for the clarity of his thinking, his lively writing, and his judicial demeanor. Gorsuch was also, by any measure, a judge with a very conservative philosophy, an originalist in the mold of Justice Scalia. One study concluded that he was more conservative than 87 percent of the other federal judges; another study found Gorsuch to be even more conservative than Justice Samuel Alito or the late Justice Scalia—as far right, it seemed, as a federal judge could possibly be.[23]

Most Democrats viewed Gorsuch as an extreme right-wing jurist. But with the exception of Robert Bork in 1987, the Senate did not reject Supreme Court nominees on the basis of ideology. Senate Democrats and grassroots Democrats were still seething at the treatment that McConnell had given to Merrick Garland the year before. "This is the first time that a Senate majority leader has stolen a seat," said Senator Jeff Merkley of Oregon. "We will do everything in our power to stop this nomination."[24]

Mitch McConnell could have told Merkley that there was nothing in his power, or the power of the Democrats, to stop the Gorsuch nomination. Back in 2013, Harry Reid had used the "nuclear option" to make federal judgeships other than the Supreme Court subject to majority approval, without recourse to the filibuster. As sure as night follows day, McConnell would move to extend the nuclear option to Supreme Court justices in order to get Gorsuch confirmed. McConnell immensely enjoyed reminding the Democrats that they had brought this on themselves. He only had to hold his Republicans together, and Gorsuch had sterling credentials and a sprinkling of liberal endorsements, including one from Neal K. Katyal, who had been acting solicitor general in the Obama administration.[25]

It is impossible to overstate the dedication of the key elements of the Republican Party to lock in a right-wing majority on the Supreme Court. The effort had begun in 1969, when Richard Nixon came to the White House with a commitment to reverse the liberal tide of decisions under the Supreme Court of Chief Justice Earl Warren.[26] Circumstances allowed Nixon to place four justices on the court—Chief Justice Warren Burger and Associate Justices Harry Blackmun, Lewis Powell, and William Rehnquist—even though the Senate rejected two of Nixon's nominees, Clement Haynsworth and G. Harrold Carswell. Nixon's record also began the long period of mounting Republican frustration when Blackmun evolved into a liberal justice (he was the author of the majority opinion in *Roe v. Wade*), and Powell, a pre-eminent corporate lawyer, turned out to be a fair-minded conservative who often came down on the side of civil liberties.

A lasting pattern was set. The Supreme Court would become markedly more conservative than the Warren court had been, as Republican presidents would fill twelve of the next fourteen Supreme Court vacancies. But somehow these nominations were never enough to satisfy the "constitutionalists," as the Republican conservative legal community liked to call itself.[27] At different times, they would be enraged by what they saw as the betrayals not only by Blackmun and Powell but also by John Paul Stevens (appointed by Gerald Ford), Sandra Day O'Connor and Anthony Kennedy (appointed by Ronald Reagan), and David Souter (appointed by George H. W. Bush), all of whom turned out to be fair-minded but not ideologically conservative justices. In 2012, the "constitutionalists" even turned their wrath on Chief Justice John Roberts, whose nomination had thrilled them, because he had the temerity to join a majority opinion that the Affordable Care Act was constitutional.[28] Despite all the justices appointed by Republican presidents, the legal right wing could not get everything it wanted because its reading of the Constitution was so extreme. Now, finally, with Trump elected, the list made public, McGahn in the West Wing, and McConnell driving the train, it would no longer be denied.

"The Senate confirmation process of Supreme Court justices has always been cabined by norms of behavior and unwritten rules," Stanford Law professor Nathaniel Persily commented shortly after Gorsuch's nomination. "With the failure to even hold a hearing on Garland, the norms have all gone out the windows." He predicted that the Democrats "now feel emboldened to try anything."[29]

Indeed, the Gorsuch hearings never could escape the cloud created by McConnell's refusal to hold such hearings for Garland. Every Democrat on the Judiciary Committee mentioned the "unprecedented treatment" of the Garland nomination; even some Republicans acknowledged that the Democrats had good reason to be upset.[30] Gorsuch, as expected, handled the hearings well; he was prepared, amicable, knowledgeable, and often folksy. Like previous right-wing justices, he proclaimed himself to be a fair-minded judge, favoring no party above the law, and he avoided commenting on any controversial legal issue or even offering a view on established Supreme Court precedents.[31]

No one disputed Gorsuch's competence; the focus had shifted to the political battle. McConnell had fifty-two Republican votes but could not possibly find eight Democrats to give him sixty, allowing him to invoke cloture and cut off debate. There was no compromise possible; Schumer was committed to fighting the nomination with a filibuster, and McConnell was determined to get Gorsuch confirmed. Weeks before, McConnell had named the date on which Gorsuch would be confirmed: April 7. On April 6, with Schumer powerless to do anything, McConnell read the series of formulaic statements that allowed him to change the Senate rules to lower the threshold for confirming a Supreme Court justice to a simple majority. "When history weighs what happened, the responsibility will fall on the Republicans' and Leader McConnell's shoulders," Schumer commented bitterly. "They have had other choices, and they have chosen this one."[32]

McConnell, unsurprisingly, saw the history quite differently. "This is the latest escalation of the left's never ending judicial war, the most audacious yet," he responded, after describing the Democrats' opposition to the nominations of Robert Bork in 1987 and Clarence Thomas in 1991. And it cannot and will not stand. There cannot be two standards: one for the nominees of Democratic presidents and another for the nominees of Republican presidents." McConnell could be seen exchanging exuberant "high fives" with Republican senators.[33] The next day, as McConnell had predicted and orchestrated, the Senate elevated Judge Neil Gorsuch to the Supreme Court by a 54–45 vote.

Having filled the vacancy that he had created, McConnell understandably took a victory lap. He was an ungracious winner, and his trips down memory lane were always a mix of fact and fiction. Although the Republican "constitutionalists" never stopped revisiting the Bork fight, every Supreme Court nominee since that time, except for Clarence Thomas, had been confirmed smoothly—until McConnell's obstructionism against Barack Obama and Merrick Garland.

In truth, Gorsuch's confirmation was inevitable, and the substitution of one qualified, extreme conservative justice for another did not alter the ideological balance of the court. Democrats were angry at McConnell for his unprecedented act of hardball against Garland, and they were angry at themselves as well. Brian Fallon, the former press secretary to Hillary Clinton's 2016 presidential campaign, had founded a political action committee, Demand Justice, after Trump's election. "Our goal," Fallon stated, "is to correct for the apathy and complacency that you saw among progressives when it comes to the Court and judges that you saw in 2016."[34] Democrats had never matched the Republicans' laser focus on the importance of the courts; with one Trump justice confirmed, the party's alliance with the Federalist Society and the Heritage Foundation was in high gear, looking forward to future fights to lock in a right-wing majority on the court.[35]

Midway through the fourth month of the Trump presidency, the cabinet was in place and Justice Gorsuch was confirmed, the House was moving ahead with legislation to repeal the Affordable Care Act, trilateral negotiations to modify the North American Free Trade Agreement (NAFTA) had begun, and the stock market was booming. All was right in the Republican world.

This period of calm and Republicans' fleeting hope for a somewhat normal presidency ended abruptly on May 10 when Trump fired James Comey, the high-profile and controversial FBI director.[36] The firing came shortly after Comey had requested additional resources to pursue the investigation of Russian interference in the 2016 presidential election,[37] but the White House claimed that Trump had acted in accordance with a recommendation by Deputy Attorney General Rod Rosenstein. The next day, Trump admitted that that he had already decided to fire Comey before hearing from Rosenstein because of "the Russia thing."[38]

One bombshell revelation followed another. The day after sacking Comey, Trump met in the Oval Office with Sergei V. Lavrov, Russia's foreign minister, and Sergey Kislyak, the Russian ambassador to the United States, excluding American press but allowing the Russian state news agency Tass to attend and take photographs. It was soon reported that Trump had revealed sensitive intelligence information in the meeting and described Comey as a "nut job," saying explicitly that removing Comey had reduced the pressure on Trump from the Russia probe.[39] Comey's firing immediately raised the question of whether the president had committed obstruction of justice, given his admission about why he had acted. Trump's shocking dealings with Russia, our leading adversary—at least the tip of the iceberg—were playing out in full sight.

In past crises involving potentially serious abuse of power by presidents, the Senate had stepped forward strongly. Bob Woodward and Carl Bernstein broke their blockbuster stories on Watergate in the fall of 1972; in January 1973, the Senate unanimously agreed to establish a select committee to investigate the issue, even though Richard Nixon had just won reelection in a forty-nine-state landslide. After revelations had emerged in November 1986 that the Reagan administration had sold arms to Iran and illegally funneled the profits to the Nicaraguan "contras," the Senate in January 1987 again unanimously created a select committee to investigate this scandal. Serious threats to the constitutional order and the country always transcended politics.

This time, again, the Senate responded strongly. Bipartisan concern about Russian interference in the presidential election had surfaced as far back as December. Schumer joined Jack Reed of Rhode Island, the ranking Democrat on the Armed Services Committee, and John McCain and Lindsey Graham in calling for the creation of a select committee to investigate. "Only a select committee that is time-limited, cross-jurisdictional and purpose-driven can address the challenges of cyber," they wrote.[40]

Schumer's involvement was a rookie mistake by the new Democratic leader, giving the request a partisan appearance that allowed McConnell to brush it aside, suggesting that any inquiry would more appropriately be handled by the Intelligence Committee.[41] Richard Burr and Mark Warner, the Republican chairman and Democratic ranking member of the Senate Intelligence Committee, immediately began to assemble a staff for the investigation.[42]

By itself, Russian interference in the presidential campaign, with the intent to undermine our institutions and affect the outcome, posed an unprecedented challenge to American democracy. The mounting evidence of Russian collusion with Trump's presidential campaign made the situation more ominous. Now, with the campaign over, the president was openly consorting with Russia's senior diplomats and telling them—and the world—why he had fired the troublesome FBI director who was investigating his conduct. "There is a smell of treason in the air," said Douglas Brinkley, a leading presidential historian.[43]

Deputy Attorney General Rosenstein, under stinging criticism from Capitol Hill for having been used by Trump, responded strongly by appointing Robert Mueller, a former director of the FBI, to serve as special counsel supervising an investigation into Russia's interference in the election and any possible connection to Trump or his campaign. Mueller's stature and integrity produced a rare moment of universal agreement that Rosenstein had made a superb choice, ensuring that the investigation would be full and fair.[44] It should have also provided a respite to Trump, who was about to make his first foreign trip.

But even as the president made headlines on successful visits to Saudi Arabia and Israel, the *Washington Post* reported that Trump had separately called Dan Coats, the director of national intelligence, and Michael Rogers, the head of the National Security Agency, and asked each man whether he could get the FBI to stop its investigation. As Jeffrey Smith, a former general counsel to the CIA, quickly noted, Trump's action mirrored precisely what Richard Nixon had done on June 23, 1972, when he asked the CIA to block the FBI investigation into the break-in at the Democratic National Committee headquarters in the Watergate. The tape recording of Nixon's statement became the "smoking gun," clear evidence of obstruction of justice that prompted Senate Republicans to abandon Nixon, bringing about his resignation.[45] This time, the revelation prompted no response from McConnell or any of the other Republicans in the Senate.

As Mueller began staffing his investigation, the Senate moved forward forcefully, with the Intelligence and Judiciary Committees

competing to see which would get Comey to tell his story in public.[46] McConnell, who had initially mocked the Democrats for "complaining about the removal of an FBI director whom they themselves
had repeatedly and sharply criticized," changed his tune, saying that
Comey should testify publicly as soon as possible.[47] "Lawmakers can
barely hide their ambition about landing what would be a grand media
spectacle," the *Washington Post* observed.[48]

Since the advent of television, Senate hearings had produced
many of America's most dramatic political moments. And on June 8,
Comey did not disappoint. An experienced witness at ease in the hot
seat, he offered a detailed, vivid depiction of five instances of President
Trump's demanding "loyalty" and pressuring him to "let Mike Flynn
go," a reference to the FBI's investigation of Trump's former national
security adviser and his questionable ties to Russian intelligence during the presidential campaign and the transition period. Comey said
the president had "lied, pure and simple" in saying that the FBI was
in disarray and that the agents had lost confidence in him, the president's stated rationale for firing Comey. He said that he had prepared
contemporaneous memos of his conversations with Trump, which he
never felt the need to do when dealing with the other presidents under
whom he had served. He acknowledged turning over the memos to
Mueller, suggesting that the special counsel would be investigating
Trump for possible obstruction of justice.

On June 13, five days after Comey's testimony, the Senate demonstrated its implacable anger toward Putin's Russia and its deep distrust
of Trump by approving, by a vote of 98–2, legislation strengthening
sanctions on Russia and making it impossible for Trump to weaken
the sanctions without congressional approval. The measure directed
sanctions toward Russia's defense and intelligence apparatus as well as
parts of its energy, mining, railways, and shipping economy. It aimed
to punish Russia not only for its interference in the US presidential
election but also for its annexation of Crimea in 2014, its continuing
military activity in eastern Ukraine, and its human rights abuses.[49]

'Trump strongly objected to the sanctions, saying that they
encroached on his ability to conduct foreign policy.[50] Sanctions are a

frequently used—indeed, overused—tool of American foreign policy, but limiting the president's ability to suspend or terminate the sanctions was a striking departure from normal practice. David Ignatius, one of the most respected commentators on national security issues, wrote, "If this were any president other than Trump, and any antagonist but Russia, Trump's argument would have carried more weight."[51] But given Trump's firing of Comey, and following the ominous revelations before that, the Senate recognized a four-alarm constitutional fire and responded with the requisite urgency. Between the sanctions, the Senate committee investigations, and Mueller's work, it appeared that the public could be confident that Trump's accommodating stance toward Russia would be fully investigated.

For those who recalled the Senate at its best and understood its special role in our constitutional framework, the response was heartening. McConnell could rightfully judge that his Senate had stepped up. He could also breathe a sigh of relief that the course of any Senate investigation would not resemble the summer of 1973, when the hearings of the Senate Watergate Committee riveted America week after week. The investigations would proceed quietly, out of the public eye, allowing the work of government, and the pursuit of Republican objectives, to go on unimpeded.

Indeed, six months into the Trump presidency, Republicans willing to look past Trump's Russia connection and aberrational behavior could find evidence to convince themselves that traditional Republican policies were being advanced under the Trump administration. Senate Republicans, led by Orrin Hatch and Chuck Grassley, had joined the business community in pushing back strongly against Trump's threat to pull the United States out of NAFTA, and Trump now seemed to be calmer about Mexico, or at least willing to channel his anger toward building the border wall rather than blowing up NAFTA. North American supply chains, essential to virtually every large company, were no longer facing imminent threat of disruption. The business community also strongly supported the administration's push for deregulation of protections for the environment, consumers, and workers. They looked forward to the tax reform legislation that

Treasury Secretary Steven Mnuchin was spearheading, and Trump's promise of a massive infrastructure program.

However, two Republican senators, who had every incentive to resolve their doubts about Trump in his favor, simply could not do it. Jeff Flake is a fifth-generation Arizonian, from a ranching family, whose politics were inspired by his hero, Barry Goldwater. A deeply religious person, raised as a Mormon, Flake had attended Brigham Young University and served two years as a missionary in South Africa and Zimbabwe. Before entering politics, he had been the executive director of the Goldwater Institute, a think tank committed to advancing Goldwater's principles including free markets, open trade, liberal immigration policy, and strong national defense. Flake was elected to the House of Representatives in 2000, and after six terms there, he won a Senate seat in 2012. Immediately after reaching the Senate, Flake became one of "the Gang of Eight," the bipartisan group negotiating the comprehensive immigration legislation that the Senate passed in 2013.

Like many Republicans, Jeff Flake spoke out strongly against Donald Trump before he was nominated. In June 2016, Flake said, "We can't support a candidate who will do to the Hispanic vote what has been done to the African-American vote for Republicans going forward."[52] After Trump was nominated, Flake continued to speak out, issuing this tweet: "America deserves far better than @Donald Trump. . . . Republicans should not be okay with @Donald Trump threatening to jail his opponent after the election . . . @Donald Trump saying that he might not accept election results is beyond the pale."

Unlike other Republicans who turned 180 degrees as soon as Trump won the presidency, Flake continued to be appalled by Trump's conduct. In July 2017, borrowing the title of Goldwater's classic 1960 manifesto, *Conscience of a Conservative*, Flake published a book without precedent in American politics: a US senator attacking a newly elected president of his own party. He began the book by noting that Trump "has a regular habit of destabilizing the American people, not just foreign leaders," and he denounced "the embrace of 'alternative facts' at the highest levels of America life," which "creates a state of confusion, dividing us along fissures of truth and falsity and keeping us in a kind of low-level dread."

Flake's statement of conscience pinpointed the special responsibility that he and other Republican senators carried. "Under our Constitution, there simply are not that many people who are in a position to do something about an executive branch in chaos," Flake wrote. "Too often we observe the unfolding drama along with the rest of the country, passively, all but saying: '*Somebody should do something*' without seeming to realize that that someone is us."[53]

In October, having enraged Trump and his Arizona Republican base, Flake announced that he would not seek reelection in 2018. "None of these appalling features of our current politics should ever be regarded as normal," he stated. "We must not allow ourselves to lapse into thinking that this is just the way things are now. If we simply become inured to this condition, thinking this is just politics as usual, then heaven help us."[54]

Perhaps Flake's Republican colleagues could dismiss him as an earnest, unrealistic moralistic backbencher; he had, after all, been a missionary in his youth. Bob Corker, however, was a different case: a successful builder who had been mayor of Chattanooga before being elected to the Senate from Tennessee in 2006. Corker had risen to become chairman of the Foreign Relations Committee—one of the four most prestigious Senate chairmanships—just eight years after coming to the Senate, which was a modern record. Consequently, Corker was a much more powerful senator than Flake, and focused intently on national security issues. He, too, spoke out publicly against Trump.

In May 2017, after the Oval Office meeting with the Russian foreign minister and the Russian ambassador, Corker expressed regret that "a really good national security team" was being undermined by the "chaos and lack of discipline" of the president. In August, Corker said that Trump "has not been able to demonstrate the stability, nor some of the competence that he needs to demonstrate in order to be successful."[55] In October, in a *New York Times* interview, Corker escalated his criticism: Trump was treating his office "like a reality show" with "reckless threats toward other countries" that could set the nation "on the path to World War III. . . . He concerns me. He would have to concern anyone who cares about the nation."[56]

In interviews with CNN and ABC's *Good Morning America* on October 24, Corker suggested he would convene hearings to examine the ways that President Trump "has purposely been breaking down relationships around the world. . . . He's obviously not going to rise to the occasion as president." If his own concerns as chairman of the Senate Foreign Relations Committee were not enough, Corker stated, "Except for a few people, the vast majority of our caucus . . . understands the volatility that we're dealing with here."[57]

Critics would say that Flake could have sought reelection as an independent, and that Corker should have run again, particularly given his prominent Senate chairmanship. But the positions they expressed were extraordinary—true profiles in courage. They undoubtedly hoped that other Republican senators would follow their lead, but the silence was deafening.

The danger posed by President Trump to our nation was crystal clear to Flake and Corker, and undoubtedly to other Senate Republicans who chose to stay silent. McConnell, an experienced hand in national security matters, undoubtedly shared many of these concerns, but he saw no point in publicly attacking a Republican president. He would instead offer private counsel to Trump and rely on the "adults in the room"—Defense Secretary James Mattis, National Security Adviser H. R. McMaster, and Chief of Staff John Kelly—to make sure that Trump did not run wild on the global stage.

McConnell's North Star remained unchanged: keeping the Senate majority. Flake could not win reelection in Arizona after his extraordinary attacks on Trump. Corker might have been able to win another term in Tennessee, but the state had become increasingly conservative, so another Republican without Corker's anti-Trump baggage would be able to hold the seat. Moreover, McConnell personally disliked Corker, who, next to McCain, was his most persistent pain in the ass. As a new senator in 2007, Corker had tried to take the lead on promoting bipartisan financial regulation; McConnell had had to slap him down, and neither of them ever forgot it.[58]

As the summer of 2017 approached, the time had come for McConnell's second priority (other than judges): repealing the hated Affordable Care Act. Here he had a steeper path to climb. Seven years after the law's passage, millions of previously uninsured Americans were now covered by health insurance. Key provisions of the ACA had also proved to be very popular. Requiring insurers to cover people with preexisting conditions was a godsend to millions. Allowing parents to keep their adult children on their insurance until age twenty-six constituted a meaningful benefit for many families. Making health insurance portable so that people could leave their jobs while still keeping their health care provided an enormous relief to workers and their families while making the economy more dynamic.[59]

Nor would it be easy for the Republicans to improve upon the ACA. "In drafting his health care plan, Barack Obama chose a moderate, market-based approach," the *New York Times* columnist David Leonhardt reminded his readers. "It was to the right of Bill Clinton's and Richard Nixon's plans, and way to the right of Harry Truman's. And yet the Republicans still wouldn't support it. The version that passed did not leave the Republicans much room to maneuver."[60]

With Donald Trump in the White House, the Republicans would now get their chance to repeal "Obamacare." They confronted the problem that once people faced the stark reality of losing the benefits they had gained, the ACA became even more popular. An Urban Institute report concluded that if the ACA were repealed, the number of uninsured Americans would rise from twenty-nine million to fifty-nine million within two years.[61] The Tea Party and the Republicans had played the fear card in opposing Obamacare in 2009 and 2010; now the law's defenders had the fear card on their side.

The House of Representatives, led by Speaker Ryan, would go first. Ryan's predecessor as speaker, John Boehner, had opposed the Affordable Care Act's passage in 2010, but even he was dubious about the Republicans' ability to build a new health-care system on the fly. "In the twenty-five years I served in the Congress, the Republicans never ever, one time, agreed on what a health care proposal should look like—not once," Boehner observed. "And if you pass repeal without replace, anything that happens is your fault. You broke it."[62] But Boehner's insight did not matter. "This is existential for Republicans," said David McIntosh, a former House member from Indiana who was now president of the Club for Growth. "If you don't repeal Obamacare and replace it, I don't think you'll stay in the majority in the next election."[63]

Ryan knew that the House Democrats would unanimously oppose Obamacare repeal, and so he had to hold virtually every House Republican, and there were still a group of Republican moderates who would not support blowing up the health-care system. But after several weeks of intense horse-trading, on May 4, by a narrow vote of 217–213, the House of Representatives passed the American Health Care Act, redeeming its pledge to remake the American health-care system without mandated insurance coverage. The extreme nature of the House legislation produced "a rare unifying moment," as doctors, hospitals, insurers, and consumer groups all expressed immediate, vehement opposition. "This is not a reform," said Michael Dowling, the chief executive of Northwell Health, a large health-care system in New York. "It is just a debacle."[64]

The action now shifted to the Senate. A complex policy issue, with impact on virtually every American, with profound political impact—it was hard to remember an issue that so deeply engaged so many senators. At least ten Republicans, led by Susan Collins, a former state insurance commissioner in Maine; Bill Cassidy of Louisiana, a physician; and Lamar Alexander, the chairman of the Health, Education, Labor and Pensions Committee, appropriately known as HELP, began floating ideas and alternative bills.

In mid-May, six Republicans sat down with three moderate Democrats and began to hammer out legislation. They shared an understanding that only a bipartisan solution would work. "I don't think there is a Democrat who would vote for repeal," said one of those Democrats, Joe Manchin of West Virginia. "But I think there are forty-eight Democrats who are willing to work on some repairing or fixing."[65]

One immovable object stood in the way of a bipartisan legislative fix: Mitch McConnell. The majority leader had given memorable speeches in 2014 and 2015 about how the Senate was the place where the parties came together to forge bipartisan agreements that would command broad support. But he made those speeches when Obama was president. Now that Trump, a Republican, was in the White House, McConnell saw no need for bipartisanship. He took a back-seat to no one in his hatred of the ACA, which he termed the "worst piece of legislation he had ever seen," and if the Democrats would not vote for repeal, he would repeal the law without them. The lesson that McConnell drew from the debacle on the House side was that stronger leadership—his—could produce a better bill and repeal the ACA on a strictly partisan basis.[66]

McConnell formed a task force of thirteen Republican senators to hammer out a bill. He excluded all five Republican women, even though three of them—Susan Collins, Lisa Murkowski, and Shelley Moore Capito—had already shown deep interest in the issue.[67] McConnell's "process" envisioned no hearings, no committee action, and, in fact, very little public exposure of the legislation being cobbled together. Speed and stealth were the essence of the strategy; McConnell promised to issue a discussion draft on June 22 and to hold a Senate vote before the July 4 recess. He sought to ram through the legislation before any of the affected constituencies could rally against it.[68] It was an astonishing approach. Experienced observers could think of no case where the Senate had dispensed with hearings on an important issue, and no issue affected more Americans than this one.

Although the Obama administration had failed to educate the public well about the ACA when it was under consideration in Congress, it very effectively mobilized support for the legislation from a wide range of affected constituencies. The ACA had become law because it had won support from insurers, hospitals, doctors, nurses, pharmaceutical companies, consumer groups, patient advocates, and senior citizens. They were invested in it; they would oppose repeal or significant changes. They would also oppose a legislative process in which they were not serious participants.

Exasperated Republican senators were pushing back as well. It was one thing to follow the majority leader in a partisan battle, but here he was asking his caucus to fall in line for legislation that would do harm to millions of their constituents. "Do you know what the health care bill looks like?" Murkowski asked reporters. "Because I don't."[69] Utah's Mike Lee, a member of the task force, complained that he didn't know what was in the bill; "it's not being written by us. It's apparently been written but apparently by a small handful of staffers in the Republican leadership."[70] Jennifer Steinhauer of the *New York Times* observed that "without hearings, committee work, or a public drafting of the bill— all marks of the original health care law—members on both sides of the [Republican] divide felt bruised and left out."[71]

McConnell's discussion "draft," released on schedule on June 22, satisfied virtually no one. The bill's prospects, already dim, worsened when the Congressional Budget Office estimated that twenty-two million additional Americans would become uninsured over the next decade than under current law.[72]

With the reality of the legislation's effects now apparent, Republicans began to defect. Collins stated her opposition first, diplomatically saying that McConnell had "done his best," but she would have handled it differently.[73] Dean Heller of Nevada, the most vulnerable Senate Republican up for reelection in 2018, joined his state's Republican governor in denouncing the bill.[74] Rob Portman of Ohio and Shelley Moore Capito of West Virginia expressed concern about the deep cuts in Medicaid proposed by McConnell's bill.[75] Jerry Moran of Kansas said that he could not support the bill as written and called for a "national debate that includes legislative hearings. It needs to be less politics and more policy." At the same time, Rand Paul of Kentucky and Ron Johnson of Wisconsin attacked the bill for containing too little reform; Paul called it "Obamacare-lite."[76] Temper fraying, McConnell, usually unflappable, lashed out at Portman, chiding him for abandoning the commitment to entitlement reform that he had favored when he had served as budget director for President George W. Bush.[77] Taking fire from both sides, McConnell wisely concluded that the time was not right to move forward before the July 4 recess.

It was a striking moment. McConnell, the supposed institutionalist, proposed to repeal the Affordable Care Act by jettisoning every traditional aspect of legislating and every commitment he had made about restoring "regular order." McConnell often seemed to care about nothing other than keeping power for himself and the Republicans, but he held some strong views. His anger at Portman was genuine; he believed the rate of entitlement growth was unsustainable, particularly the explosive growth of Medicaid. He hated the fact that under the ACA, the federal government would assume the overwhelming share of the responsibility for Medicaid in those states that chose to accept the funds provided by the legislation.

McConnell showed no concern that many state budgets were buckling under the weight of Medicaid costs, or that Medicaid had become the essential provider of health care for the working poor, which included much of Trump's political base and a significant part of the population of Kentucky, one of the nation's poorest states. McConnell's obsession with the ACA and his desire for a Republican victory seemed to blind him to the magnitude of the issue and its impact on the people represented by the Republican caucus. During his long tenure as leader, McConnell had routinely sacrificed the Senate in pursuit of his partisan objectives. But he had not previously asked Republican senators to walk the plank in so blatant and public a way.

On July 17, McConnell conceded that "the effort to repeal and immediately replace the failed Obamacare will not be successful." Instead, he would ask the Senate to repeal the ACA now and work to replace it over the next two years.[78] This was another jaw-dropping idea; would McConnell really compound his failure by forcing his caucus to cast a vote that would cause chaos in the health-care system?

Having seemingly admitted defeat, McConnell regrouped to mount an enormous, all-out offensive. He probably concluded that he had no choice. The Koch brothers and the network of groups they financed were determined to shred the ACA, and they formed a key part of the Republican donor base. Paul Ryan, a weak leader, had rammed a bill through the House, and Trump was goading the Senate Republicans to act. McConnell, the strongest leader in memory, did not like to show any evidence of weakness. Circumstances combined to produce a moment of extraordinary drama for the Senate and the country.

On July 25, John McCain returned to the Senate after eye surgery that had revealed the same incurable brain cancer that had taken the life of another Senate giant, Ted Kennedy, during the 2009 fight to pass the ACA. With almost every senator present in the chamber, McCain gave an impassioned speech in which he repeatedly disparaged McConnell's terrible process, predicted that the current effort would fail, and urged a return to "regular order": legislating through hearings and a thoughtful committee process.

He then broadened his comments to reflect on the increasingly tribal and fractured nature of the Senate. "We've been spinning our wheels on too many important issues," McCain declared, "because we keep trying to win without help from across the aisle." He talked about the importance of things other than winning: "incremental progress," "compromise," and "just muddling through."[79]

Unmoved by McCain's logic, passion, or courage, McConnell pressed the Senate to vote on one version of repeal after another, repeatedly falling short of the fifty votes needed for passage. (Vice President Mike Pence would then provide the tiebreaking fifty-first vote.) McConnell's last-gasp effort was an eight-page "skinny repeal" that abolished the mandate for individuals and employers to buy insurance, as well as some of the taxes that funded the ACA. The "skinny repeal" immediately received scathing criticism from many senators. Lindsey Graham called it a "disaster" and a "fraud" and said he would only vote for it if Paul Ryan agreed that the House would not accept it and that the legislation coming back from conference would be much different.[80] The Republican health-care drive had come full circle; the idea of the Senate improving the House bill was a distant memory. Still, McConnell, counting votes closely, thought he would get the fifty votes he needed.

Events conspired to make Thursday, July 27, one of the most memorable nights in Senate history, when a decision of enormous political consequence combined with a moment of tremendous emotional power. John McCain, dying of brain cancer, but holding the deciding vote, came to the Senate floor after midnight, talked to several of his colleagues, and, when his time to vote came, flashed a thumbs-down, joining Collins and Murkowski in defecting from McConnell, to defeat the "skinny repeal" by a 51–49 vote. McConnell, tight-lipped and face flushed, took the floor to offer an understated observation: "This is clearly a disappointing moment." He then criticized the Democrats for not participating in a process from which they had been completely excluded.[81]

The "blame game" for the Republican debacle began quickly. On August 7, McConnell made a speech in Louisville in which he observed that President Trump, "who has not been in this line of work," had "excessive expectations" about the speed with which Congress could pass major legislation. This matter-of-fact observation enraged the thin-skinned president, who blasted out in a series of tweets, suggesting that if McConnell could not deliver on major legislation, he should step down as leader.[82]

In truth, McConnell was undoubtedly correct in thinking that Trump had failed to provide any meaningful presidential leadership in this major fight, in stark contrast to the way Obama battled for the ACA. But it was also true that McConnell had failed Trump in a fundamental way. The neophyte president needed the counsel of the veteran majority leader. McConnell should have understood that it is extraordinarily difficult to take away a benefit once given. He should have recognized early on that he could not hold fifty of the fifty-two Republican senators to repeal and replace the ACA. McConnell had made every key strategic and tactical decision, and so his attempt to shift the blame to Trump was embarrassing.

One of McConnell's guiding principles, which he had demonstrated brilliantly during the Obama years, is that the party in power gets blamed when things go wrong. Consequently, he should have been looking for a bipartisan approach. If an Obamacare "fix" proved popular, the Republicans could take the credit. If the fix proved unpopular, or if premiums and deductibles soared, or if the insurance markets crashed, the Democrats would share the blame. McConnell's fixation with repealing the ACA blinded him to the political realities and the human costs, causing him to overreach.

McConnell had committed legislative malpractice on a grand scale, and yet, remarkably, he almost succeeded. At least ten Republican senators who had clearly expressed reservations stood with McConnell in voting for several versions of ACA repeal—with or without a replacement. It provided a clear measure of the intense tribal politics dividing the nation, their loyalty to McConnell, and their fear about getting crosswise with Trump. The Senate Republicans were lemmings, walking with eyes wide open into the sea. They voted to do grave damage to the health-care system of America and millions of their constituents, all to fulfill the obsession of the majority leader, some key Republican donors, and Trump, who (without any real understanding of the health-care system) had signed on to their plan.

The repeal battle also taught a clear lesson about McConnell. His willingness to cast aside Senate norms and customs plainly extended well beyond Supreme Court nominations. He would stop at nothing to win. And despite the painful defeat, in McConnell's "long game" there would be other opportunities to undermine the ACA. In the meantime, he would turn to an issue that would unite all Republicans. He urgently needed to deliver major legislation; the only antidote to the ACA failure that could calm the Republican donor base was a massive tax cut for business and the wealthiest individuals.

In 1981, Ronald Reagan had made an enormous supply-side tax cut the centerpiece of his domestic program. In 2001, George W. Bush had done the same. The Republican Party also claimed credit for the 1986 tax reform legislation, the centerpiece of Reagan's second-term agenda, which brought about a historic simplification of the tax code, accomplished with broad bipartisan support. For thirty years, the Republicans had pounded the Democrats for their willingness to consider raising taxes under any circumstances. Now it was time for Trump to match or surpass the work of his Republican predecessors.

The federal tax code, riddled with loopholes, privileges, and complexity, certainly needed reform. There was a powerful case to be made that the 35 percent corporate tax rate had become uncompetitive as other nations cut their rates to attract investment. It was also causing many American companies to leave hundreds of billions in profits overseas to avoid US taxation. Repatriating that money was a high priority for the Obama administration, which did not succeed in accomplishing it, largely because of McConnell's opposition.[83]

The economic case for a tax cut was not compelling. The previous Republican tax cuts came during times of recession. In contrast, "Mr. Trump is proposing to cut taxes during one of the longest economic expansions in American history," economics reporter Binyamin Appelbaum observed in the *New York Times*. "It is not clear that the economy can grow much faster; the Federal Reserve has warned that it will seek to offset any stimulus by raising interest rates."[84]

There was certainly a case to be made for tax relief for low-income and working-class people; America had the highest level of income inequality of any developed nation. Instead, the proposed tax cut that McConnell championed exacerbated the problem. It was primarily a business tax cut, with its central provision cutting the corporate tax rate to 21 percent. It also disproportionately benefited wealthy individuals—the top 1 percent—by reducing the top individual income tax rate from 39.6 percent to 37 percent for married couples with incomes over $600,000. It doubled the estate tax exemption that the wealthiest households could pass on tax-free to their heirs. And it was a windfall for those who had "pass-through" income (income from businesses such as partnerships, S corporations, and sole proprietorships that business owners claim on individual tax returns); these taxes were cut by 20 percent. The top 1 percent of taxpayers would receive 61 percent of the benefits of the legislation, while the bottom two-thirds of households would see just 4 percent.[85]

These inequities did not concern Mitch McConnell. The $2.1 trillion Tax Cut and Jobs Act sped through both houses of Congress, thanks to the budget reconciliation process, passing the House on November 16 by a 227–205 vote and the Senate on December 2 by a 51–49 vote. The "usual suspects"—Flake, Collins, Murkowski, and Corker—raised serious concerns, but ultimately all were satisfied by concessions, other than Corker, who opposed the legislation as an unacceptably large addition to the federal debt. The Reagan and Bush tax cuts had attracted significant bipartisan support, but this one passed on a party-line vote.[86]

Cutting the corporate tax rate and allowing businesses to fully and immediately write off the costs of equipment and other expenses produced an immediate jump in corporate investment. Economists and analysts described the effect of the law as temporary, a "sugar high," which proved to be accurate.[87] Democrats assailed the legislation for providing little benefit to poor, working-class, or middle-class Americans, and polls showed the legislation to be unpopular. McConnell did not let these polls stand in the way of his satisfaction. Delighted to have a major legislative achievement, he repeatedly called the legislation a "once in a lifetime opportunity" that would benefit "hard-working middle-class people," the actual impact notwithstanding.[88]

McConnell had another reason to celebrate. Folded into the thousand-page bill was a provision to eliminate a core component of the Affordable Care Act, the requirement that most people have health insurance or pay a penalty if they did not buy it. He failed to repeal the ACA directly but returned to weaken the law substantially in December. And Collins, Murkowski, and McCain all voted for it. McConnell was ending the year with a major victory on the two issues that mattered most to him.[89]

· 4 ·

Saving Brett Kavanaugh

$\mathcal{A}$s 2018 began, President Trump was in a rage about Rex Tillerson, his secretary of state, after press reports—which the secretary did not deny—that he had called Trump a "moron." This was an unfortunate match from the start: a president with no governing experience choosing a secretary of state with the same absence of qualifications. They had clicked exactly once—the day they met, when Trump, impressed by Tillerson's recently completed tenure as the CEO of ExxonMobil; endorsements from Condoleezza Rice and Robert Gates, who both served on the company's board; and Tillerson's silver hair, offered him the job on the spot.[1] Although Washington columnists frequently grouped Tillerson with Secretary of Defense James Mattis and Chief of Staff John Kelly as the "adults in the room" restraining Trump from following his worst impulses, there was no evidence that Tillerson had any impact on Trump (or on anything else). Despite his executive experience, Tillerson's lack of interest in management and unwillingness to protect the foreign service demoralized the State Department.[2] On March 13, Trump fired Tillerson, giving him the dubious honor of the shortest tenure of any secretary of state in US history. In truth, Tillerson's only achievement was preventing Trump from picking Newt Gingrich or Rudy Giuliani to be secretary of state, which did constitute a significant service to the nation.

CIA director Mike Pompeo would be the new secretary of state. Pompeo had built a good relationship with Trump through his conduct of the president's daily intelligence briefings.[3] He was a former tank commander, first in his class at West Point, and a Harvard Law graduate—a smart, tough warrior whom Trump admired and probably wished he could have been. Pompeo had also served in the House of Representatives, where he had earned strong support from Republican hard-liners and Freedom Caucus members for his role in the endless investigations of Hillary Clinton's role regarding the 2012 attack on the US diplomatic compound in Benghazi. Every president needs a secretary of state in whom he has confidence, and Pompeo seemed to fit that bill for Trump.

In the wake of Pompeo's arrival, Trump embarked upon a series of forceful and unorthodox foreign policy decisions—virtually a bombshell every week. On March 22, Trump announced that he would impose tariffs on a broad range of products from China.[4] In April, the administration announced that its hard-line immigration policy would now feature family separations at the border.[5] In early May, Trump announced that the United States was withdrawing from the Iran nuclear deal.[6] And on May 31 Trump invoked the national security emergency powers under Section 232 of the 1962 Trade Expansion Act to justify imposing steel and aluminum tariffs on Canada, Mexico, the European Union, and Japan.[7] The announcements on trade and the Iran deal caused the G-7 in Quebec to dissolve in acrimony on May 30, captured in an indelible photograph of Trump, sitting with arms crossed, glowering at German chancellor Angela Merkel and the other G-7 leaders.[8] Sixteen months into his presidency, Trump's "America First" seemed increasingly like "America alone." His disruptive presidency had isolated America from its traditional allies.

In one area, however, the Trump presidency remained focused, strategic, subtle, and successful. Trump never forgot how well he had played the Supreme Court issue in the 2016 campaign, and he loved the accolades he received for putting Neil Gorsuch on the court in 2017. Trump was champing at the bit to nominate another justice; "I think I'm going to get five," he liked to tell people.[9]

There was good reason to believe that his second opportunity would come soon. Justice Anthony Kennedy, now eighty years old, had been on the court since 1988, and it was one of the worst-kept secrets in Washington that Justice Kennedy's wife wanted him to retire. "Will Kennedy step down?" became a virtual parlor game starting in the fall of 2017. Kennedy, although generally a conservative jurist, had aligned with the court's liberal wing on several important cases. He had cast the deciding vote in 5–4 decisions protecting abortion rights, establishing the constitutional right to gay marriage, and preserving affirmative action. Consequently, replacing Kennedy with a more reliable right-wing justice, locking in a conservative majority on the key social issues, was the highest priority for the Federalist Society and Republicans generally.

Historically, justices appointed by Republican presidents had timed their departures so that another Republican president could nominate their successors. And the Senate Republicans were not shy about their intentions. In early May, Chuck Grassley, the Judiciary Committee chairman, put it bluntly on the conservative pundit Hugh Hewitt's radio show: "My message to any of the nine Supreme Court justices: if you're thinking of quitting this year, do it yesterday."[10]

In fact, Justice Kennedy had requested a private moment with the president on April 10, 2017, after coming to the White House to preside over the swearing-in of Gorsuch, his former law clerk. Kennedy thanked Trump for picking one of his former clerks and then urged him to consider another of his clerks, Judge Brett Kavanaugh, for the next vacancy. "The justice's message was as consequential as it was straightforward, and it was a remarkable insertion by a sitting justice into the distinctly presidential act of judge picking," Ruth Marcus of the *Washington Post* would later observe.[11] Trump and Don McGahn, the White House counsel, who had consolidated power over judicial nominations, got the message. Kennedy was planning to retire, but they could ensure it would happen soon if they anointed his chosen successor.

On June 27, 2018, as the Supreme Court ended its session, Justice Kennedy announced his decision to retire from the court. On July 9, President Trump announced that he would nominate Brett Kavanaugh to succeed Justice Kennedy. Commentators noted that Trump, not known for his subtlety, had handled Kennedy quite deftly: winning his confidence by nominating Gorsuch and then making it clear that he was considering two other Kennedy clerks to replace him. It also became clear that the president and the justice had closer ties than previously known, since Kennedy's son, Justin Kennedy, was the former head of Deutsche Bank's global real estate capital markets. Deutsche Bank was the largest creditor and frequent lifeline for the Trump Organization as it constantly teetered on the edge of the financial abyss.[12]

The stakes for the country could not be higher. Mitch McConnell immediately guaranteed that Kavanaugh would be confirmed in the fall. Minority Leader Chuck Schumer, reflecting the continuing Democratic bitterness about the Garland nomination, said that the nomination should be voted on after the midterm elections. It was destined to be a contentious September. McConnell undoubtedly saw it as wonderful timing: an assured victory, thanks to the Democrats' inability to filibuster a Supreme Court nomination, and a battle that would energize the Republican base in the run-up to the midterm elections, where turnout might otherwise drop sharply.

Indeed, it was a moment when Senate Republicans might have convinced themselves that Trump was delivering on his populist platform for his base—a hard line on immigration and trade, bashing allies, denigrating minorities and women—while meeting the highest priorities for the Republican Party's business supporters: tax cuts, deregulation, and conservative judges. The judges also helped to hold the third wing of the Republican coalition, religious conservatives, whose desire to overturn *Roe v. Wade* was paramount. With the economy booming, Trump's disruptive presidency seemed to be working. And even though Robert Mueller was conducting his investigation and the Treasury Department was imposing sanctions on high-ranking Russians, it was possible for most Republicans to forget Trump's disconcerting relationship with Putin and Russia.

The Russia issue would return to center stage soon enough. Mueller's task force presented to a grand jury detailed evidence of a cyber-attack by an arm of the Russian military during the 2016 presidential election and was ready to request that the grand jury issue a sweeping indictment. But with President Trump scheduled to meet with Vladimir Putin in Helsinki, Finland, in July, Mueller and his team faced a dilemma. They understandably did not want the release of the indictment to create diplomatic difficulties between the United States and its leading adversary, but they also did not want to delay the indictment for what could be perceived as political reasons. Confronted with this difficult clash between legal process and diplomacy, Mueller instructed his staff to take the unusual step of checking with the White House to see whether there were any objections to the timing of the indictment. The answer came back: not necessary to delay.

The indictment was announced on July 13,[13] and three days later Donald Trump and Vladimir Putin held a joint press conference in Helsinki. When asked about Russia's disruption of the election, Trump said that Putin had denied such interference and that he took the Russian president at his word. By that time Trump had received the original assessment of the intelligence community and the corroboration of Mueller's team. Still, Trump said, "Putin was extremely strong and powerful in his denial," and that was apparently good enough for him.

Trump's statement, made standing side by side with Putin and accepting his denial against the overwhelming evidence compiled by the US law enforcement and intelligence communities, provoked a firestorm. "Today's press conference in Helsinki was one of the most disgraceful performances by an American president in memory," said John McCain. "No prior president has ever abased himself more abjectly before a tyrant." Even Newt Gingrich, one of Trump's fiercest supporters, urged the president to clarify his statement, calling it "the most serious mistake of his presidency."[14] The conservative *Wall Street Journal* editorial page called it "a national embarrassment."[15] In the Senate, Richard Burr, the chairman of the Intelligence Committee, was deeply involved in reviewing the question of Russian interference in the 2016 election. Burr forcefully stated that the committee had full confidence in the conclusion of the intelligence community: "Any statement by Vladimir Putin contrary to these facts is a lie and should be recognized as one by the President."[16]

Eliot A. Cohen, a former foreign policy adviser to George W. Bush, said, "The word treason is so strong that we must use it carefully. But that press conference has brought the President of the United States right up to that dark, dark shore."[17] Trey Gowdy, a retiring House member, gently suggested that the intelligence community should be able to convince Trump that acknowledging Russian interference in the election did not delegitimize his victory. When Trump later attempted to clarify his statement by saying that he had misspoken—"in a key sentence in my remarks, [relating to Russia's interference] I said the word 'would', instead of 'wouldn't'"[18]—the best that Senator Rob Portman could manage in response was "I wish he had said it in front of President Putin and the world, but yeah, I take him at his word if he said he misspoke."[19]

Of course, Trump did not misspeak or commit a careless error. Since winning the election, Trump had repeatedly and publicly attacked the intelligence and law enforcement communities for their conclusion that Russia had interfered in the presidential campaign. Throughout his presidency, Trump would lie endlessly, but he was also quite transparent. In accepting Putin's denial, Trump was simply restating his deeply held view.

Special Counsel Robert Mueller, shocked by what he was seeing, confided to his team that if Trump was in the tank with Putin, "it would be about money"—Trump seeking to make millions in Russia.[20] But even if Trump simply hated the fact that Russian interference called into question the legitimacy of his election, that was serious enough. The American president was compromised in dealing with the nation's foremost adversary. And Trump's unwillingness to acknowledge Russia's interference in the 2016 election would also make it impossible for him to recognize, and then combat, potential Russian interference in the 2018 or 2020 elections.

Mitch McConnell reacted tersely: "As I have said repeatedly, the Russians are not our friends, and I agree with the assessment of the intelligence community."[21] McConnell, a hard-liner on Russia, was undoubtedly appalled by Trump's behavior. His stature, and some degree of self-respect, required him to condemn the Russians and support the intelligence community. But McConnell saw nothing to be gained from attacking Trump; there was every reason to turn the page by moving on to a better topic for the Republican Party, an issue with profound long-term impact where he could work with Trump, not against him. It was time to clear the decks to confirm a second Supreme Court justice.

Judge Brett Kavanaugh, age fifty-three, was in many ways a nominee from central casting. Educated at Yale College and Yale Law School, Kavanaugh had served a series of prestigious judicial clerkships, culminating in his work for Justice Kennedy. He had been deeply involved in Republican politics and government, including stints as associate White House counsel and staff secretary for George W. Bush. Indeed, Kavanaugh had become even closer to the Bush family by marrying President Bush's personal secretary, Ashley Estes. Bush had appointed Kavanaugh to the D.C. Circuit Court of Appeals, the second most powerful federal court, where he had served for twelve years and had earned respect as a serious, capable judge. He had an academic bent and had taught at Yale and Harvard. He was popular with his legal colleagues, including Justice Elena Kagan, who had been dean of the Harvard Law School when Kavanaugh taught there. Kavanaugh had a lovely family, coached his daughters' basketball teams, and was active in his church.[22]

Yet despite these glittering credentials, Kavanaugh had not been included in the list of possible Supreme Court nominees that the Federalist Society prepared for Trump during the 2016 presidential campaign. Leonard Leo, the longtime vice president of the Federalist Society and a powerful force in the conservative legal movement, regarded Kavanaugh as too much of a creature of the Washington, D.C., "swamp," who would be susceptible to political and media pressure that might cause him to "go liberal" once on the court. Leo was determined to avoid any possibility of another David Souter, John Paul Stevens, Anthony Kennedy, or Sandra Day O'Connor—that is, another justice nominated by a Republican president who turned out to be receptive to liberal arguments.[23]

It was hard to understand Leo's reservations. Kavanaugh's record established him as an ideological warrior with strong right-wing views.

A vocal critic of "unenumerated" rights, Judge Kavanaugh posed a clear threat not only to *Roe v. Wade* but also to the line of cases before and since *Roe* that had guaranteed a right of privacy to women (and men) to make the most personal life decisions. He had said that states cannot ban AR-15 assault weapons, although the Supreme Court had held that the Second Amendment protected the private right to own a handgun but permitted reasonable regulations. Kavanaugh had also expressed the view that the strict wall between church and state is "wrong as a matter of law and history."

Just as significant, Kavanaugh had championed the controversial constitutional doctrine of the "unitary executive"—an expansive view of presidential power. His view went well beyond the reasonable position that a sitting president cannot be indicted while in office; he argued that "we should not burden a sitting President with civil suits, criminal investigations or criminal prosecutions." Had this been the law in the 1970s, the Supreme Court would never have had the chance to rule on *U.S. v. Nixon*, the case that forced Richard Nixon to surrender the Watergate tapes, leading directly to his resignation as president. "It is an *especially* dangerous time to have a Court that supports executive supremacy," observed the historian Timothy Naftali, the former director of the Nixon Presidential Library.[24]

A data-driven study of Judge Kavanaugh's writing found that his opinions and rhetoric were more extreme and polarizing than those of Samuel Alito, Neil Gorsuch, and Robert Bork when they were nominated to the court. "More so than his colleagues," the authors noted, Kavanaugh "has expressed dislike toward Congress and the federal government, as well as working-class groups (labor unions and farmers)." After summarizing the evidence, the authors concluded, "Kavanaugh is an outlier judge; he would not be your average justice. On the evidence derived from the content of his decisions, he would be more radical than his colleagues. . . . [He] is much like the man who selected him—highly divisive in his decisions and his rhetoric."[25]

After Donald Trump's election, Kavanaugh had campaigned, not very subtly, for a nomination to the court. In a February 2017 keynote address at the Notre Dame Law School in a symposium honoring

Justice Scalia, Kavanaugh said, "I loved the guy. Justice Scalia was and remains a judicial hero and a role model to many throughout America. He thought carefully about his principles, he articulated his principles, and he stood up for those principles. As a judge, he did not buckle to political or academic pressure from the right or the left."[26] That was regarded as a signal to the Federalist Society: Brett Kavanaugh would not be one of those Republican nominees to the Supreme Court who turned out to be a centrist.

Kavanaugh was also a familiar and controversial figure to the Senate. As a young lawyer, he had found his way to the midst of virtually every major political battle during the Clinton and Bush presidencies. He served under Kenneth W. Starr, the independent counsel who investigated President Clinton, examining the suicide of deputy White House counsel Vincent W. Foster, and he drafted some of the most salacious parts of the report that led to Clinton's impeachment by the House after his affair with Monica Lewinsky. When the 2000 election between George W. Bush and Al Gore deadlocked for thirty-six days over the virtual tie vote in Florida, Kavanaugh was one of the Republican lawyers working on the recount litigation. During the Bush administration, Kavanaugh worked on the selection of federal judges and legal issues arising from the 9/11 terrorist attacks.

He was "the Zelig of young Republican lawyers," Chuck Schumer said in 2004. "If there was a partisan political fight that needed a good lawyer in the last decade, Brett Kavanaugh was probably there."[27] His own nomination to the D.C. Circuit Court of Appeals was held up for almost three years by the senior Democratic senators Patrick Leahy and Richard Durbin, who believed that Kavanaugh had lied to the Judiciary Committee about his role in controversial nomination fights. McConnell, who never shied away from a partisan fight, made clear in multiple phone calls with Trump and McGahn that other nominees would be easier to confirm.[28]

Ultimately, however, Trump got excited about Kavanaugh. As one White House official recalled, Trump would ask, "Why didn't anyone tell me he had been on the court for twelve years? Why didn't anyone tell me that he clerked for Kennedy, went to Yale and said all these nice things about executive power?" Trump particularly liked the fact that Kavanaugh was a fighter who had spent several years going after Bill and Hillary Clinton.[29]

It took Chuck Schumer less than a half hour after Kavanaugh's nomination was announced to declare his all-out opposition.[30] Far more was at stake than when Gorsuch was nominated. This was the opportunity that McConnell, the Federalist Society, the Christian Right, and the Republican Party had sought for thirty years: the chance to tilt the Supreme Court majority decisively to the right. With the filibuster no longer available for Supreme Court nominations, McConnell could get the Senate to confirm Kavanaugh with only the fifty-two Republican votes, and there were several moderate Democrats—Joe Manchin, Claire McCaskill, Joe Donnelly, Heidi Heitkamp, and John Tester—facing tough reelection fights in states that had voted for Trump in 2016, who might also support Kavanaugh. McConnell's principal challenge was likely to be holding the votes of Susan Collins and Lisa Murkowski, who were independent by nature and pro-choice. The opposition to Kavanaugh from supporters of abortion rights was fierce from the start. They believed, with clear justification, that Kavanaugh posed a threat to *Roe v. Wade* and the 1992 decision in *Planned Parenthood v. Casey*, a 5–4 decision in which Kennedy had been in the majority.

If there was a path for the Democrats to defeat the nomination, it was the playbook from the epic battle against Robert Bork in 1987, when the retirement of Justice Lewis Powell had opened up the swing vote on the court. Led by Judiciary Committee chairman Joe Biden and Ted Kennedy, the Democrats successfully portrayed Bork, a brilliant legal scholar and judge, as a judicial extremist whose constitutional views were sufficiently outside the mainstream that his nomination to the court should be rejected. Of course, Bork helped their cause by rising to the bait and speaking at length about his judicial philosophy, which was in fact quite extreme. It also helped that the Democrats had just retaken the Senate majority, the Reagan presidency was rocked by the Iran-contra scandal, and there were a handful of moderate Republicans who were open to opposing Bork.[31]

Now, thirty years later, Supreme Court nominees had learned the lessons of Bork's experience and tap-danced through their confirmation, invoking the "Ginsburg rule"—"no forecasts, no hints"—to avoid all difficult questions.[32] Kavanaugh would be extremely well prepared. The Senate was in Republican hands, and the politics were far more tribal. Moreover, the Republicans had learned bitter lessons from the Bork experience, and the Federalist Society had spent thirty years creating the political and financial infrastructure to prevent another such defeat. McConnell was on a personal mission to remake the Supreme Court, and he would stop at nothing to win. The Democratic strategist Ron Klain, who had worked on the selection or confirmation of eight justices over his career, grimly observed, "You had this sense of impending doom from moment one."[33]

Working closely with Judiciary chairman Chuck Grassley, Lindsey Graham, and Don McGahn, McConnell dealt with the problem of Kavanaugh's voluminous record by running roughshod over every precedent. It was customary that the National Archives curate the documents and submit what was relevant to the Judiciary Committee members and their staffs. This time, however, the documents were vetted not by the Archives staff but by William Burck, a lawyer chosen by the White House who had previously worked for Kavanaugh. When Elena Kagan had been nominated to the court in 2010, she was serving as solicitor general in the Obama administration, and the White House waived "executive privilege," allowing internal documents to be considered by the committee. This time, the White House invented a new claim of "constitutional privilege," preventing the committee from seeing more than 100,000 pages of documents without requiring the White House to invoke executive privilege. The Democrats objected vehemently, but McConnell didn't mind. One of his favorite sayings is "When you're arguing about process, you're losing."[34] Some liberal groups agreed. "Chuck Schumer is bringing a FOIA request to a knife fight," said Elizabeth Beavers, the associate policy director of Indivisible, a grassroots Trump-resistance group. "Most ordinary constituents are not enraged and spurred to action by process."[35]

Chuck Grassley would preside over Kavanaugh's confirmation hearings, as he had done for Neil Gorsuch the year before. Grassley had been elected to the Senate in 1980, riding Ronald Reagan's landslide victory, and he was now serving his seventh six-year term. He was a conservative Republican, but his interests were wide ranging and his views often unpredictable; he frequently cosponsored legislation with liberal Democrats. Grassley had also emerged as a leading champion of criminal justice reform, starting with legislation that would change the harsh, mandatory sentences that had crowded US prisons with young men, mostly black and brown, convicted of minor drug crimes. "I consider myself a law-and-order Republican," Grassley would say. "I'm also a taxpayer watchdog. And I believe in the redemptive power of rehabilitation."[36]

Grassley was a steadfast defender of whistleblowers in the government; he had first written legislation protecting whistleblowers in 1989. He was also the principal champion of the inspectors general serving as watchdogs in the major federal agencies. In 2017, less than three weeks after Trump took office, Grassley wrote to the president that whistleblowers could help him accomplish his goal to "drain the swamp." "Whistleblowers are brave, patriotic people who tell the truth about what is going on in our government. They help us identify waste, fraud and abuse in a vast and unwieldy federal bureaucracy," Grassley argued. "Whistleblowers speak up about violations of law, rule and regulation, and about gross mismanagement, abuses of authority and threats to public health and safety. They often do so at the peril of their own careers, reputations and even health. They put Americans first." He noted that he had introduced legislation to protect whistleblowers from retaliation.[37]

Despite his independence, Grassley was unstintingly conservative where judges were concerned. He and his staff ran the judicial conveyor belt that moved federal court nominations through the Senate as rapidly as possible. He would do the same for Kavanaugh under the bright lights and national attention that Supreme Court confirmations received. Grassley was experienced and tough enough to handle this important task; he was also smart enough to know that every important decision would be made in conjunction with McConnell and McGahn.

Part of Ron Klain's "sense of impending doom" was the feeling that the Senate Democrats were hopelessly outgunned. The ranking Democrat on the Judiciary Committee, California's Dianne Feinstein, had had a storied career and a record of tough independence, but she was now eighty-five years old, and she had unmistakably lost more than a step. Many of her colleagues were quietly chagrined that she had chosen to seek reelection to a fifth full term in 2018. Feinstein could not provide the leadership that the Democrats needed, but her pride and Senate mores did not allow her to turn over her leadership role to someone who could.[38] The committee's Democrats included an impressive group of experienced lawyers, including former prosecutors and state attorneys general Pat Leahy, Dick Durbin, Amy Klobuchar, Kamala Harris, Richard Blumenthal, and Sheldon Whitehouse. But the committee rules, which limited each senator to five minutes of questioning, put a premium on the ability of the group to coordinate their questions, and the Democrats proved unable to do so. Will Rogers's famous quip—"I'm not a member of any organized political party; I'm a Democrat"—had found new relevance a century later.

Despite its power and prestige, the Senate only rarely takes center stage and seizes the attention of the American public. The powerful and effective Senate of the 1960s and 1970s won the confidence of Americans because of its handling of those historic moments: breaking the two-month Southern filibuster to enact the Civil Rights Act of 1964; the Foreign Relations Committee hearings, chaired by J. William Fulbright, which showed the country the flawed assumptions of the escalation of the Vietnam War (1966); the Watergate committee exposing the abuses of the Nixon administration (1973); and overcoming intense partisanship to approve the bitterly controversial Panama Canal treaties (1978). In recent decades, however, the Senate had forfeited public confidence by its disastrous handling of the confirmation of Clarence Thomas after the accusations of workplace sexual harassment by Anita Hill (1991) and the rush to judgment giving President George W. Bush the authority to send US forces into Iraq (2002). Now, with America already angrily divided over the Trump presidency, with the swing seat on the Supreme Court on the line, the weakened and polarized Senate was about to fail America in a profound way.

The Judiciary Committee hearings on Brett Kavanaugh's confirmation were chaotic from the first moment, "less regular order than a senatorial roller derby, with Kavanaugh as a bystander in the fury erupting around him,"[39] in the words of the *Washington Post*'s Ruth Marcus. Kamala Harris interrupted Chairman Grassley's opening statement six seconds into his first sentence, complaining about the treatment of the documents, arguing for a postponement. Six of her Democratic colleagues followed immediately, one after the other. "What are we trying to hide?" asked Leahy, who had chaired the committee for ten years. "Why are we rushing?" He charged that Kavanaugh's nomination had received "the most incomplete, most partisan, least transparent vetting for any Supreme Court nominee that I've ever seen, and I have seen more of those than any person serving in the Senate." Leahy offered a long list of objections to the handling of the documents, concluding that "nothing about this is normal." Feinstein, struggling to maintain some order, interjected weakly, "I really regret this, but I think you have to understand the frustrations on this side of the aisle."[40]

This continued for nearly ninety minutes, and the anger of the Democratic senators was matched by the protestors in the audience. "This is a mockery and travesty of justice," shouted one. "Cancel Brett Kavanaugh," yelled another. Viewers around the country witnessed the spectacle of protestors being dragged from the hearing room into the corridors of the Senate office building, which were already jammed with women dressed in scarlet *Handmaid's Tale* outfits.[41]

Playing to the television cameras, and proving their anger to the Democratic base, was a high-risk strategy. The Senate Republicans were happy to use the chaotic scene, accusing the Democrats of descending into "mob rule," as John Cornyn of Texas put it. "That the senators interrupted the chairman at the start of his opening statement was a shocking, if understandable, breach of decorum. Combined with the screaming audience members being forcibly removed, it made the

Democrats look like an unruly, even unhinged, pack," Ruth Marcus wrote.[42]

The volume of documents from Kavanaugh's White House years created a significant challenge, but over the years, committee chairmen and ranking members had found compromises to countless problems of this type. Grassley and Feinstein had served more than a quarter of a century together. Traditionally, such long and deep relationships established trust and made the Senate able to work through difficult problems. But the magnitude of what was at stake—the swing vote on the Supreme Court—combined with the Senate's steep decline to make compromise impossible. Given those realities, the Democrats should have considered simply refusing to attend the hearing, which would have forced the Republicans to accept a delay and offer a compromise or to proceed on their own, violating the Judiciary Committee's own rules, which require at least one member of the minority party to be present in order for business to be transacted.

While all of this was going on, Brett Kavanaugh sat and waited. He was well prepared for the committee's questioning, and, like all nominees since Bork, he was "adept at showing familiarity with doctrine without tipping his hand about any of his own views," in the words of Ruth Marcus.[43] In fact, Kavanaugh's numerous opinions, plus his willingness to expound on his views in articles and speeches, had given the Democrats plenty of ammunition and left very little doubt that he was fiercely conservative. Ultimately, Kavanaugh and the president who nominated him were counting on McConnell to hold the Republicans together and deliver fifty-one votes, or fifty plus Vice President Pence's tiebreaker. Barring a catastrophic storm of unforeseen magnitude, Brett Kavanaugh would be confirmed in time for the court's next session on the first Monday in October.

Of course, although neither Kavanaugh nor the committee members knew it, the catastrophic storm had already arrived.[44] Christine Blasey Ford, a professor of psychology from California who specialized in measuring the aftermath of trauma, had, after weeks of agonizing indecision, called the district office of Representative Anna Eshoo to tell her that Judge Kavanaugh had sexually assaulted her at a party when they were high school students in Maryland thirty-five years before. Ford also reached out to the anonymous tip line at the *Washington Post* and left two messages about the assault, the second of which named Kavanaugh. Inexplicably, almost two more weeks passed before Eshoo's district office director met with Ford on July 18.

Two days later, on July 20, Eshoo met with Ford and then called Senator Feinstein.[45] "You know this is very serious," Feinstein told Eshoo. "Have her write a letter to me."

Ford, still torn between her desire to expose Kavanaugh's action and an equal desire to keep the whole thing private, took ten days to produce the letter. During that time, Feinstein did nothing to follow up, nor did she inform her staff. Once the letter arrived, with its alarmingly detailed description of the incident, Feinstein immediately arranged a call with Ford, and she and a staff member questioned Ford about the allegations. Feinstein came away believing Ford but also assured her that she would protect her privacy—which was something she could not guarantee, given the fact that Ford was discussing it widely with friends and had shared it with the *Washington Post* tip line.

Feinstein also told her staff she wanted Ford's accusation investigated, but not in a partisan way. There was an obvious solution to the problem: Senate committee process 101, sharing it with Grassley. But Feinstein did not do that, fearing that he would share the letter with the White House. Nor, remarkably, did Feinstein seek the counsel of any of her Democratic colleagues, including Durbin and Schumer, extraordinarily experienced senators whose advice would have been helpful. When rumors of the letter prompted her colleagues to ask Feinstein to share it, she refused.[46]

Feinstein made a series of unforgivable errors. Of course this was a sensitive matter, but it was not rocket science or a question of national security. Once Ford had conveyed her story, Feinstein's obligation was to the Senate and the country. She should have told Ford that she had waived her privacy in coming forward and that, as ranking member of the Judiciary Committee, she was obligated to share the information with Grassley. Feinstein could promise to do her best to protect Ford's confidentiality, but she should have told Ford that she could not guarantee it.

For the Democrats, the result would be a nightmarish repeat of the confirmation of Clarence Thomas in 1991, when at what seemed to be the end of contentious hearings, Anita Hill came forward to accuse Thomas of sexual harassment when she worked for him at the Equal Employment Opportunity Commission. The mishandling of Hill's allegation disgraced the Senate, as the Republicans attacked her viciously and the Democrats defended her feebly. The debacle cast a long shadow over Joe Biden, who was then Judiciary Committee chairman. Diane Feinstein had won her Senate seat in 1992 in part because of the surge of activism in the "year of the woman" following the Thomas hearings. Now, twenty-seven years later, a Senate with twenty-five female senators, including four on the Judiciary Committee, in the midst of the #MeToo movement, faced a similar situation and produced its own massively failed response.

As rumors of Ford's story began to surface, Dick Durbin insisted on a meeting of the Judiciary Committee Democrats. When they met, Feinstein, in the words of one senator, was "agitated and defensive." She kept insisting that she had done the right thing, honoring Ford's repeated requests for confidentiality, and would continue to do so.

But Durbin insisted that this was impossible. "Dianne, stop, stop, listen to me," he said. "This is incredibly important. We have to get this right. You cannot keep this to yourself anymore." It had been "a huge mistake" to have sat on the letter. "You must give this to the FBI," he repeated. "I respect your motives, but you cannot withhold this." Feinstein gave in and sent the letter to the FBI.[47]

When Christine Blasey Ford recognized that the story could no longer be contained, she authorized Emma Brown, the *Washington Post* reporter with whom she had been speaking, to use her name and publish the details of her letter. When the *Post* story broke, overnight Brett Kavanaugh's confirmation lost its sense of inevitability. Jeff Flake, a key committee vote, told the *Washington Post*, "I'm not comfortable moving ahead with the vote on Thursday if we have not heard her side of the story or explored this further." Bob Corker also called for a delay, saying that "it would be best for all involved, including the nominee. If she does want to be heard, she should do so [speak up] promptly." Susan Collins, always regarded as a key vote, tweeted, "Professor Ford and Judge Kavanaugh should both testify under oath before the Judiciary Committee."[48]

In a tense conference of Republican senators, McConnell and Grassley initially opposed a hearing on Ford's allegations, but they reluctantly concluded that it could not be avoided.[49] And the Republicans were wise enough to know that in the #MeToo era, Ford had to be treated respectfully. In 1991, the Republicans on the Judiciary Committee had brutalized Anita Hill; Alan Simpson later acknowledged being a "monster" to her.[50] When Trump, who had been uncommonly restrained, lashed out at Ford, questioning why she had not filed charges thirty-six years earlier, Collins described herself as "appalled by the president's tweet." Flake called it "incredibly insensitive," and McConnell called Trump to urge him to stop.[51]

In the White House, the pressure was extraordinary. Ivanka Trump and Jared Kushner were urging Trump to find a new nominee. Leonard Leo shocked the White House and Grassley's staff by suggesting that it was time to abandon Kavanaugh. Leo argued that there were other excellent nominees for whom he could raise the money that would ensure that the Supreme Court would be a major issue in the midterm elections, and the nominee could be confirmed afterward. In the maelstrom, two people stayed cool: Don McGahn and Mitch McConnell. McGahn simply refused to answer the phone when President Trump called him. "I don't talk to losers," McGahn reportedly said. He then turned to McConnell to stiffen Trump's spine. "You can ditch Kavanaugh if you really want, but don't think you can play a switcheroo here and I'm going to get it done before the election, because I'm not," McConnell told the president.[52] Later that day, Trump asked McConnell whether he was determined to see Kavanaugh confirmed. "I'm stronger than mule piss" on Kavanaugh, McConnell replied, a phrase that probably had never been said to any president before.[53]

On September 27, Grassley gaveled the Judiciary Committee to order for one of the most memorable days of testimony in the long history of the Senate. The courteous, friendly relationship between Grassley and Feinstein was long past. He ripped her for failing to share Ford's letter, which he referred to as "the ranking member's secret evidence." He reviewed several opportunities when Feinstein could have brought the matter to his attention. Feinstein responded strongly, attacking the majority's failure to investigate Ford's allegation and castigating it for rejecting the request for an FBI investigation or for hearing testimony from any other witness. She called these actions "an inexcusable rush to judgment."[54]

Christine Blasey Ford's prepared statement was emotional, gripping, human, and convincing. "I am here today not because I want to be. I am terrified. I am here because I believe it is my civic duty to tell you what happened to me when Brett Kavanaugh and I were in high school," she said. In less than twenty minutes, she described the assault by Kavanaugh and Mark Judge, two drunken high school seniors. Ford was precise on certain memories, vague on other details, which made her seem more credible, underscoring that she had been in shock. Leahy asked her what she remembered most of the evening. Ford, the psychologist whose expertise was victims' trauma, responded, "Indelible in the hippocampus is the laughter" of Kavanaugh and Judge, "the uproarious laughter between the two, and their having fun at my expense."[55]

Ford was eminently believable; the overwhelming reaction among Republicans was despair. "Almost all of us were saying 'it's over,'" Jeff Flake recalled. "Had there been a vote right after her testimony, it would not have been good for Kavanaugh," Bob Corker stated. On Fox News, Chris Wallace called Ford's testimony "extremely emotional, extremely raw and extremely credible," adding, "This is a disaster for the Republicans."[56]

Kavanaugh's nomination hung by a thread. Trump was shaken, asking those around him, "Do you think this guy is too damaged to be confirmed? And if I pull him, can I salvage it and get another guy through?" Ultimately, the two strongest voices steadied the ship.

McConnell reassured the president, "We're only at halftime." McGahn played an even stronger role. Kavanaugh had done a previous interview on Fox News in which he sounded both robotic and weak, which was not the way to keep Trump's support. Now speaking to Kavanaugh with only his wife present, McGahn urged Kavanaugh to defend himself forcefully because his reputation and career were at stake.[57]

When the committee reconvened to hear from the nominee, Kavanaugh rose to McGahn's challenge. In a forty-five-minute tirade, he denied every aspect of Ford's accusation; the incident she described, he said, never occurred. He then went further. "This confirmation process has become a national disgrace," Kavanaugh raged. "The Constitution gives the Senate an important role in the confirmation process, but you have replaced advise and consent with search and destroy."

"The behavior of several of the Democratic members at my hearing a few weeks ago was an embarrassment," Kavanaugh asserted, "but at least it was just a good old-fashioned attempt at Borking. These efforts didn't work. When I did at least okay enough at the hearings that it looked like I might actually get confirmed, a new tactic was needed. Some of you were lying in wait and had it ready." In Kavanaugh's telling, Feinstein's decisions were part of a nefarious plot to hold Ford's allegations unless and until they were needed, and then make them public and follow them with those of other accusers to destroy him.

"This whole two-week effort has been a calculated and orchestrated political hit, fueled with apparent pent-up anger about President Trump and the 2016 election. Fear that has been unfairly stoked about my judicial record. Revenge on behalf of the Clintons. And millions of dollars from outside, left-wing opposition groups," Kavanaugh continued. "This is a circus. You may defeat me in the final vote. But you'll never get me to quit. Never."[58]

To objective observers, Kavanaugh's rant did nothing to change the essential fact that Ford, coming forward reluctantly with a painful story that she had told only to her therapist, her husband, and a few friends, was far more credible than Kavanaugh, who had every incentive to lie about his drunken behavior thirty-five years earlier, to save his career and his reputation. But Kavanaugh's performance had worked; Trump loved his fight and was reassured and energized. And Kavanaugh's rage sparked Lindsey Graham, whose political identity vacillated between being an independent maverick on the model of his late friend John McCain and the right-wing prosecutor who had gone after a Democratic president in Bill Clinton's impeachment twenty years earlier.

"If you wanted an FBI investigation, you could have come to us," Graham charged. "What you want is to destroy this guy's life, hold this seat open, and hope you win in 2020. . . . Boy, all you want is power. I hope you never get it. I hope the American people can see through this sham. That you knew about it and held it. You had no intention of protecting Dr. Ford, none. She's as much of a victim as you are."

"God, I hate to say it, because these have been my friends, but let me tell you, when it comes to this, if you're looking for a fair process, you came to the wrong town at the wrong time, my friend," Graham concluded.[59]

When the brutal day's hearing came to an end, Grassley announced the committee would vote on the nomination the next day. However, the troubled group of undecided or uncommitted senators—Flake, Collins, Murkowski, and Manchin—met for dinner and found themselves still dissatisfied that the allegations of Ford and others had not been adequately investigated. Of the four, only Flake served on the Judiciary Committee. The next morning, Flake, at the prodding of Chris Coons, the Delaware Democrat who was his close friend, insisted on an FBI investigation. McConnell, Grassley, and the White House had no choice; without Flake's vote, the nomination would fail in committee.

An agreement was hammered out that the FBI would have a week to investigate the allegation more fully, but with strict parameters (set by McGahn) on what the FBI could investigate. Experienced lawyers and investigators immediately realized that under these limitations the investigation was destined to fail: too brief, and lacking independence. Ultimately, the FBI questioned only four people and did not interview Ford or Kavanaugh. The FBI also failed to question at least one universally respected Washington public policy expert—Max Stier, the president and CEO of the Partnership for Public Service—who would have

confirmed previous obscene acts by Kavanaugh when he drank exces-
sively.[60] But McConnell and the White House never considered a serious investigation. They would do only as much as needed to be done
to satisfy Flake, Collins, and Murkowski, and thereby secure fifty votes.

The dramatic day of testimony produced remarkable reactions
across the nation. The Jesuit publication *America* withdrew its previous endorsement of Kavanaugh,[61] and more than twenty-four hundred
law professors joined an open letter opposing his confirmation. Calling
his testimony "intemperate, inflammatory and partial," the law professors stated, "Judge Brett Kavanaugh displayed a lack of judicial temperament that would be disqualifying for any court, and certainly for
elevation to the highest court in the land."[62] The National Council of
Churches, an organization representing thirty million Catholics, said
that Kavanaugh had "exhibited extreme partisan bias and disrespect
for certain members of the committee and thereby demonstrated that
he possesses neither the temperament nor the character essential for a
member of the highest court in our nation. . . . We believe he has
disqualified himself and should step aside immediately."[63] Kavanaugh's
extraordinary tirade, which law professors and religious leaders saw
as clearly disqualifying, would ultimately affect the vote of only one
Republican senator.

Jeff Flake, a man of genuine conscience, was appalled at the state of
American politics. He had shown his courage by speaking out against
Trump early and often, ending his career in politics. Chris Coons had
hammered away at his friend, raising his concern about Kavanaugh's
excessive deference to presidential power. Nor was Flake impressed by
Kavanaugh's fiery defense, which he found completely lacking in judicial temperament.[64] He was positioned to strike a blow against Trump,
by denying him a second Supreme Court justice. But Flake was a conservative Republican, with strongly held pro-life views. At the end of
the day, Flake would not derail the opportunity to lock in a conservative majority on the Supreme Court.

For Susan Collins, the issues were different. She was an independent player who hated what the Senate had become. She had shown
plenty of courage in the past, breaking with McConnell on two of his

highest priorities: Obama's economic stimulus in 2009 and the repeal of the Affordable Care Act in 2017. No one had studied the issues more intently than Collins, a nonlawyer who had been briefed by nineteen outside attorneys.

But from the beginning, Collins signaled that she intended to vote for Kavanaugh, notwithstanding the fact that she was a staunch defender of a woman's right to choose, whereas he was an opponent of abortion rights. She may have had good karma with him from his time in the Bush White House or from his earlier confirmation to the Court of Appeals. After a long discussion with him, Collins accepted Kavanaugh's assurance that he believed in *stare decisis*; in other words, he would not overrule *Roe v. Wade*. Calls from President George W. Bush and conversations with Rob Portman, who had served with Kavanaugh in the Bush White House, plainly helped satisfy her that the nominee was a mainstream conservative who would be an open-minded, even-handed justice.

On this matter Collins often seemed to be on an island of her own. Everyone else on both sides of the fierce fight understood what was at stake. *America*, the most influential Jesuit magazine, had endorsed Kavanaugh early, specifically citing his antiabortion views: "Anyone who recognizes the humanity of the unborn should support the nomination of Judge Kavanaugh."[65] The whole point of the Federalist Society list was to ensure the nomination of Supreme Court justices who were pro-life. That was why so many pro-life advocates were jubilant that Kavanaugh had been chosen.

Nor was there anything in Kavanaugh's record that was consistent with Collins's views on gun control, the separation of church and state, presidential power, or environmental regulation. Nonetheless, she liked him and trusted him. And in private statements, and then in her decisive floor speech, Collins made clear her anger at the degree of pressure she had received from women's rights groups. A significant "tell" was that in her closing speech, Collins made no reference to Kavanaugh's tirade or the issue of judicial temperament that it posed. When she encountered an issue that she could not, in good conscience, resolve in his favor, Collins simply chose to ignore it.[66]

Susan Collins's vote ensured that Brett Kavanaugh would be confirmed to be a Supreme Court justice, even though Lisa Murkowski, after agonized deliberation, voted against him. In the days that followed, where another president might have tried to bring people together, Trump lashed out, calling Kavanaugh "a man who did nothing wrong, a man that was caught up in a hoax that was set up by the Democrats, using the Democrats' lawyers."[67]

Collins may have summarized it best: "Today, we have come to the conclusion of a confirmation process so dysfunctional, it looks more like a caricature of a gutter level political campaign than a solemn occasion."[68] Given the frightening damage done to the Senate, McConnell might have chosen to applaud Kavanaugh's confirmation, express confidence that he would be a fair-minded justice, and tone down the political rhetoric. Instead, he taunted the opposition for the "great political gift" they had given to the Republicans. "I want to thank the mob," McConnell said, "for energizing our base." McConnell went on to note, "Nothing brings home the importance of the Senate like a court fight and nothing unifies the Republicans like the courts. Whether you're a Trump Republican or a Bush Republican or whatever kind of Republican you are, we all think putting strict constructionists on the courts is important."[69]

The midterm election results confirmed the stark political divide in America. The resistance to Donald Trump's presidency sparked an unprecedented level of off-year voting and produced a "blue wave" in the House of Representatives, where the Democrats gained forty seats to regain the majority by a comfortable margin. Nancy Pelosi, who had made history in 2007 by becoming the first woman speaker, would regain the gavel that she had lost in 2010. The Senate, however, remained in Republican hands even though the Democrats won 60 percent of the votes cast in Senate races across the country.[70] Heidi Heitkamp, Claire McCaskill, and Joe Donnelly went down to defeat in North Dakota, Missouri, and Indiana, and Republicans Rick Scott and Ted Cruz won election narrowly in Florida and Texas, the two races that were most fiercely contested. The results would further erode confidence in the Senate's lack of legitimacy, but that was a long-term problem. For now, the results confirmed McConnell's keen political judgment and his stranglehold on the functioning of American government.

Nonetheless, the postelection period presented the opportunity for a remarkable bipartisan accomplishment. For several years, consensus had been building that the harsh criminal sentencing provisions of the 1990s, imposing mandatory minimum sentences in place of judicial discretion, had proved to be a disastrous mistake. By 2015, more than 1.5 million Americans were incarcerated, disproportionately black and brown Americans, many of whom had received sentences for minor drug offenses. The staggering cost of locking up nonviolent offenders without preparing them to reenter society had produced a broad coalition, from the American Civil Liberties Union on the left to the Koch brothers on the right, that favored major legislative change.

In 2015, Chuck Grassley, joined by Dick Durbin and Mike Lee, had introduced major sentencing reform legislation that had won the support of the Obama administration and strong majorities in both parties. However, Jeff Sessions, then still in the Senate and a strong advocate of harsh sentencing, vehemently opposed the legislation. McConnell, recognizing a division among Republicans and unwilling to give Obama a legislative victory in an election year, had refused to bring the bill to the Senate floor. "It's one of the things that makes this a frustrating place to work," said Senator John Cornyn of Texas, the number-two Republican in the Senate, who became a believer in the new approach to criminal justice after seeing the benefits in his home state.[71]

After Trump's election, Grassley, Durbin, and Lee persisted. "Mandatory minimum sentences were once seen as a strong deterrent," Durbin observed. "In reality, they have too often been unfair, fiscally irresponsible, and a threat to public safety." The unlikely coalition of supporters broadened and deepened. Jared Kushner, Trump's son-in-law, whose father had been imprisoned, became a driving force behind the legislation, working hard to sell it to Trump, directly and by enlisting those whose voices mattered to the president, including Sean Hannity of Fox News.

With the 2018 midterm elections behind him, Trump became enthusiastic about the possibility of signing legislation that would be a genuine bipartisan accomplishment. "Criminal justice has gone from being the ultimate wedge issue to the most meaningful area of bipartisan agreement," said Michael Waldman, the president of the Brennan Center for Justice at the New York University School of Law and a frequent critic of Trump on policy. "It's a strange and ironic twist to have the president's support push it over the finish line."[72]

One obstacle remained: McConnell. The majority leader had refused to bring the bill to the Senate floor before the election, and he remained unwilling to bring it up afterward.[73] Estimating that the legislation would require ten days on the Senate floor, McConnell told the president and Grassley that the time would be better spent on his highest priority: confirming additional federal judges. As McConnell consolidated and wielded power, he collected some memorable nicknames, including "the Grim Reaper" and "Moscow Mitch," but the most consistently accurate might have been "Dr. No."

Grassley went ballistic. For two years, he had turned the Judiciary Committee into a conveyor belt for Trump's judicial nominations, and he had persevered through the brutal Kavanaugh fight. McConnell had promised him a floor vote if he could show that the legislation would receive more than sixty votes, and he had many more than that. Now McConnell was telling him there was no floor time for his legislative priority, which had broad bipartisan support and the president's endorsement. "I think it deserves a floor vote, and McConnell should honor his indication that he gave us that he would bring it up if we could show the votes," Grassley tweeted. ("McConnell," he said pointedly, not "the majority leader.") A few days later, Grassley called McConnell. "I have been there for you," Grassley said, according to aides who were in the room. "I would hope this is something you would help me make happen."

Libertarian supporters of the legislation lobbied McConnell constantly. "We are keeping up the pressure on him to make sure he is good on his word," said Jason Pye, the vice president of legislative affairs for FreedomWorks.[74] Rand Paul, in an interview, asked

McConnell to "look at the people who are coming at this from all walks of life and hear all our voices saying we want this legislation."[75]

On December 11, McConnell reversed his course, announcing that he would allow the First Step Act to come to a vote. "When you have a president do something that seems out of political character, it can sometimes make a historic difference," Durbin said.[76] McConnell had feared that the legislation would take up ten days of floor time; the debate was completed in an afternoon. Grassley, Durbin, and Lee had promised to produce at least sixty votes; the legislation passed by an overwhelming vote of 87–12.

Jared Kushner also received accolades for his tireless efforts to bring his father-in-law along. "There was a constant back-and-forth with Sessions, and Kushner won that battle," said Representative Hakeem Jeffries, a rising star among House Democrats. "Getting meaningful criminal justice reform over the finish line . . . would not have occurred without substantial leadership from Jared Kushner." Grassley and New Jersey senator Cory Booker, who had been at sword's point during the Kavanaugh hearings, embraced. The celebration was a reminder of what bipartisan legislative accomplishment felt like.[77] "The bill in its entirety has been endorsed by the political spectrum of America," Durbin said exultantly. "I can't remember any bill that has this kind of support, left and right, liberal and conservative, Democrat and Republican."[78]

A deeply divided Capitol had come together for the first time in years, to address a fundamentally serious failure in the way that our country enforced our laws and administered justice. A vital aspect of effective governance is to look realistically at its performance, acknowledge problems, and work to rectify them. Legislation often produces unanticipated results; government needs to be able to respond, even if slowly, to offer needed changes. In this case, many politicians, after much soul-searching, realized that the well-intentioned solutions to crime adopted in the 1990s had proven to be wrong. They had listened to the judges whose hands had been tied by sentencing guidelines, the prisoners who had been subjected to excessive and discriminatory punishments, the families that had lost hope that their sons would be treated fairly, and the advocacy groups who were on the front lines every day, working to help those who had been imprisoned to reenter society. They admitted their mistakes and crafted legislation to make important changes in the system.

It was an inspiring moment for everyone—except Mitch McConnell. Although he ultimately voted for the legislation, there is no evidence that he cared about the deep and complex problems that Grassley, Durbin, Lee, and the others worked for years to address. He cared only about keeping the Senate Republican caucus together. McConnell had worked for eight long years to obstruct government from acting while Obama, a Democrat, was president. His basic political calculation was sound; gridlock would hurt the Democrats and help the Republicans. But now, with a Republican president, McConnell was still locked in concrete; it took an enormous, unified, last-minute effort by everyone up to and including President Trump to move him. It was almost as if he hated the idea that the Senate should respond at all to the nation's problems.

That singular moment of bipartisan accomplishment stood in stark contrast to the turbulence and conflict as Trump finished his second year. On November 7, Trump fired Attorney General Jeff Sessions. Trump valued loyalty above all else, and he had never forgiven Sessions for recusing himself from the investigation of Russia's interference in the election. On December 8, Trump nominated William Barr, who had served as attorney general in the administration of George H. W. Bush, to do the job a second time. Barr, a familiar mainstream figure who had become wealthy as Verizon's general counsel, struck Republicans as a reassuring choice. However, Democrats were troubled that Barr had sent an unsolicited memo to the White House, expressing an expansive view of presidential power, in which he questioned whether Mueller could investigate Trump for obstruction of justice.[79] To many, it looked like a job application in which the applicant was making a promise to put the president's personal interests ahead of those of the nation.

On December 18, the same day the Senate passed the First Step Act, Secretary of Defense James Mattis, the most respected member of the cabinet, resigned in protest over the president's decision to withdraw all US troops from Syria, a decision that had triggered a firestorm of opposition from Republicans as well as Democrats. Mattis's departure removed from the administration the single strongest constraint on Trump's impulsiveness in the national security area. Military leaders feared that a precipitous withdrawal would jeopardize the territorial gains made against ISIS, essentially repeating what had happened when Barack Obama had withdrawn US troops from Iraq in 2011. Lindsey Graham, who had become one of Trump's strongest supporters, called it "Iraq all over again. . . . If Obama had done this," Graham said, "we'd be going nuts right now; how weak, how dangerous."[80] The decision was also seen as a betrayal of the Syrian Kurds, who had been our strongest allies in the fight against ISIS, and as ceding a crucial region to Russia and Iran.[81]

At the same time, Trump advised the country that he was prepared to shut down the government unless the Democrats provided $5.7 billion for his border wall. When Senate Democrats resisted, Trump pressed the Senate to eliminate the filibuster so that the border funding could be accomplished with fifty votes. McConnell, who had repeatedly predicted that there would be no shutdown, showed no interest in changing the legislative filibuster.[82] The Democrats continued to reject Trump's demand, and on December 21 the federal government shut down. "The shutdown is an appropriate end to a period of unified Republican rule of the White House and both chambers of Congress that has been marked by dysfunction and infighting, and a mercurial president whose shifting positions and whims have scuttled legislative deals," the *New York Times* reported.[83]

The first year of the Trump presidency had ended on a triumphant note, but year two ended with the federal government shut down, the Justice Department and the Pentagon leaderless, Robert Mueller and his team working intently, and a Democratic House set to arrive that would pose a constant threat to the president. Amid the chaos, the one constant remained Mitch McConnell, celebrating the Kavanaugh confirmation and running an unprecedented number of ideological and young right-wing judges through the Senate.

· 5 ·

To Impeach or Not to Impeach

$\mathcal{A}$s Congress returned in January 2019, Mitch McConnell faced a transformed political landscape. With the arrival of a Democratic majority in the House, President Donald Trump faced for the first time the imminent prospect of serious congressional oversight backed up by the subpoena power wielded by House committees. The chances that Trump would be impeached had gone from zero when the Republicans ran the House to eminently possible, if not probable, with the Democrats in charge.

Trump's political and personal fate depended on the interaction of the leaders of the Democratic House and the Republican Senate: Nancy Pelosi and Mitch McConnell. They were, and remain, the yin and yang of American politics—fiercely competitive, strong-willed politicians, superb strategists and tacticians, committed party builders, and tireless fundraisers. They had been facing off as leaders for a historically long time, beginning after the 2006 midterm elections.

Pelosi had had four years in the majority, followed by eight in the minority; McConnell's arc was precisely the reverse. During their first Congress as leaders, Pelosi and McConnell had made a promising start, working together after the Lehman crash to pass the consequential and controversial Troubled Asset Relief Program (TARP) in October 2008. But since then, they had crossed swords many times, particularly in the fierce battles over the Affordable Care Act. It would be difficult to find a single issue they agreed on; they personified the divide between Democrats and Republicans. There might have been mutual respect between two old pros, but McConnell was increasingly disinclined to respect anyone; in his 2016 memoir, he mocked Pelosi for reciting her talking points endlessly, with the message always being "Don't forget the children."[1] As he often did, McConnell showed real insight. Pelosi, with five children and nine grandchildren, approached politics guided by a burning concern for children and their futures, which played no part in the calculus of McConnell or Trump.

Pelosi, the first woman to serve as speaker, had her own issues with her caucus. She and her principal deputies, Steny Hoyer and James Clyburn, were all seventy-five or older, and many House Democrats, including some incoming members, thought it was time for a generational change. Two weeks after the 2018 midterm elections, sixteen newly elected House members announced their opposition to Pelosi as leader. "We are thankful to leader Pelosi for her years of service to our country and our caucus," their letter stated. Now, it went on, "the time has come for new leadership."

Pelosi wasted no time beating back the rebellion. With her characteristic thoroughness and forcefulness, she persuaded potentially strong opponents not to run and easily defeated those who did.[2] Eager to legislate after eight years out of power, Pelosi cranked up the machinery and started advancing legislation across the full spectrum of Democratic priorities.

McConnell's agenda was clear enough. With the House in Democratic hands, few (if any) Trump legislative initiatives were likely to succeed, but, in fact, there were few (if any) Trump legislative initiatives at all. Trump had promised a trillion-dollar infrastructure package, which could have had bipartisan appeal, but it never seemed to materialize. Hard-fought compromises about NAFTA 2.0 and treatment of the Dreamers (undocumented immigrants who had arrived as children) might be possible, but certainly not in the early months of the year. McConnell's principal role would be to kill every piece of legislation that the House sent over. Speaking in Kentucky in April, he promised to be the "grim reaper" for all progressive policies, such as the "Green New Deal."[3]

Since his Senate would have no legislative agenda, McConnell focused the chamber on his highest priority, and the one issue the Senate could handle without Pelosi's cooperation: confirming federal judges. Of course, this had been his priority since day one of the Trump administration, but now there was nothing to compete for Senate floor time. For the first two years, McConnell had given priority to confirming Trump's nominees for the courts of appeals. Now he turned his attention to confirming a flood of federal district judges. In 2017, the Senate confirmed only six district court judges. In 2018, the pace picked up as the Senate confirmed forty-eight. The year 2019 would see eighty nominees for federal district judgeships confirmed.[4]

At the same time, the central drama of the Trump years was coming to a head; Special Counsel Robert Mueller and his team were bringing their work to its conclusion. Under the existing regulations for a special counsel, Mueller would submit his report to the attorney general, William Barr, who would be confirmed as Jeff Sessions's replacement on February 12. Barr was inheriting a department demoralized by Trump's interference in the law enforcement process and would face the challenge of rebuilding confidence that the Justice Department was not simply a political arm of the White House. Many prominent lawyers who had worked with Barr thought he was well suited to right the ship. But others shared the concern that Barr had virtually applied for the job by submitting his nineteen-page memo expressing a remarkably broad view of presidential power, which undoubtedly appealed to Trump.[5]

In the Senate, Lindsey Graham had become the chairman of the Judiciary Committee, succeeding Chuck Grassley, and he would have the responsibility for confirming Barr, working with him, and overseeing the Justice Department. Graham was a chameleon, having gone from being a member of the House team of managers who zealously prosecuted Bill Clinton's impeachment trial to an independent maverick who was John McCain's best friend and wingman and scathing

Trump critic, to being Trump's strongest defender and golfing buddy. Barack Obama, in his memoir, would describe Graham as completely untrustworthy. "You know how in the spy thriller or the heist movie, you're introduced to the crew at the beginning?" Obama told Rahm Emanuel, his chief of staff. "Lindsey's the guy who double-crosses everyone to save his own skin."[6]

Political observers puzzled over what had happened to Graham. Some speculated that Graham, who grew up poor and lost his parents early, needed an older brother or father figure to look up to.[7] Others felt that the best part of Graham had died with John McCain. But the answer was less complicated. Graham, by his own admission, liked to be "relevant."[8] He took delight in being Trump's new best friend, believing, with some justification, that he could have special impact by talking privately to the president. Moreover, Graham was up for reelection in 2020, and he would likely face a strong, well-financed challenge. Nor had it escaped his notice that Trump was much more popular in South Carolina than he was. Graham needed to anticipate defeating any Republican primary challenger who came after him for being too independent, and Trump could be brutal to any Republican who crossed him. Graham had every incentive to stay close to Trump; he thrust himself into the center of many key debates, having discovered long before that reporters love to quote senators. In the turbulent months ahead, it would often seem as if there were only two Senate Republicans: McConnell, who was the leader, and Graham, who never stopped talking.

The first order of business was to reopen the government. Trump's temper tantrum in December had resulted in the longest shutdown of the federal government in history, even though the Republicans controlled both houses of Congress. With Pelosi now in command in the House, Trump's leverage was dramatically reduced. When McConnell, who had opposed the shutdown, called the White House, Trump proved eager to find a way to end the impasse. On January 25, Trump simply capitulated, agreeing to a compromise to reopen the government until February 15, which included no money for the border wall. It was essentially the same approach he had rejected in December, which enraged some of his hard-line supporters but was welcomed by many Republican senators. "None of us are willing to go through this again," said Lisa Murkowski. "We've already lost," said Georgia's Johnny Isakson. "It's a matter of the extent that we want to keep losing." Shelley Moore Capito, coming from West Virginia, one of the nation's strongest pro-Trump states, observed, "There are a lot of strategies we could employ that would work better" than a shutdown.[9]

Attention now turned to the Mueller investigation, which after more than a year and a half was drawing to an end. On March 12, Mueller sent his 448-page report to the attorney general, as required by law. A week earlier, Mueller had briefed Barr on the contents of the report and the approach he had taken to the key issues. Recognizing that the report was dense reading, Mueller and his team had prepared comprehensive summaries of its two major subjects: possible Russian interference in the 2016 election and possible obstruction of justice committed by President Trump. Mueller assumed that Barr would release the summaries to the public. Instead, Barr issued a four-page letter in which he offered his own "summary" of the report, though it was in fact a misleading characterization of the Mueller team's work.

Part I of the Mueller report documented extensive evidence of Russia's efforts to interfere in the 2016 presidential election. Although the report stated that it had not found evidence of criminal conspiracy involving Trump campaign officials, it documented numerous examples of Russia's outreach to the Trump presidential campaign and the clear willingness of the Trump campaign to accept Russian assistance. Part II documented ten instances in which Trump had taken actions that seemed intended to obstruct the investigation into Russian interference in the election. Mueller did not reach a conclusion about whether the president had committed an indictable offense; rather, he laid out the evidence for Congress and the public to assess.

Barr's letter emphasized that Mueller had found no criminal conspiracy—which would have required "probable cause"—between Trump campaign officials and Russia, without acknowledging the mass of evidence showing coordination of efforts. Barr was even more disingenuous in dealing with the issue of obstruction of justice. He knew that Mueller was working under the constraint of legal guidance from the Justice Department's Office of Legal Counsel that a president cannot be indicted while in office. Mueller told Barr that he would not make a finding suggesting that Trump had obstructed justice because the president would have no chance to respond to it in court. But the report spelled out ten specific acts by the president that sounded very much like obstruction of justice. Despite knowing Mueller's rationale, Barr stated that Mueller had not been able to reach a conclusion, leaving it up to the attorney general to do so—which he did, exonerating Trump.

"It was obvious that Barr had spun our findings for political gain at best, and lied for the president at worst. . . . It contained so many deceptions, it was hard to take them all in," said Andrew Weissmann, a respected senior member of Mueller's team. "Some were delicately worded obfuscations. Some were unbridled lies."[10] Mueller had explained to Barr his complete thinking on the issues of collusion and obstruction, but Barr had betrayed his confidence by deliberately distorting what the report said. Playing by what he thought were the rules, Mueller called Barr's office the next day. Receiving no response, Mueller then wrote to Barr on March 27, showing his unmistakable anger. "The summary letter the Department sent to Congress and released to the public late in the afternoon of March 24 did not fully capture the context, nature and substance of this Office's work or conclusion," Mueller wrote. "There is now public confusion about critical aspects of the results of our investigation. This threatens to undermine a central purpose for which the Department appointed the Special Counsel: to assure public confidence in the outcome of the investigation."[11]

But public confidence in the outcome of the investigation was not Barr's goal. Having undercut Mueller's findings, Barr was now in no rush to release the full report. "A critical three weeks passed between when you delivered the letter with the focus on the principal conclusions and when we ultimately got the redacted report," Senator Chris Coons said when Barr testified before the Judiciary Committee. "My concern is that gave President Trump and his folks more than three weeks of an open field to say 'I was completely exonerated.'"[12] The impact of Barr's letter became clear immediately. The *New York Times* called it "a significant political victory for Mr. Trump [that] lifted a cloud that has hung over his presidency since before he took the oath of office."[13]

On April 18, the day before he finally released Mueller's report, Barr held a press conference and once again mischaracterized the report, piling on one misstatement after another, including the remarkable assertion that Trump had fully cooperated with Mueller's investigation, even though the president had refused to be interviewed, his son Donald Jr. had refused to be interviewed, and Trump had encouraged many witnesses not to cooperate.[14]

Mark Twain famously observed that "a lie can go halfway around the world while the truth is putting on its shoes." On April 18, speaking in Louisville hours after Barr's statement, McConnell said that the Mueller report should make President Trump "feel good," while acknowledging that he had not yet read it. McConnell noted that Barr had "an outstanding reputation in Washington circles. . . . There is no chance that at his age and his status within the profession that he's going to go in there and be some sort of political hack for this administration. . . . I trust Bill Barr."[15]

McConnell's water-carrying for Barr and Trump intensified in the weeks that followed. "The special counsel's finding is clear: case closed," McConnell said mockingly on May 7. "This ought to be good news for everyone but my Democratic colleagues seem to be publicly working through the five stages of grief."[16]

"With an exhaustive investigation complete, would the country finally unify to confront the real challenges before us?" McConnell queried, "Or would we remain consumed by unhinged partisanship, and keep dividing ourselves to the point that Putin and his agents need only stand on the sidelines and watch as their job is done for them?"

"Regrettably," he continued, "the answer is obvious."

Chuck Schumer responded to McConnell, saying, "It's not done," and he accused the majority leader of "whitewashing" Trump's conduct and attempting to protect him from accountability. "The leader says:

'Let's move on.' It's sort of like Richard Nixon saying let's move on at the height of the investigation of his wrongdoing," Schumer said.[17]

After initially indicating an intention to invite Barr and Mueller to testify before the Judiciary Committee, Lindsey Graham pivoted to join the "case closed" contingent. "He's done his job, and I'm not going to retry the case," Graham said in an interview. "I'm all good. I'm done with the Mueller report." When questioned about Mueller's finding that Trump had tried to order White House counsel Don McGahn to fire Mueller while the probe was under way, Graham added, "I don't care what he said to Don McGahn—it's what he did. The President never obstructed."[18]

Not only was he done with Mueller, but Graham also stated his readiness to go on the offensive. Republicans were interested in getting a better handle on what he called "the other side of the story": investigating the 2016 campaign and whether the FBI, the Department of Justice, and Hillary Clinton's campaign engaged in efforts to hurt Trump.

Even those Republican senators facing difficult reelection bids who might have benefited from distancing themselves from Trump refused to do so. Cory Gardner of Colorado, widely seen as the most endangered Republican Senate candidate, said, "It's time for Congress to move forward and get to work on behalf of the American people." Gardner said he would seek punishment for Russia's efforts to interfere in the election but stopped short of any criticism of Trump. Thom Tillis of North Carolina said that "pursuing the path of endless investigations and impeachment would be a bitterly partisan move that would further divide the country." But two independent-minded Republicans did express criticism of Trump. Mitt Romney, recently elected to the Senate from Utah, said that he was "sickened" by the report's description of Trump's behavior, and Susan Collins called the portrayal of Trump "unflattering." But Romney indicated that the lack of charges on obstruction of justice resolved the matter for him. "The business of government can move on," he said.[19]

The full story would emerge and become the subject of fierce debate, but for the moment, the congressional Democrats who had been waiting for Mueller's report faced the challenge of how to deal with Trump's assault on the rule of law and his continued inexplicable attachment to Vladimir Putin. The House Democrats were fully committed to oversight hearings that would shed light on the corruption and abuse of power by Trump, his family, and his administration. They faced the overriding issue of whether Trump's conduct warranted an impeachment inquiry.

While many of the House Democrats had vehement and clashing views, ultimately, only one Democrat was "the decider." Nancy Pelosi took a back seat to no one in her contempt for Trump, her belief that he was abusing his power and violating his oath of office, and her fear of the damage he could do to the country. She questioned his fitness for the presidency, describing him as unethical, anti-intellectual, incurious, dishonorable, and uninformed. "This is a strain of cat that I don't have the medical credentials to analyze nor the religious credentials to judge," Pelosi said. She called him "the most dangerous person in the history of the country."[20]

At the same time, the speaker was an extraordinarily savvy, practical politician with a keen sense of the national climate and what her caucus would support. Barr's handling of Mueller's report had deprived it of the impact that it might otherwise have had. The ball was now in Pelosi's court, without the strong validation of an impeachable offense by the special counsel. Polls showed support for impeachment weakening,[21] and Pelosi was well aware that her majority resulted from moderate Democrats having won narrow victories in closely balanced districts that could easily swing the other way in 2020. Pelosi's moderates wanted Congress to focus on practical matters—ensuring access to health care, reducing college costs, and creating jobs—not impeachment. They were not ready to support it, and therefore neither was she.

Pelosi's reluctance to impeach Trump went beyond her political calculus. After first becoming speaker in 2007, she had faced pressure from Democrats to impeach George W. Bush over the increasingly disastrous war in Iraq. Pelosi was fiercely opposed to the war; she thought the invasion of Iraq was "the biggest mistake our country has ever made." But she did not believe that a president should be impeached based on policy differences, and she worried about the implications of impeaching Bush after Clinton had been impeached.[22] Now, twelve years later, considering Trump, she remained cautious.

"I'm not for impeachment," she told the *Washington Post* in mid-March. "Impeachment is so divisive to the country that unless there is something so compelling and overwhelming and bipartisan, I don't think we should go down that path, because it divides the country," Pelosi said. "And he's just not worth it," she concluded.[23]

It was a memorable one-liner, but Pelosi's position would become increasingly unconvincing. Notwithstanding Barr's distortions, the case for impeaching Trump clearly met her standard of being "so compelling" and "overwhelming." In June, more than a thousand former prosecutors, Democrats and Republicans, joined an open letter declaring that Trump would have been indicted on multiple counts of obstruction of justice if he were not the sitting president.[24] By insisting that impeachment could proceed only with bipartisan support, Pelosi was giving Trump impunity by granting McConnell and the Senate Republicans absolute veto power on whether the House should move forward. Her moderates were afraid of impeaching Trump, but that should not have been decisive if the country was facing a dangerous president running roughshod over the Constitution. Throughout the Trump years, Democrats and liberal pundits would constantly criticize the Senate Republicans for lack of political courage in failing to put the national interest over their political fortunes. But the House moderates would be showing the exact same lack of courage if they prevented impeachment from being pursued. At some point, they would need to step up.

Mueller, who had been virtually invisible since his appointment, finally appeared in public, testifying in the House on July 27, more than four months after having submitted his report. The partisan divide was deeper than ever, with the Democrats split over how to proceed and the Republicans united behind the false narrative that Trump had been exonerated.

Mueller had one chance to cut through the partisan warfare and stand up for his report, whose impact had been blunted by Barr's mischaracterization of it and by the delay in its release. He testified for seven hours, appearing first before the House Judiciary Committee and then before the House Intelligence Committee. He was plainly a reluctant witness, who steadfastly avoided making statements that went beyond the text of the report. Mueller declined to answer nearly two hundred questions put to him and offered the most cryptic answers possible to many others. He created confusion on his views about the rationale for his decision not to say that Trump had obstructed justice. He also refused to be critical of Barr's handling of the report. Even so, the Democrats' persistent questioning did get him to confirm the most damaging elements of his findings: that Trump had not been cleared of obstructing justice and that the president had been untruthful in some of his responses to the probe.[25]

But overall Mueller did not convey the urgency about a corrupt president abusing his power and jeopardizing our democracy in a way that would have influenced an open-minded viewer. He chose to appear alone, when it would have been perfectly reasonable for him to be flanked by his principal deputies, to whom he could have deferred on particular questions. And he was not an impressive witness; he looked old, hesitant, and frequently befuddled.[26]

Adam Schiff, the chairman of the House Intelligence Committee, was able to get Mueller to acknowledge that accepting foreign assistance to influence the outcome of a presidential election was unethical—possibly a crime, Mueller noted—and certainly unpatriotic. When the hearing ended, Schiff observed that the special counsel had submitted his report; now, it was up to the House to determine how to respond.[27] Schiff was one of Pelosi's most trusted lieutenants, and the ball was plainly in the speaker's court.

Although Mueller's testimony inflicted no perceptible damage on Trump, this last week of July would prove to be fateful for the Trump presidency. Dan Coats, the respected director of national intelligence, resigned, removing one of the few experienced foreign policy advisers willing to give Trump unwelcome news.[28] And on July 25, the Senate Intelligence Committee released the first volume of what would be a five-volume report on Russian "active measures" that had interfered with the 2016 presidential election, a comprehensive, bipartisan under-taking steered by the committee's Republican chairman, Richard Burr, and its Democratic vice chairman, Mark Warner. Burr and Warner came to their assignment with a real personal friendship, which helped keep the committee's work on track.[29] Their friendship did much to restore the Intelligence Committee's tradition of bipartisanship, which had been rocked by fierce divisions over the committee's five-year investigation into the CIA's detention and enhanced interrogation practices at Abu Ghraib during the Bush administration.[30] Now, the sobering nature of what the committee members were learning about Russian "active measures" and the evidence of collusion with the Trump campaign kept them committed to their task.

But the Intelligence Committee report would take a back seat to another development that same day. On July 25, President Trump placed a call to Ukraine's president Volodymyr Zelensky, asking him to investigate Hunter Biden, the son of former vice president Joe Biden, and his ties to the Burisma Company, on whose board he served, if Ukraine wanted to receive $400 million in military assistance that had already been appropriated by Congress. Apparently, Zelensky was not sufficiently responsive. That same day, the Office of Management and Budget formally withheld military aid to Ukraine.[31]

Throughout the Trump presidency, observers would wonder what lessons the president was taking away from his experiences. In private life, Trump had successfully brazened, bullied, lied, and liti-gated through every situation, repeatedly avoiding disaster and com-ing out ahead. Now he was the president, wielding great power that he saw as virtually unconstrained. Plainly, Trump's experience with Mueller did not chasten him; his takeaway was that nothing could stop him. The call to Zelensky was blatant, rather than private; at least seven other administration officials were on the call. One who heard the call was sufficiently disturbed that he or she filed a whistleblower complaint on August 12.

Ukraine desperately needed the military aid to combat a military invasion by Russia, which had already seized Crimea and the east-ern part of Ukraine. On September 3, a bipartisan group of senators, including Jeanne Shaheen, Rob Portman, Dick Durbin, Ron Johnson, and Richard Blumenthal, all of whom had championed the aid for Ukraine, demanded to know why it was being held up.[32] On September 20, the *Wall Street Journal* ran a bombshell story reporting that in a July phone call, Trump had repeatedly pressured the Ukraine president to investigate Hunter Biden's tie to Burisma, urging Zelensky about eight times to work with Rudy Giuliani, Trump's personal lawyer, and Attorney General Barr to probe whether former vice president Biden had acted improperly. Trump defended his call with Zelensky as "totally appropriate"; he would later characterize the call as "perfect."[33]

Unlike the complex interaction between the Trump campaign and Russia, which came to light over a two-and-a-half-year period and multiple investigations, Trump's pressure on Zelensky exploded into public view virtually overnight. On September 24, the White House, responding to the press and congressional pressure, released a transcript of the phone call, which clearly showed Trump's call to be a shakedown of the Ukrainian president, who was in desperate need of military support.[34]

That morning, Nancy Pelosi initiated impeachment proceedings against President Trump. Her resistance had ended when she realized that Trump was incorrigible and that he would defy Congress's appropriation of military aid and jeopardize the security of an American ally, advancing Russia's interests in order to serve his own personal political ends. Indeed, Pelosi quickly saw that her argument against impeachment—let the voters give their verdict on Trump at the next election—made no sense if Trump was abusing his office to ensure his reelection by damaging his most formidable likely opponent.

Within twenty-four hours, 57 House Democrats endorsed impeachment, a number that quickly rose to 196. Pelosi was undoubtedly moved by a powerful op-ed piece in the *Washington Post* by seven freshman Democrats with experience in the military and the defense and intelligence agencies—precisely the moderates that she wanted to protect—endorsing the impeachment inquiry. "This flagrant disregard for the law cannot stand," the op-ed stated. "To uphold and defend our Constitution, Congress must determine whether the president was indeed willing to use his power and withhold security assistance funds to persuade a foreign country to assist him in an upcoming election. If these allegations are true, we believe these actions constitute an impeachable offense."[35]

By this point, though, Pelosi harbored no realistic hope that impeachment could be bipartisan. Trump tweeted angrily, "Presidential harassment." McConnell had previously said that he was "never given an explanation" for why Ukraine aid was held up, even though he had pressed for one.[36] Now, however, the majority leader moved quickly to get his talking points out. "Speaker Pelosi's much-publicized efforts to restrain her far-left conference have finally crumbled. House Democrats cannot help themselves," McConnell said. "Instead of working together across party lines on legislation to help American families and strengthen our nation, they will descend even deeper into their obsession with re-litigating 2016."[37]

Lindsey Graham, who not long ago had demonstrated a deep commitment to Ukraine and strong support for military aid to allow Ukraine to resist Russian aggression, now lined up to defend the president's behavior. Just weeks before, Graham had joined Dick Durbin in threatening to withhold $5 billion from the Pentagon unless the aid to Ukraine was restored, but none of that history mattered now. Pelosi's decision launched Graham into a rant. "Impeachment over this? What a nothing (non-quid pro quo) burger? Democrats have lost their mind when it comes to President Trump," Graham vented. "If you are underwhelmed by this transcript, you are not alone or 'crazy.' Those willing to impeach the president over this transcript have shown their hatred for President Trump. . . . In the phone call everybody is talking about, there is not one scintilla of evidence that the President threatened Ukraine with withholding money because they wanted him to do Trump's political bidding. That did not happen."[38]

Graham's passion notwithstanding, the facts of what Trump had done were clear. The audiotape of Trump's call with Zelensky was truly the proverbial smoking gun. The pressure Trump had put on Zelensky was enormous. He was holding something of great value to Ukraine: desperately needed military aid. He was defying the will of

Congress, which had appropriated the funds. His desire to have Zelensky do political harm to Biden was undeniable. "I need a favor," Trump said, making it crystal clear that he was seeking a quid pro quo.

McConnell was certainly right in saying that many Democrats had wanted to impeach Trump for a long time. But they had not done so, and after Mueller's report and congressional appearance fizzled, Pelosi and most other Democrats had given up on impeachment, turning their attention and energy to legislation and to the fierce election coming up in 2020. They reversed course only because of Trump's shocking act. Moreover, the whistleblower complaint that made Trump's phone call public was an act of conscience by a career foreign service officer. The witnesses who gave testimony that built the case for impeachment were not political people. They were almost all career foreign service officers, who had been in government for fifteen to thirty years, serving Republican and Democratic administrations. They knew what normal government policy looked like and the way normal presidents behaved. All of them believed that Trump's behavior was shockingly aberrational and an abuse of his office. They came forward and risked their careers, out of a sense of commitment to the Constitution.

Evidently, nothing that Trump could do would diminish McConnell and Graham's reflexive, unyielding support. However, several Senate Republicans responded more soberly, expressing concern about Trump's conduct. "It remains troubling in the extreme. It's deeply troubling," Mitt Romney said after reading the transcript. "Republicans ought not to be rushing to circle the wagons and say there's no 'there' there when there's obviously a lot that is very troubling there," observed Nebraska's Ben Sasse. Still, most of the Senate Republicans, however uneasy, downplayed the seriousness of what Trump had done, even as they questioned the wisdom of releasing the transcript.[39]

In the intense few weeks that followed, various Republicans would try out several mitigating defenses: Trump had momentarily overstepped and made a "bad call"; the military aid had been held up for a variety of reasons not related to investigating the Bidens; the aid was ultimately disbursed, so no real harm had resulted. But as the House inquiry and the press coverage continued, none of these defenses held water. The effort to smear Joe Biden and his son had started months before; Rudy Giuliani had publicly announced in May that he was traveling to Kiev to urge the Ukrainian government to investigate Hunter Biden's involvement with Burisma and the origins of interference in the 2016 presidential election.[40] Trump's phone call was not a one-off error; it was part of a concerted effort by the administration to block the military aid to Ukraine, despite congressional pressure to provide the aid that had been appropriated. The administration released the funds only after the scheme to block it became public.

The House investigation moved forward rapidly, and subpoenas were issued to Giuliani, Secretary of State Pompeo, Secretary of Defense Mark Esper, and Acting Budget Director Russell Vought.[41] But White House counsel Pat Cipollone (who had succeeded Don McGahn) responded that the administration would not comply with the subpoenas.[42]

Throughout November, the House investigation moved forward. Senior foreign service officers were deposed behind closed doors before testifying in public. William Taylor, the top US diplomat in Ukraine, a thirty-year foreign service officer, directly tied Trump to the quid pro quo. Marie Yovanovich, the former US ambassador to Ukraine, offered riveting testimony that she had been replaced by Trump at Giuliani's urging because of her persistent efforts to combat corruption in Ukraine. But John Bolton, Trump's former national security adviser, and Mick Mulvaney, Trump's acting chief of staff and the former director of the Office of Management and Budget, refused to appear for their depositions, continuing the stonewalling by Trump's political appointees.

Gordon Sondland proved to be the one exception. Sondland, whose sudden involvement in Ukraine policy was troubling to the career diplomats (he was a wealthy hotel owner and Republican donor who had become Trump's ambassador to the European Union), initially testified that there was no quid pro quo. But on November 20, apparently having considered that his statements under oath had placed him in legal jeopardy, he "updated" his testimony, forthrightly acknowledging that he had told Ukrainian officials that the military aid and a presidential visit were conditioned on the investigations that Trump demanded. His testimony also implicated Trump, Pence, Pompeo, Bolton, Mulvaney, and Giuliani as the other central players in the drama.[43]

With the facts emerging clearly, on December 4 the House Judiciary Committee convened its first impeachment hearing to evaluate whether the Ukraine quid pro quo met the historic standard for impeachment under the Constitution. Four law professors—Noah Feldman from Harvard, Pamela Karlan from Stanford, Michael Gerhardt from the University of North Carolina, and Jonathan Turley from George Washington University—agreed on the bedrock principle: the president, unlike the king of England, was not above the law.

"Congress could oversee the president's conduct, hold him accountable and remove him from office if he abused his power," Feldman stated. They agreed that impeachable offenses were acts that "abused the public trust" and "relate chiefly to injuries done immediately to the society itself." Karlan noted that "the essence of an impeachable offense is a president's decision to sacrifice the national interest for his own private ends."[44]

The combination of two of the framers' core concerns—foreign influence on the president and threats to the integrity of elections—can create a combustible problem, Karlan observed:

> In his farewell address, President Washington warned that "history and experience prove that foreign influence is one of the most baneful foes of republican government." And he explained that this was in part because foreign governments would try and foment disagreement among the American people and influence what we thought. The very idea that a president might seek the aid of a foreign government in his re-election campaign would have horrified them. But based on the evidentiary record, that is what President Trump has done. . . . Put simply, a candidate for president should resist foreign interference in our elections, not demand it.[45]

The constitutional law professors were not impressed with the argument that the decision about Trump's stewardship must be left to the voters. "The framers believed that elections were not a sufficient check on the possibility of a president who abused his power by acting in a corrupt way," Feldman stated. "They were especially worried that a president might use the power of his office to influence the election in his favor. They concluded that the Constitution must provide for the impeachment of the president to assure that no one would be above the law."[46]

Feldman, Karlan, and Gerhardt, all of whom had been invited by the Democrats, concluded that the evidence of impeachment was overwhelming. Turley, the Republican invitee, disagreed: "If the House proceeds solely on the Ukrainian allegations, this impeachment would stand out among modern impeachments as the shortest proceeding with the thinnest evidentiary record, and the narrowest grounds ever used to impeach a president." Ironically, Turley's point, which McConnell and other Republicans would repeatedly cite, was the exact reason that many Democrats thought Trump should have been impeached for inviting Russia's interference in the 2016 presidential election, engaging in obstruction of justice, and not combating another round of Russian interference in 2020. Still, even Turley noted that "the use of military aid for a quid pro quo, if proven, can be an impeachable offense."[47] To acquit President Trump, the Senate Republicans would have to disregard both the damning facts and the clear intentions of the nation's founders. No one doubted that they would meet the challenge.

The day following the legal scholars' testimony, Pelosi instructed the Judiciary Committee to draft articles of impeachment, and on December 9 the lawyers for the Judiciary and Intelligence Committees presented two impeachment articles, accusing the president of abusing his office and obstructing Congress in its efforts to investigate and hold him accountable. These articles were debated and approved by a fiercely divided Judiciary Committee, on a straight partisan vote of 23–17, on December 12. "It's a horrible thing to be using the tool of impeachment, which is supposed to be used in an emergency," Trump told reporters, an ironic formulation from a president who had cried "emergency" to justify funding the border wall despite Congress's votes to the contrary and slapping tariffs on steel and aluminum imports from friendly nations.

Five days later, with his impeachment imminent, Trump unleashed a single-spaced letter, which ran more than five pages. "The Articles of Impeachment introduced by the House Judiciary Committee articles are not recognizable under any Constitutional theory, interpretation, or jurisprudence. They include no crimes, no misdemeanors, no offenses at all. You have cheapened the importance of a very ugly word, impeachment," Trump wrote. He claimed without justification that his rights had been denied and accused the whistleblower of lying. He attacked Pelosi for "declaring open war on democracy. . . . You are offending Americans of faith by continually saying 'I pray for the president' when you know it is not true, unless it is meant in a negative sense." Trump raged on, repeating his anger about the 2016 election and what he called the "witch hunt" conducted by Mueller. But he could not halt the process that his July 25 phone call had set in motion.

On December 18, Speaker Pelosi gaveled the House to order to vote on the articles of impeachment, which resulted in virtually straight party-line results: 230–197 for the first article and 229–198 for the second. As the votes were being cast, Trump took the stage at a campaign rally in Battle Creek, Michigan. In an extraordinary scene, he railed against the Democrats as thousands of his supporters responded in real time to the vote. It was the only time in American history that a president held a political rally of his supporters while being impeached. More than six thousand supporters, who had braved the cold, cheered as Trump bragged about Republican unity. "The Republican Party has never been so affronted, but they've never been so united," he bellowed.[48]

Year three of the aberrational Trump presidency had come to an end, with Donald Trump now the third president in American history to be impeached. Yet the US government continued to function. Less than twenty-four hours after the impeachment vote, the House voted, 385–41, to approve historic legislation to implement the new US-Mexico-Canada trade agreement (USMCA). Months of tough, substantive, honest negotiations between United States trade representative

Robert Lighthizer and the House and Senate trade committees had produced a remarkable result. NAFTA, bitterly controversial for almost thirty years, was modernized and changed in a way that won broad support from business, labor, and nongovernmental organizations. Progressive Democrats endorsed the deal after a series of concessions on key issues of importance to them, including new requirements on rules of origin and wage rates that would benefit autoworkers in the United States and Canada. "On every conceivable front, we have improved the old NAFTA," said Richard Neal, the chairman of the House Ways and Means Committee. Senator Sherrod Brown of Ohio and Congresswoman Rosa DeLauro, two of the harshest Democratic critics of free trade deals, supported the new USMCA.[49] Frustrated Democrats, who had seen Mitch McConnell block Senate consideration of more than 275 House-passed bills in the past year, could take pride in a singular accomplishment.[50] So could Senate Republicans, who once feared that Trump's antitrade policy would end NAFTA and undermine North American supply chains.

In the same week, the Senate broke a months-long logjam to pass a $738 billion defense bill by an overwhelming vote of 86–8. The legislation contained several victories for Trump, including the authorization of the Space Force that he had proposed as a sixth branch of the American military. The bill also provided twelve weeks of paid parental leave for civilian federal employees, a Democratic priority that had also been embraced by Jared Kushner. And it contained a series of provisions rebuking Russia, China, and Turkey, nations that had aroused bipartisan anger on the Hill. "Let the vote be so overwhelming that there isn't a military family in America who could doubt our commitment to them," proclaimed Senator James Inhofe of Oklahoma, the chairman of the Armed Services Committee. "Let's use our vote to send a message to Russia and China that we're revitalizing America's power so we can win the competition for influence that will shape the kind of world our children and grandchildren are going to live in."[51] The overwhelming votes on both pieces of legislation showed that the congressional process could still work when capable legislators and administration officials engaged in good-faith negotiations to attack the nation's problems.

It was, in many respects, a fitting end to Trump's third year. His presidency continued to move on two distinct tracks. On one track, he led an administration whose policies were disruptive and often extreme but could be debated, contested, compromised about, or ultimately reversed through intense but normal political engagement. American voters could pass judgment on Trump's record on trade, immigration, education, health care, the environment, race, and policies toward China, Iran, and Israel. But on the second track, Trump was conducting an unprecedented assault on the rule of law and the Constitution, jeopardizing national security, and undermining assumptions about shared facts and reality.

· 6 ·

The Sham Trial

$\mathcal{T}$he bipartisan moment that produced the USMCA and the defense spending bill ended as abruptly as it appeared. The Senate—both judge and jury in the impeachment trial—seemed likely to be as divided on partisan lines as the House had been. Inevitably, Americans would be subjected to one more tour de force by Mitch McConnell.

On December 19, the day after the House approved the articles of impeachment, McConnell criticized Chuck Schumer for "angrily negotiating through the press" and creating an "impasse" over the rules of the trial. It was remarkably early in the process to proclaim an impasse, but McConnell wanted to send a clear message. "In 1999, all 100 senators agreed on a simple pre-trial resolution that set up a briefing, opening arguments, senators' questions and a vote on a motion to dismiss," McConnell recalled, speaking of the impeachment trial of President Bill Clinton. "Senators reserved all other questions, such as witnesses, until the trial was underway. . . . If 100 senators thought this approach was good enough for President Clinton, it ought to be good enough for President Trump."[1]

McConnell also charged that the House "seems to have gotten cold feet and be unsure whether they even want to proceed to a trial."[2] This claim also seemed premature, but it would acquire unexpected force in the weeks that followed. Pelosi, following the counsel of Harvard law professor Laurence Tribe, decided that she could put pressure on the

Senate by delaying the transmittal of the articles of impeachment.[3] This gambit could work over the Christmas break but did not seem like a promising long-term strategy. The speaker had crossed the Rubicon by deciding that Trump's abuse of power required the House to impeach regardless of whether the Senate would convict. But she moved onto thin ice with an effort to somehow control the proceedings of a Senate trial, beyond the responsibility of the House managers to present the case against Trump. McConnell rarely found himself on the moral high ground, but this time Pelosi had given him the opportunity to claim it.

"The House Democrats' turn is over. It's the Senate's turn now—to render sober judgment as the framers envisioned. But we can't hold a trial without the articles," McConnell intoned. "If they ever muster the courage to stand behind their slapdash work product and transmit the articles, it will be time for the United States Senate to fulfill our founding purpose."[4] On January 8, McConnell spoke on the Senate floor about the rules for the impeachment trial and his view that the House was encroaching on the Senate's constitutional role. "There will be no haggling with the House over Senate procedure. There is a reason the Constitution reads the way it does," McConnell stated. "'The House has sole power of impeachment.' They have exercised it. But it is the Senate to whom the founders gave 'the sole power to try all impeachments.' End of story."[5]

On January 15, Pelosi gave her assent for the articles of impeachment to be transmitted to the Senate, but McConnell was still in attack mode. "We have a 230-year tradition of rejecting purely political impeachments; it died last month," he said. "Speaker Pelosi and the House have taken our nation down a dangerous road. If the Senate blesses this unprecedented and dangerous House process by agreeing that an incomplete case and a subjective basis is enough to impeach a president, we will almost guarantee the impeachment of every future president of either party. This grave process of last constitutional resort will be watered down into a kind of anti-democratic recall measure that the founding fathers explicitly did not want."[6]

The commencement of an impeachment trial was a solemn and historic occasion that certainly warranted the majority leader invoking the Founding Fathers and describing the Senate's special role and responsibility. But McConnell's record undercut his moral authority. He had already established himself as the most partisan Senate leader in modern history; more than any other person, McConnell had erased the fundamental difference between the two houses by turning the Senate into a partisan instrument. Moreover, claiming that Pelosi had engineered the first partisan impeachment in history was demonstrably false. The House Republicans, twenty-one years earlier, had impeached President Bill Clinton on a purely partisan basis, for lying about his sexual relationship with Monica Lewinsky. At that time, the Senate, led by Republican Trent Lott and Democrat Tom Daschle, stepped up to its responsibility by managing to hold a respectable trial of the blatantly political indictment presented by the House Republicans. In 2020, the two houses would reverse their roles. The House impeached Trump for compelling reasons that were historically justified; the Senate would rush to a partisan, preordained conclusion that Trump should not be removed from office.

The memory of Clinton's impeachment trial hung over Trump's in an unfortunate way. If the House Republicans had not impeached Clinton, Trump's impeachment trial would have been the first in more than 150 years, and only the second in American history. It would be the first serious consideration of impeachment since Richard Nixon in 1974, nearly fifty years earlier. But because of the Clinton experience, commentators fretted that impeachment had now become routinely used, posing a danger to democracy.[7] Ultimately that concern did not determine the Senate Republicans' votes; they were in the tank from the beginning. But it did affect the national debate.

On January 23, 2020, the impeachment trial of President Donald J. Trump began, with all one hundred senators at their desks and Chief Justice John Roberts presiding. Pelosi had chosen a diverse team of seven managers to present the case, led by Adam Schiff, who was not only the chairman of the House Intelligence Committee but also Pelosi's most trusted lieutenant. A former California prosecutor, Schiff combined an impressive courtroom style with a mastery of the complex case. Although all seven House managers would present part of the case, Schiff dominated the proceedings, starting with a meticulously reasoned, powerful, two-hour opening statement laying out the facts of the complex matter and clearly showing that Trump had demanded that President Zelensky investigate the Bidens in order to receive the military aid specifically allocated, by a bipartisan Congress, to Ukraine for its defense.

Schiff and the other House managers hammered home the fact that Trump had allowed aid to flow freely to Ukraine until former vice president Biden had emerged as a political threat to his reelection. They refuted the contention by Trump's defense team that he was simply engaged in typical diplomacy. As Michael McFaul, a former US ambassador to Russia, noted, it was quite normal to use the promise of a presidential visit or even military aid to obtain diplomatic objectives. What was unacceptable was the nature of the favor that Trump asked of Zelensky: digging up dirt against his principal opponent, influencing the American presidential election. "Trump used his public office—the most sacred office in our country—to try to pursue his private electoral interests," McFaul tweeted. "That's the definition of corruption."[8]

Schiff urged the Senate to be the tribunal that Alexander Hamilton had envisioned: "a body able to rise above the fray." The House managers used video clips and PowerPoints to present their case with a riveting clarity to the Senate and the American public. But none of the testimony mattered to the overwhelming majority of the Senate Republicans, who grew increasingly bored and irritated as the trial forced them to give up other important work, such as raising funds for reelection. Lindsey Graham, as usual, was the most vocal. Graham was a resident expert on partisan impeachments, having been one of the House managers who had prosecuted Bill Clinton at his impeachment trial. Now Graham seemed irritated when Schiff and Jerrold Nadler, another House manager and the chairman of the House Judiciary Committee, showed tapes of his presentation at Clinton's trial arguing that impeachment did not require a literal crime. When Nadler accused the Senate Republicans of being "complicit" with Trump's cover-up, Graham shot back in the press. "I'm covering up nothing," he said. "I'm exposing your hatred of this president to the point you would destroy the institution."[9]

The House managers faced a roadblock when it came to the question of calling witnesses to testify directly to the Senate. Chuck Schumer and his fellow Democrat, Doug Jones of Alabama, vigorously argued that hearing from additional witnesses was the sine qua non for a fair trial.[10] This became a difficult argument to sustain as the House managers built an extremely powerful case based on video clips from the witnesses they had already interviewed. "I have to say this. Schiff is very, very effective," James Inhofe, one of the most conservative Republicans, admitted.[11] The debate over witnesses focused primarily on John Bolton, Trump's former national security adviser, who had written a yet-to-be-published tell-all memoir reportedly containing a detailed description of Trump's Ukraine shakedown. No one doubted that Bolton's testimony would be a major embarrassment for Trump. But the Republicans were determined not to bring Bolton in. They suggested that the price for Bolton's testimony would be calling Joe Biden and Hunter Biden as witnesses, but their true strategy was not to extend the trial. If no witnesses were called, the trial would end sooner. The Democrats needed to win four Republican votes to prevail. Holding the key votes, as always, were the last standing independent Republicans: Collins, Murkowski, Romney, and Lamar Alexander, probably the most respected Republican, who was serving his final year in the Senate. (He had announced his retirement at age eighty, after a half century of public service.) Alexander's refusal to state a position lent suspense to the vote, although his long friendship with McConnell made it difficult to envision him breaking ranks on this crucial issue.[12]

On January 31, the Democrats' push for more witnesses and documents fell short by a vote of 51–49. Collins and Romney joined the Democrats; Murkowski and Alexander did not. "America will remember this day, unfortunately, where the Senate did not live up to its responsibilities, when the Senate turned away from the truth, and went along with a sham trial," Schumer said. "If the president is acquitted with no witnesses, no documents, the acquittal will have no value because Americans will know that this trial was not a real trial."[13]

Notwithstanding Schumer's passion, the failure to call witnesses did not make it a sham trial. What made it a sham trial was that forty-nine of the fifty-two Republican senators would never even consider voting to remove Trump from office, regardless of the strength of the case presented. "Will the Senate Republicans ever step in against this president and say, 'Enough?'" mused Carl Hulse of the *New York Times*, who had covered the Senate for thirty years. "In pressing inexorably toward their preordained vote of acquittal, Senate Republicans made it clear they see their fortunes and future intertwined with the president's and are not willing to rock the 2020 boat."[14]

This had not always been the case. During the first two years of Trump's presidency, some Senate Republicans had expressed serious reservations about Trump's character and conduct in office. But those days were past; Jeff Flake and Bob Corker were gone, and other Republican senators, led by the shameless Graham, were working feverishly to get in lockstep with Trump. "Their party is a cult of personality at this point," said Senator Chris Murphy of Connecticut.[15]

Still, despite the gravitational pull of Trump's popularity among Republicans, and the pressure from McConnell and Graham, a small but significant group of Senate Republicans understood that Trump had indeed abused his power by shaking down Zelensky. Most of them followed the logic of Lamar Alexander, who seemed to relish being center stage. "It was inappropriate for the president to ask a foreign leader to investigate his political opponent and to withhold United States aid to encourage that investigation," Alexander said. "But the Constitution does not give the Senate the power to remove the president from office and ban him from this year's ballot simply for actions that are inappropriate. The framers believed there should never, ever be a partisan impeachment. . . . If this shallow, hurried and wholly partisan impeachment were to succeed, it would rip the country apart, pouring gasoline of the fire of cultural divisions that already exist. It would create the weapon of perpetual impeachment to be used against future presidents whenever the House of Representatives is of a different party."[16]

Of course, if one party decides that it will oppose impeachment irrespective of the serious political crimes that have been committed, then, by definition, the impeachment is "partisan." The framers envisioned senators who would have the stature and independence to provide a check against both a renegade president and the misuse of partisan impeachments. There was nothing "shallow" about the impeachment of Donald Trump, which the House managers documented in their compelling case. In fact, Alexander's use of the term "inappropriate" to describe Trump's abuse of power was itself "inappropriate." Lisa Murkowski, in a statement announcing her vote against impeachment, was closer to the mark, calling Trump's abuse of power "shameful and wrong."[17]

Moreover, "let the voters decide" is not an adequate response to a president who repeatedly demonstrated a willingness to solicit foreign interference to help his reelection efforts. In an eloquent closing statement, Schiff warned, "You know you can't trust this president to do what's right for the country. You can trust he will do what's right for Donald Trump. He'll do it now. He's done it before. He'll do it in the election if he's allowed to. That is why if you find him guilty, you must find that he should be removed."

And Schiff said prophetically, "You may be asking how much damage can he really do in the next several months until the election? A lot. A lot of damage."[18]

Leading Republicans professed not to see the danger. "I believe the president has learned from this case," said Susan Collins. "The president has been impeached. That's a pretty big lesson." Lamar Alexander shared that view: "Enduring an impeachment is something nobody would like. I would think you would think twice before doing it again."[19]

But other Republicans, outside the Senate, saw it differently. "I think [Trump] will just have been given a green light and he will claim not just acquittal but vindication and he can do those things and they can't impeach him again," said Mickey Edwards, a former Republican congressman now teaching at Princeton. "I think this is going to empower him to be much bolder. I would expect to see him even more let loose."[20]

One Senate Republican stood alone: Mitt Romney. He had only served one year in the Senate, but of course he had special stature as the Republican Party's presidential nominee in 2012. Now he would become the first senator in history to vote to convict a president of his own party in an impeachment trial. "The grave question the Constitution tasks senators to answer is whether the President committed an act so extreme and egregious that it rises to the level of a 'high crime and misdemeanor,'" Romney said in explanation of his vote. "The President asked a foreign government to investigate his political rival. The President withheld vital military funds for an American ally at war with Russian invaders. The President's purpose was personal and political. Accordingly, the President is guilty of an appalling abuse of the public trust. What he did was not 'perfect'—no, it was a flagrant assault on our electoral rights, our national security interest, and our fundamental values. Corrupting an election to keep oneself in office is perhaps the most abusive and destructive violation of one's oath that I can imagine."[21]

As always, McConnell had the last word. One week after the Senate voted against conviction, McConnell went to the Senate floor to offer his reflections on impeachment. "We cannot forget the abuses that fueled this process," he began, but the abuses he had in mind were not those committed by Donald Trump. "We cannot make light of the dangerous new precedents by President Trump's opponents in their zeal to impeach at all costs. House Democrats brought their war on institutions to this chamber. From the first evening it was clear the House managers would not even try to persuade a supermajority of Senators, but simply sought to degrade and smear the Senate itself before the nation. . . . The Senate did its job. We protected the long-term future of our Republic. We kept the temporary fires of factionalism from burning through the bedrock of our institutions. . . . But impeachment should never have come to the Senate like this. This most serious constitutional tool should not have been used so lightly, as a political weapon of first resort, as a tool to lash out at the basic bedrock of our institutions because one side did not get its way."[22]

The impeachment trial was another partisan triumph for McConnell and another disgrace for the Senate. In 1999, in Clinton's case, a weakened Senate, already in decline, struggled with the first impeachment in 130 years but rose to the occasion: writing bipartisan rules for the first impeachment trial in a television age; debating and resolving the difficult issue of how many witnesses to have and how to treat Monica Lewinsky; and giving the House managers ample time to present their case without tying up the Senate for months. Continuous bipartisan conversation between leaders Lott and Daschle, but also many other members, marked a good-faith effort to satisfy the nation that justice was done. Nothing like this happened in the impeachment trial of Donald Trump. McConnell and Schumer despised each other. There was no return to the historic old Senate chamber for a heart-to-heart meeting of all the senators. The feuding factions remained feuding factions. The impeachment trial did not ease the partisan divide; it amplified it.

Was there a better way forward? Joe Manchin, the most conservative Democrat from perhaps the strongest Trump state, floated the idea of censuring Trump, rather than voting on whether to convict. "I do believe a bipartisan majority of this body would vote to censure President Trump for his action in this matter. Censure would allow this body to unite across party lines," Manchin said. "Censure would allow a bipartisan statement condemning his unacceptable behavior in the strongest terms."[23] During the Clinton trial, a handful of senators had looked at alternatives, including censure, that could have prevented votes on the three articles of impeachment that the House had approved against Clinton. Based on the history of the impeachment clause, the senators had concluded that a vote on each article of impeachment was required.[24] However, that did not foreclose the idea of considering a censure motion against Trump after the articles of impeachment were rejected. Whether Alexander, Rob Portman, or any other Senate Republicans would have supported censure remains unknown; McConnell would never have let it happen, knowing that Trump would lash out against any criticism. As always, McConnell would choose to win rather than pursue an alternative course that might help educate the country about the singular danger Trump posed to our democracy.

Less than forty-eight hours after being acquitted by the Senate, Trump fired Gordon Sondland and the National Security Council staffer Colonel Alexander Vindman, clearly retaliating against them for testimony they had given during the House impeachment inquiry. Vindman, a decorated Iraq War veteran, was marched out of the White House by security guards. His brother Yevgeny, an army officer who also served on the NSC staff, was sacked as well.[25] At the same time, Trump attacked Joe Manchin for voting to convict him. "I was told by many that Manchin was just a puppet for Schumer & Pelosi," Trump tweeted. "That's all he is."[26] He also called on the House to "expunge" his impeachment, "because it was a hoax . . . a total political hoax."[27]

Democrats expressed alarm at the purge and the president's ranting, which confirmed their fear that Trump would be unleashed, rather than chastened, by the outcome of the impeachment trial. But it was understandable why Trump—or any president—would be unwilling to continue working with people who provided testimony in support of his impeachment. Although Sondland had acted out of self-preservation, Vindman and the other high-ranking foreign service officers— Marie Yovanovitch, Bill Taylor, and Fiona Hill—had acted out of conscience, told the truth, served their country, and paid a high price. What America needed were acts of conscience and courage from people of stature who did not work for Trump: the Senate Republicans. Their failure to act would have profound consequences in the coming year.

A Politicized Pandemic

$\mathcal{O}$n January 16, 2020, as the Senate prepared to begin the historic impeachment trial, Tom Cotton, a fiercely conservative Republican senator from Arkansas, was studying disturbing news reports from China about the discovery of a novel, highly infectious virus in Hubei Province. Cotton focused on the discrepancy between the Chinese government speaking confidently about its handling of the virus and the increasingly urgent steps being taken to stop its spread. "That's when it really crystallized for me," Cotton later said. "Those two things obviously do not match."[1]

Nearing the end of his first term, Cotton had earned a reputation as the most hawkish and one of the nastiest senators, which in McConnell's Senate was no small achievement.[2] Cotton also detested China's communist regime, which might call into question his objectivity in assessing what was going on in China. But even Cotton's strongest critics acknowledged his brainpower, and he brought to his work the background and insight from serving on both the Intelligence and the Armed Services Committees.

Cotton began pressing the White House to ban travel from China immediately. He worked the phones incessantly, calling, among others, President Trump, Jared Kushner, and Alex Azar (secretary of health and human services), alerting them to the dangers of the virus and urging them to ground all flights to and from China. Within days,

Cotton's views became so well known that White House officials understood what he meant when he pointed to the ground: his grim signal for getting the planes down.[3]

Aa Cotton placed urgent calls to the White House, President Trump was already downplaying the virus. "We have it totally under control," Trump said on January 22. "It's one person coming in from China, and we have it under control. It's going to be fine."[4]

Early as he was in recognizing the threat, Cotton was not the first public official to become alarmed. In early January, Matthew Pottinger, the deputy national security adviser, received a call from a Hong Kong epidemiologist who was a longtime friend. The doctor's message was blunt and urgent. A ferocious new outbreak that appeared similar to the SARS epidemic of 2003 had emerged. It had spread far more quickly than the government was admitting, and it would not be long before it reached other parts of the world. The virus, which started in the city of Wuhan, was being spread by people who showed no symptoms. "You need to be ready," his friend stated.

Pottinger soon found that specialized corners of the intelligence community were producing similarly chilling reports, warning that the novel coronavirus was likely to spread across the globe, causing a pandemic. Within weeks of getting the initial information early in the year, biodefense experts within the NSC felt the need to begin planning what it would take to quarantine a city the size of Chicago. Pottinger began convening daily meetings of agency experts. On January 28, Robert O'Brien, Trump's national security adviser, recommended to the president that he impose limits on travel from China. On January 29, Peter Navarro, Trump's aggressive trade adviser and a longtime hawk on China, circulated a memo endorsing a travel ban, saying that failure to confront the outbreak could lead to hundreds of thousands of deaths and trillions of dollars in economic damage.

The leading public health experts were initially opposed to a travel ban, arguing that such bans were usually counterproductive because they prevented doctors from reaching affected areas while causing people to flee, which could spread the disease faster. But on January 30, the public health officials, led by Dr. Robert Redfield, the head of the Centers for Disease Control and Prevention, and Dr. Anthony Fauci, the longtime director of the National Institute of Allergy and Infectious Diseases, told Azar that they had changed their minds. The World Health Organization had declared a global health emergency, and American officials had identified the first case of person-to-person transmission in the United States. In an email to medical experts around the country, Dr. Carter Mecher, a senior medical adviser at the Department of Veterans Affairs, was blunt. "Any way you cut it, this is going to be bad," he wrote. "The projected size of the outbreak already seems hard to believe."[5]

On January 31, President Trump banned travel from China, an early action that he would cite proudly in the coming year. Although he had previously downplayed the threat, Trump's action represented a relatively rapid response to the crisis posed by the novel coronavirus. It suggested a president who at least grasped the essence of the damage that the virus threatened if unchecked and who was prepared to take strong steps to protect the American people.

Over the next year, Trump's repeated, worsening failures of leadership would condemn hundreds of thousands of Americans to needless deaths. Even Trump's harshest critics did not anticipate the catastrophic magnitude of his failure when it was so obvious that strong leadership was in Trump's political self-interest as well as in the public interest. And Trump was not alone in this; the US Senate also failed to show the courage, vision, independence, and steadiness to help steer our nation through the devastating harm caused by a once-in-a-century pandemic.

Among Trump's many lies, two of the most damaging would be his assertions that no one could have anticipated a pandemic and that he "inherited practically nothing" in pandemic preparedness from the Obama administration. In fact, the serious possibility of a pandemic had been widely discussed for at least fifteen years, going back to the original SARS coronavirus. Bill Gates gave a talk at the TED conference in 2015 about the threat of a pandemic that received twenty million views on YouTube. Gates said that a pandemic is "the most likely thing, by far, to kill over 10 million excess people in a year" and then forecast a "better than 50/50 chance" that we would see a global pandemic that kills more than thirty million people in his lifetime.[6]

To his lasting credit, President George W. Bush became alarmed by the threat of a pandemic during his term in office, and he took vigorous action to protect the United States and the world community against such a catastrophe.[7] Bush addressed the United Nations on the need for global cooperation to combat potential pandemics and pressed for legislation to prepare the United States. In December 2006, Congress enacted the Pandemic and All-Hazards Preparedness Act, whose sections include "national preparedness and response leadership, organization and planning," "public health security preparedness," "all-hazards medical surge capacity," and "pandemic and biodefense vaccine and drug development"—unmistakably clear indications of the threat that the Bush administration and Congress anticipated the need to meet.

The Obama administration began building on the legislation immediately after coming into office in 2009. At Obama's first meeting with the President's Council of Advisors on Science and Technology (PCAST) in June of that year, he asked what his administration needed to do to prepare for an influenza pandemic. He met frequently with John Holdren, the White House science adviser, and ordered an interagency task force to work on a pandemic preparedness plan. Over the course of Obama's presidency, a pandemic infrastructure was put in place.[8]

The administration faced the challenge of a potential Ebola outbreak in 2014, and two years later Ron Klain, the administration's Ebola czar, wrote an article on the persistent threat: "As the next President maps out plans to combat war and climate change, terrorism and ethnic conflict, humanitarian challenges and sectarian strife, he or she should make a high priority of the national security threat that has killed more humans than all wars, terrorist attacks, and natural disasters *combined*: infectious diseases. . . . The single most likely cause of a nightmare scenario is not any of the oft-discussed threats, but an oft-overlooked one: pandemic illness."[9] During the transition in 2016–2017, the Obama administration handed the incoming Trump team a sixty-nine-page playbook, written to coordinate a response to an emergency disease threat anywhere in the world.[10]

Donald Trump chose to take the opposite course. "Beginning the morning after his inauguration, a spectacular science-related tragedy has unfolded. The Trump administration has systemically dismantled the executive branch's scientific infrastructure and rejected the role of science to inform policy," wrote Dr. Jason Karlawish, professor of medicine and bioethics at the University of Pennsylvania. With his passion for using a wrecking ball on all of Obama's accomplishments, Trump dismantled PCAST on his third day in office. He also chose not to appoint a White House science adviser until his third year in office, and PCAST was not reconstituted until November 2019. At a PCAST meeting on February 3 and 4, four days after Trump banned travel from China, there was no discussion of the novel coronavirus that had prompted the ban.[11]

Congressional leaders were aware of the wide-ranging economic and security impacts posed by infectious diseases. The House Intelligence Committee had included a specific provision on pandemics in the Intelligence Authorization Act encompassing 2018, 2019, and 2020, requiring the director of national intelligence to submit a report "on the anticipated geopolitical effects of emerging infectious disease . . . and pandemics, and their implications on the national security of the United States." Nevertheless, many of the programs created under the Pandemic and All-Hazards Preparedness Act had their funding cut to dangerously low levels even before Trump took office. The Strategic National Stockpile, funded at levels 50–60 percent of what was needed, was seriously short of masks and ventilators when the pandemic hit.[12]

On January 24, at the urging of Senator Lamar Alexander, administration officials came to the Senate to provide a classified briefing. Only fourteen senators attended, in part because the briefing was scheduled on short notice, and in part because that was the day on which their impeachment questions had to be submitted. A White House official expressed surprise at the "incredibly" poor attendance, noting that it came "even though the amount of concern expressed then was rather intense." Alexander and three Republican colleagues issued a bland statement thanking the administration for the briefing but conveying no real sense of alarm or urgency.

Nevertheless, on January 28, Chuck Schumer and Washington's two Democratic senators, Patty Murray and Maria Cantwell, wrote to Azar, demanding to be kept apprised of "the latest information regarding the severity of the disease, the country's capacity to diagnose cases, what steps were being taken to prepare U.S. health care workers, what screening systems were in place at U.S. airports, and the status of a novel coronavirus vaccine." At the time, just five cases of coronavirus had been identified in the United States. A week later, at a briefing with Azar on February 5, Democrats began pushing for emergency supplemental funds to combat the virus. "They aren't taking this seriously enough," Senator Chris Murphy tweeted after leaving the briefing, referring to his Republican colleagues. "Notably, no request for ANY emergency funding, which is a big mistake. Local health systems need supplies, training, screening staff etc. And they need it now."[13] He would later recall, "Senate Republicans were not using February to pressure the president to get serious about an early supplemental [appropriations] request."[14]

February was the crucial month, and the Senate missed the opportunity to work with the administration or to use its own powers to pressure the administration to act. Some senators who were in positions to exert leadership focused instead on financial self-interest. Richard Burr had done a distinguished job of leading the Intelligence Committee's investigation into Russia's interference in the 2016 presidential campaign; he also had a long and commendable record in supporting pandemic preparedness, through his service on the Senate Health Committee. But his actions when news of the pandemic emerged did not have the public's interest in mind. On February 13, Burr and his wife sold thirty-three stocks worth between $628,000 and $1.7 million, including several hundred thousand dollars of stock in hotel chains.

At the same time, Burr wrote an opinion piece for Fox News suggesting that the United States was "better prepared than ever before" to combat the virus, but he conveyed his actual view two weeks later to the Tar Heel Club, a nonpartisan North Carolina business group visiting Washington. Burr warned the group that the virus would soon cause a major disruption in the United States. "There's one thing I can tell you about this. It's much more aggressive in its transmission than anything we have seen in recent history," said Burr, in a recording obtained by NPR, which reported his remarks. "It's probably more akin to the 1918 pandemic." He added, "Every company should be cognizant of the fact that you may have to alter your travel. You may have to look at your employees and judge whether the trip they're making to Europe is essential or whether it can be done on video conference."[15]

Burr, at least, had a record of some distinction in the Senate against which his decision to sell stocks based on confidential information could be balanced. In contrast, Kelly Loeffler, a multimillionaire businesswoman, had recently been appointed to the Senate by Georgia's governor to fill the seat vacated when Johnny Isakson resigned because of ill health. Loeffler had been in the Senate barely two months before she took advantage of confidential information about the virus to sell stock.[16]

The novel coronavirus would spread exponentially; before long, there would be thousands of additional infections, illnesses, and deaths. During the crucial weeks in January and early February, Mitch McConnell's focus was on the impeachment trial. After Trump was acquitted on February 5, McConnell took his victory lap and then turned back to his highest priority: the conveyor belt that carried right-wing lawyers onto the federal bench. For the next three weeks, McConnell made no public statements about the virus. If he was exercising any leadership behind the scenes, it was not reported.

On February 27, McConnell did speak thoughtfully about the virus on the Senate floor. "The continued spread of Covid-19 has the world on notice. Here in the United States, we are fortunate not to be facing an immediate crisis," he stated. "But obviously, as our public health experts remind us, a nation of nearly four million square miles and more than 300 million people cannot be hermetically sealed off from the rest of the world. There seems to be little question that

Covid-19 will eventually cause some degree of disruption here. . . . In Congress, it's our job to ensure that funding is not a limiting factor as public health leaders and front-line medical professionals continue getting ready." But McConnell then attacked Schumer, who had been pushing for urgent action, for "reflexive partisanship . . . moving the goal posts . . . and a strange and clumsy effort to override the normal appropriations process." This was no time, McConnell commented dryly, for "performative outrage." He was confident that the necessary funding legislation would be considered by the Senate in two weeks.[17]

COVID-19 became the dominant reality in American life in the week starting on March 9. In just a few days, with shocking speed, America went from normal life to a complete standstill, as schools, airports, subways, businesses, and restaurants all shut down. The Centers for Disease Control urged Americans to refrain from flying. On March 13, the House rushed to pass a significant coronavirus relief package, which was hammered out in intense negotiations between Speaker Pelosi and Treasury Secretary Steven Mnuchin, a package that included free testing, paid emergency leave for a limited time, unemployment insurance, and increased funds for food stamps. Trump proclaimed a national emergency, which he described as "two very big words."[18]

McConnell chose not to be involved, leaving the negotiations to Pelosi and Mnuchin. "The Secretary of the Treasury will have ball control for the administration. I expect he will speak for us as well," McConnell commented.[19] Undeterred by the CDC guidance and the rapidly escalating crisis, McConnell recessed the Senate for the weekend and flew to Lexington to attend the swearing-in of Justin Walker to be a federal district judge for the Eastern District of Kentucky. Walker had some excellent credentials, having graduated from Harvard Law School and clerked for Brett Kavanaugh on the D.C. Circuit and for Anthony Kennedy on the Supreme Court. But because he was only thirty-seven years old and had never tried a case, the American Bar Association gave him an "unqualified" rating for a federal judgeship. However, Walker was the son of a leading McConnell donor and an outspoken right-wing legal thinker and a darling of the Federalist Society, in which he had held leadership roles ever since law school.

Justice Kavanaugh also took the time to fly to Kentucky for the swearing-in, which became something of a right-wing pep rally. "What can I say that hasn't already been said on Fox News?" Judge Walker said, minutes after being sworn in. "In Brett Kavanaugh's America, we will not surrender while you wage war on our work, or our cause, or our hope, or our dream. . . . Although we are winning, we have not won. Although we celebrate today, we cannot take for granted tomorrow—or we will lose our courts and our country to critics who call us terrifying and who describe us as deplorable."[20]

Mid-March was a dystopian nightmare for America, with empty streets, shuttered businesses, and rapidly filling hospitals and morgues. Frontline workers were struggling to cope despite shortages of personal protective equipment, and the country was flying blind about the scope of the problem because of grossly insufficient testing. Immediate government action on a massive scale was needed. Pelosi, Schumer, and the Democrats had been providing leadership, along with Mnuchin. It took another week before McConnell finally recognized the magnitude of the crisis and the danger of being a leader who was missing in action. He mobilized the Senate Republicans to formulate a comprehensive bill, with a stunning $1 trillion price tag, which was introduced on March 19.

Over the next week, Americans would see their politicians working at their best in a frenetic effort to produce an unprecedented response to an unprecedented crisis. Each side took its share of partisan shots. "She's the Speaker of the House, not the Speaker of the Senate," McConnell said. "And we were doing fine before her intervention."[21] Schumer and Pelosi criticized McConnell's proposal for "putting corporations way ahead of workers."[22] Senator Richard Blumenthal of Connecticut excoriated McConnell's proposal for funneling hundreds of billions of dollars to private companies without requiring binding commitments to preserve jobs and wages. McConnell repeatedly cited a statement by Representative James Clyburn, the number three Democrat in the House, overheard in a private call, that the pandemic provided "a tremendous opportunity to restructure things to our vision."[23] Schumer led the Democrats in refusing McConnell's "take it or leave it" offer to increase small business loans by $500 billion, because it did not include $150 billion for hospitals.

But generally, partisanship was kept under control because of the need to respond to the crisis. In a private meeting with Republican senators, McConnell told them they would have to accommodate "Cryin' Chuck," Trump's derisive nickname for Schumer. With a Democratic House and a closely divided Senate, he knew that the only way forward was bipartisan compromise.[24]

On March 27, the Senate unanimously approved the CARES Act, a $2 trillion economic stabilization plan to respond to the coronavirus pandemic through a combination of direct payments and benefits for individuals, money for states, and a huge bailout fund for businesses. The legislation would send direct payments of $1,200 to millions of Americans earning up to $75,000 and an additional $500 per child. It substantially increased jobless aid, providing an additional thirteen weeks and a four-month enhancement of benefits, with an extra $600 per week on top of the ordinary state benefits. The package also provided unemployment benefits for the first time to freelancers and gig workers. The measure offered $377 billion in federal guaranteed loans to small businesses and established a $500 billion government lending program for distressed companies, including allowing the government to take an equity stake in the airlines that were devastated by the abrupt loss of more than 90 percent of their passengers. The legislation also provided $100 billion to hospitals on the front lines of the pandemic.

It was a stunning result; the negotiators had acted with extraordinary speed, creativity, and generosity, coming through for the American people with the largest economic relief program in history, almost three times larger than the economic stimulus in early 2009. In the coming months, analysts would show that billions of dollars went to companies that did not need the money and that the Trump administration undercut the oversight that Congress had built into the legislation by establishing a special inspector general. But there is no doubt that CARES provided a lifeline to millions of Americans facing economic disaster because of the virus.

When the legislation passed, fewer than one thousand Americans had died of COVID-19. CARES was the third legislative response to the pandemic. No one doubted that further action and much more money would be needed. Pelosi instructed the relevant House committees to begin formulating a fourth legislative package.[25]

McConnell and his Senate had proven that it could legislate for the country—at least when Trump was being rational, recognizing the crisis, and empowering Mnuchin to negotiate. Unfortunately, America needed senators and a Senate that could step up when Trump was irrational, which was most of the time, and a bad period was about to start. Within days after the enactment of the CARES Act, as infections from the virus exploded, Trump was still talking about opening the country up by Easter. He took over the daily briefings of the White House coronavirus task force, expressing optimism that had no basis, spreading disinformation, and advocating quack cures, such as injecting disinfectant. Disclaiming any responsibility for leadership, Trump said that the governors were in charge of the response. On April 17, in the middle of what was supposed to be a thirty-day extension of the initial fifteen-day period of lockdown to "slow the spread," Trump went on a rampage against several Democratic governors, tweeting "Liberate Minnesota," "Liberate Michigan," "Liberate Virginia."[26]

Rather than speaking out against Trump's rants, McConnell returned to partisanship. On April 22, McConnell issued a strong statement opposing any kind of aid to states, saying that those suffering revenue shortfalls should consider bankruptcy. This was an explicit rejection of the Democrats' plea to help state governments. Underscoring McConnell's partisan point, his staff issued a news release titled "Stopping Blue State Bailouts."

Andrew Cuomo, the Democratic governor of New York, criticized McConnell for distinguishing among states based on their political leanings, rather than "states where people are dying. . . . Not red and blue. Red, white and blue. They're just Americans dying." But McConnell made it clear that he was approaching any additional relief funding very cautiously. "We'd certainly insist that anything we'd borrow to send down to the states is not spent on solving problems they created for themselves over the years with their pension programs," the majority leader said.[27]

By late April, it was clear that the strategy of containing the novel coronavirus through testing and contact tracing was not going to work. The virus could be stopped only by the development of an effective vaccine. If history provided any indication, that could take several years, although the massive global effort underway was already showing great promise. Until a vaccine could be developed, slowing the virus would depend on relatively simple, common-sense steps: wearing a mask and social distancing.

While McConnell was sharpening the red-blue divide, he tried to provide some common sense and responsible leadership about wearing masks and social distancing. "There is no stigma to wearing a mask. There is no stigma to staying six feet apart. . . . You have an obligation to others," McConnell said at an event aired in Kentucky in late May. He described masking and maintaining social distance as a means of bringing the country back to normal.[28]

Unfortunately, Trump hated the idea of masks. He did not like the way he looked in a mask, so he chose to mock those who wore them, particularly his likely general election opponent, Joe Biden. He accused a Reuters reporter of being "politically correct" for not removing his mask when asking a question in the White House briefing room. He visited a Ford plant and took off his mask, telling reporters that he didn't want to give them the pleasure of seeing him wear it.[29]

The results were immediate and predictable. No one could deny the intense loyalty of Trump's millions of followers, and masks, improbably and disastrously, became the central issue in the political culture war. Masks were seen as unmanly and an imposition on personal freedom. Most Republican governors quickly joined the opposition to masks, either because they agreed with Trump or because they lacked the courage to differ with him.

Starting around Memorial Day, people began shaking off the restraints of COVID and congregating without masks around the country. Many gathered outside, which reduced the transmission of the virus, but there were such large crowds in bars and around swimming pools that infections spread. By June, large parts of the South and the Midwest faced a second wave of surging infections.[30]

By late June, virtually all the Republican senators had begun wearing masks and speaking out about their importance. Tim Scott of South Carolina tweeted that wearing a mask "is one of the simplest and easiest ways to help stop the spread of #Covid-19." Chuck Grassley, the second-oldest member of the Senate, posted a photo of himself on Instagram wearing a mask, with the caption "everybody's got to do their share." Shelley Moore Capito said, "We're going to be required to wear it. . . . I think [President Trump] should be leading the effort, yeah." Rick Scott, one of the president's strongest supporters, said, "I think mayors, governors, the president, they have a responsibility . . . to be talking about masks more, and social distancing."[31]

At a June 30 hearing, Lamar Alexander, the Senate Health Committee chair, plaintively urged Trump to end the "political debate" around face coverings: "Unfortunately, this simple life saving practice has become part of a political debate that says: If you're for Trump, you don't wear a mask. If you're against Trump, you do. That is why I have suggested that the president occasionally wear a mask even though there are not many occasions where it is necessary for him to do so. *The president has millions of admirers. They would follow his lead*" (emphasis added).

It was actually as simple as that. Had Trump endorsed mask wearing as a useful protective step to reduce transmission of the virus, his millions of admirers would have worn masks. Not every one of them, but probably 90 percent. By this time, even Sean Hannity and Steve Doocy, two of Trump's most fervent Fox News supporters, had joined the ranks of mask advocates. Republican governors would not have gone against Trump; the virus could have been contained and hundreds of thousands of lives would have been saved.

At least Hannity and Doocy were trying—better late than never. The shocking truth, which concerned Senate Republicans should have grasped, was that there was never a time to talk reason to Trump. "I'd prefer he do it [wear a mask]. You know he's not going to do it," said

Florida's Marco Rubio. America was in the grip of a mad king, and the situation was about to get worse.

Every biography about Trump (including the one written by his niece, Mary Trump, a psychologist) makes it clear that he grew up without a capacity for empathy. There is not a shred of evidence that Trump cared about the several million people who were ill or dying from COVID. He was angry that the pandemic had ruined "the greatest economy in U.S. history" and threatened his reelection.[32] Of course, Trump still had a path to win in November, particularly given the miraculous pace at which vaccines were being developed, but that path required calling for masks and social distancing to limit the spread of the virus until a vaccine would be available. Brad Parscale, Trump's campaign manager, came up with an alternative approach: Trump would excite his base by holding the rallies he loved, which would also provide a contrast to Joe Biden, who was staying in his home in Delaware and wearing a mask on the few occasions he came outside.[33]

Parscale invited a million of Trump's admirers to a massive indoor rally in Tulsa, Oklahoma. The rally was originally scheduled for June 19, a particularly tone-deaf choice since it was the anniversary of the brutal 1921 riots in which more than three hundred African Americans were murdered and hundreds of businesses destroyed in the Greenwood district of Tulsa. Across the country, American cities were rocked by Black Lives Matter demonstrations triggered by the murder of George Floyd by a Minneapolis policeman on May 25. The Trump campaign was quite willing to exploit racial tensions for political gain, but in this case, Parscale decided to put off the rally by a day, rescheduling it for June 20.

Across Oklahoma, a state Trump won in 2016 by thirty-six points, there was shock that the president would invite his followers to a massive indoor rally during a pandemic. Officials in Tulsa warned that the planned rally was likely to worsen an already troubling spike in cases and could become a disastrous "super-spreader" event. They pleaded with Trump to cancel the event, or at least move it out of doors.

"It's a perfect storm of potential over-the-top disease transmission," said Bruce Dart, the executive director of the Tulsa Health

Department. "There's nothing good about this, particularly in an enclosed arena," said Karen Keith, a Tulsa county commissioner. "I don't want people to lose a family member over this."[34] Oklahoma governor Kevin Stitt asked Trump and Vice President Pence, who planned to attend the rally, to consider a large outdoor venue instead.

Trump tweeted that forty thousand people would be attending, and that "Almost One Million people" had requested tickets. He said the news media was "trying to Covid shame us on our big Rallies" and accused the media of a double standard since they had not criticized the George Floyd rallies occurring around the country as possible COVID spreaders. The Trump campaign, ever prudent, required attendees to sign a waiver saying they would not sue if they contracted the virus at the rally.[35]

Trump had failed catastrophically in his leadership in the previous six months, with the notable exception of his commitment to Operation Warp Speed, the accelerated development of a vaccine. He had been derelict in his duties: negligent, irresponsible, and guilty of spreading dangerous misinformation. He continually refused to accept the advice of public health officials, and he could not bring himself to endorse masks and social distancing, which would have had a profound effect on the transmission of the virus. Now he had crossed another line, actually inviting his followers to a potential super-spreader event. When America most needed a focused, effective president, drawing on the public health and economic advice available, the occupant of the White House acted more like the leader of an apocalyptic cult.

Trump's followers were fervent, but they were not completely oblivious to the danger of an indoor rally. On June 20, the arena looked like an ad for social distancing, with many empty seats, though most of the crowd did not take the precaution of wearing masks. An outdoor stage, set up to accommodate the expected overflow crowd, went unused. Trump, who drew strength from adoring crowds, was plainly thrown off by the low turnout. He gave a disjointed seventy-four-minute speech in which he congratulated himself for a "phenomenal job" fighting the pandemic. He railed about the "left-wing radicals," whom he falsely charged with rioting in cities all around the country.[36] The most recognizable person in the audience was Herman Cain, the former chairman and CEO of Godfather's Pizza, one of the few prominent black Republican leaders, who had run a surprisingly strong campaign for the GOP presidential nomination in 2012. Sadly, on July 30 Cain died from COVID-19, almost certainly contracted at Trump's rally.

The July 4 holiday marked a grim milestone, as the number of coronavirus infections in America reached three million. In the Senate, Mitch McConnell and his fellow Republicans could comfort themselves by pointing to their statements encouraging Trump to endorse mask wearing. It is interesting to consider what more they could reasonably have been expected to do. One possibility for increasing their impact would have been a joint statement by many, if not all, of the Republican senators. Alternatively, they could have acknowledged the reality that nothing would change Trump, and therefore he needed to be restrained in some way or even removed through another impeachment trial or by the cabinet invoking the Twenty-Fifth Amendment on the grounds of presidential disability.[37] McConnell was particularly well situated to explore such action, since his wife, Secretary of Transportation Elaine Chao, was perhaps the most experienced person in Trump's cabinet. But if impeachment or the Twenty-Fifth Amendment were a bridge too far, McConnell and his Republican colleagues could have pressed Trump to let Vice President Pence take responsibility for the administration's response to the virus, allowing the president to focus on other issues, including his reelection campaign.

Viewing the "chaos president" three years earlier, Jeff Flake had expressed frustration and fear: "Congress was designed to assert itself in just such moments. . . . Too often we observe the unfolding drama along with the rest of the country, passively all but saying 'someone should do something' without seeming to realize that someone is us." If America had been attacked by an unexpected but lethal adversary, would the Senate Republicans leave a completely irrational president in the White House with hundreds of thousands of American lives at risk? We know the answer: they would and they did.

Lindsey Graham had been vocal on virtually every issue, particularly when it came to defending Trump and casting doubt on the investigation of Russia's interference in American elections. But Graham, to his credit, was trying to use his close relationship with Trump in the summer of 2020 to move the president to a more rational position on the virus. Trump spent hours at night on the phone, feeling sorry for himself and talking to people, like Rudy Giuliani, who reinforced his worst instincts, and Graham was a frequent caller. Graham, however, worried that Trump was not willing to own the coronavirus problem and told him, "You need to explain to the country, we're not helpless against the virus. Here's the game plan to beat the virus." Graham told Trump that his opponent wasn't Biden; it was the virus. "People will have a hard time attacking you if you follow the advice of Birx and Fauci and stay in close touch with governors about a plan to open up the economy."[38]

The Senate Republicans could also have joined in the effort to pass a further coronavirus relief package. The House passed a $3.5 trillion HEROES relief package in May. Now, at the end of June, the Senate began to consider what they would be willing to do. The $600 weekly unemployment benefits were scheduled to end on July 31; so was the moratorium on housing evictions. These had been lifelines for millions of Americans; the need for further legislation was pressing.[39]

But McConnell had other priorities: his own reelection campaign and the judicial conveyor belt. He again left the negotiations to Pelosi, Schumer, and Mnuchin, weighing in only occasionally to criticize their work when they appeared to be making progress. "The Speaker of the House and the Democratic leader are continuing to say our way or the highway. These are not the tactics that would build a bipartisan result. About twenty of my members think we've done enough," McConnell told the PBS news anchor Judy Woodruff in late July.[40] He expressed concern about the mounting national debt and prioritized an immunity shield to protect businesses from COVID lawsuits. Once again, as with Grassley's criminal justice reform bill, McConnell seemed to want to pass legislation only if all his Republican colleagues were on board. It was impossible to find a solution that would be acceptable to right-wing senators like Ted Cruz that was also acceptable to Pelosi and Schumer. Consequently, nothing happened, and the Republicans faced the possibility of significant political damage.

On July 31, as new jobless claims exceeded one million for the nineteenth straight week, expanded unemployment benefits expired, reducing the average unemployment check by almost two-thirds.[41] On August 8, the Paycheck Protection Act expired, with almost $138 billion unspent.[42] The desperate situation facing millions of Americans prompted President Trump to issue executive orders using $44 billion from the Disaster Relief Fund to provide extra unemployment benefits, continuing student loan payment relief, deferring collection of employee Social Security payroll taxes, and identifying options to help Americans avoid eviction and foreclosure.[43]

Most Senate Republicans recognized that many of their constituents desperately needed help. They also realized their political fate might depend on whether a massive pandemic relief package could be enacted. But McConnell was unmoved. When the August recess came, the senators went home without having taken any action. It had been five months since the House had passed the HEROES act.

September began with the bombshell revelations from Bob Woodward, the legendary *Washington Post* journalist and author of twenty-two books, that Trump had deliberately downplayed the danger of the virus. "This is deadly stuff. . . . It's so easily transmissible you wouldn't believe it," Trump had told Woodward in February and April interviews. "I always wanted to play it down, because I don't want to create a panic."[44] Many commentators criticized Trump for hiding the truth from the American people. Others, who tended to be Trump supporters, found it comforting to find out that he knew the virus was serious.

By mid-September, the United States had recorded its two hundred thousandth death from COVID-19. And while there were exciting, reliable reports of remarkable progress in vaccine development, the public health and economic consequences of the virus for America were devastating. In Kentucky, polls showed McConnell with a large lead over his Democratic challenger, Amy McGrath, and he seemed poised to secure his seventh term in the Senate.[45] Yet, despite the national crisis, McConnell and his Republican hard-liners continued to block urgently needed relief. Like Trump, McConnell was missing the empathy gene. The powerful majority leader seemed curiously disengaged, indifferent to the suffering sweeping the country. He was waiting for a challenge worthy of his full energy, and he would not have to wait any longer.

· 8 ·

The Banana Republic Confirmation

$\mathcal{A}$s always, October in Washington, D.C., and its surrounding suburbs was stunningly beautiful, with perfect weather and beautiful foliage. But that was the only thing that was familiar and normal. In Washington, as in many of the world's great cities, an eerie, quiet calm continued seven months after the arrival of the novel coronavirus. A small number of people could be found on the streets, sometimes with their partners, often with their dogs. The Metrorail system was operating but carrying only about 10 percent of its normal traffic. Riders often found they had a subway car virtually to themselves. The glass-box office buildings on K Street were deserted, as lawyers, lobbyists, and consultants worked virtually from their homes. People donned masks, maintained their social distance, washed their hands, and followed reports of the extraordinarily rapid development of the vaccines, on pace to be a scientific miracle. In the Washington metro area, like the rest of America, people waited for the vaccine and watched for the feared second wave of COVID-19 cases.

The quiet in the streets was deceptive. Millions of Americans were suffering disease and death from COVID, as well as profound economic dislocation as the virus and the shutdown rocked industry after industry. And there was boiling anger on both sides of the political debate and the racial divide. There had never been any doubt that the presidential election would be contested with fierce intensity; Trump's disruptive presidency had sparked resistance from the outset.

Despite the naïve hopes of Susan Collins and Lamar Alexander, Trump learned no lessons from his impeachment, other than concluding that he could do anything with impunity because of the protection provided by the Republicans in the US Senate. And as the year 2020 progressed, Trump's actions took on an increasingly authoritarian cast. On May 25, Minneapolis police officers killed a black man in their custody, George Floyd, when one officer kneeled on his neck for an excruciating nine minutes while Floyd pleaded for his life and three other officers stood by. A bystander recorded the killing on her phone, and circulation of the video led to massive protests against police brutality and systematic racism all over the country. Trump, rather than acting as a peacemaker, imitated authoritarian governments, sending federal forces—sometimes in unmarked vehicles and without identification—to disrupt protests and yank protestors off the street. Those actions came to a head on June 1, when Attorney General William Barr called in military forces to clear protestors from Pennsylvania Avenue and Lafayette Park so that Trump could cross the street from the White House and pose with a Bible in front of St. John's Episcopal Church. Muriel Bowser, the mayor of the District of Columbia, was outraged; she struck back by painting the words "Black Lives Matter" in ten-foot-high yellow letters on Sixteenth Street, near the site of the confrontation.

As protest activity waned in D.C., an uneasy calm returned. In contrast to most of the city, the Capitol in October was a beehive of activity, particularly around Mitch McConnell's palatial offices. Restrictions on travel made it difficult for McConnell to return to Kentucky to campaign for what looked like an easy reelection, so he devoted his political wiles and formidable energy to things that mattered most to him. Ordinarily, that would mean a single-minded focus on helping other Senate Republican candidates, to ensure that he would retain his position as majority leader. Now, however, that paled in importance compared to the historic opportunity that had been created by the death of Supreme Court justice Ruth Bader Ginsburg on September

18. McConnell was on the verge of realizing the highest priority of the Republican Party and right-wing constitutional movement: locking in a lasting conservative 6–3 majority on the Supreme Court.

Any opening on the Supreme Court was enormously consequential, but nothing could compare to replacing Ruth Bader Ginsburg with a reliable conservative nominated by Donald Trump. Ginsburg had been a formidable liberal jurist, increasingly known for her superb dissents against the 5–4 conservative majority on the Roberts court. She had attained iconic status in recent years, becoming known as "Notorious RBG" (a play on the name of rapper "Notorious B.I.G."), revered for her intellect and passion and for the indomitable spirit with which she fought several forms of cancer.

Justice Ginsburg desperately wanted to stay alive until a Democratic president was elected and could name her successor. In that fight, she was not able to prevail, passing away at the age of eighty-seven, six weeks before the presidential election.[1] Her death was a hammer blow to women and liberals across the United States. Poignantly, Justice Ginsburg, who was Jewish, died just before the first night of Rosh Hashanah, the Jewish new year. Many rabbis across the country who began their Rosh Hashanah services expressing confidence that this new year had to be better than the one just completed may have wanted to correct their statement an hour later with the grim news. The following week, Ginsburg became the first woman to lie in state in the US Capitol, and the first Jewish person to do so.

Five days before her death, Justice Ginsburg had dictated a statement to her granddaughter Clara Spera: "My most fervent wish is that I will not be replaced until a new president is installed."[2] In fact, that was her most futile wish; Mitch McConnell, legendarily unsentimental, must have laughed out loud at that thought. Within hours of the news of Justice Ginsburg's death, McConnell announced his intention to confirm as her successor a nominee put forward by President Trump. The Republicans were jubilant about the opportunity to confirm a third justice nominated by Trump; they were almost as delighted to be able to change the subject from Trump's failed handling of the pandemic to a battle over the Supreme Court.

For McConnell, this would be the fourth time in four years that he would get to shape the Supreme Court. In 2016, after the death of Justice Antonin Scalia, he had stepped forward with similar speed to announce that the Senate would not consider any nominee put forward by President Barack Obama because it was a presidential election year; the seat should be left to the next president to fill. This unprecedented act outraged Democrats and left some Senate Republicans uneasy, but McConnell never wavered, and he won his bet when Trump was elected president and nominated Neil Gorsuch to fill the vacancy. Unlike the confirmation battles over Gorsuch and Brett Kavanaugh, replacing Justice Ginsburg was a different case entirely: a great liberal would be replaced by an extreme conservative, and the balance of the court could be dramatically shifted for a generation. Within hours of Justice Ginsburg's death, McConnell was on the phone with President Trump. "This will be the hardest fight of my life," the majority leader said. "We have to play this perfectly."[3] According to his former chief of staff, Josh Holmes, McConnell told Trump, "First, I'm going to put out a statement that we're going to fill the vacancy. Second, you've gotta nominate Amy Coney Barrett."[4]

Trump needed no prodding; there was never any doubt about who the nominee would be. At one point during the heated Kavanaugh debate two years earlier, Don McGahn, the White House counsel, had said, "If you don't confirm Kavanaugh, you're going to get Amy Coney Barrett."[5] It was the most ominous threat to Democrats that McGahn could make. After Trump nominated Kavanaugh, he told several advisers that he was "saving her [Barrett] for Ginsburg's seat."[6] She was the nominee who would pose the clearest threat to a full range of constitutional rights that had been protected by a closely balanced Supreme Court.

Amy Coney Barrett had been one of the first wave of judges that Trump had nominated to the federal court of appeals in 2017. She had an appealing personal profile; forty-eight years old, she was the mother of seven school-age children, including one with special needs. Barrett had spent most of her career as a law professor at Notre Dame, where she had been voted professor of the year three times. She was a

Midwesterner, a crucial political battleground, and a graduate of Notre Dame Law School, which many people would find a welcome departure for a court monopolized by the graduates of Harvard and Yale Law Schools.[7]

But what mattered most to Trump and McConnell was that Barrett was a committed originalist, in the tradition of Justice Scalia, for whom she had clerked. She had criticized Chief Justice Roberts for voting to uphold the Affordable Care Act, and she had once signed on to an ad calling for overturning *Roe v. Wade* and its "barbaric legacy."[8] Of course, Barrett would pay lip service to being a judge, not a legislator, as Roberts himself had described a judge's role during his own confirmation hearings in 2005: "an umpire, just calling balls and strikes." And with respect to routine legal issues, Barrett might function that way. But only the most consequential issues reached the Supreme Court, and Barrett was being nominated for her unmistakably clear views on those.

She was forthrightly and fiercely conservative, to the point that her legal philosophy seemed inextricably linked to her deeply felt Catholicism. During Barrett's confirmation hearings for the Seventh Circuit, Senator Dianne Feinstein observed, "The dogma lives loudly within you."[9] Politically, this was an unfortunate statement, which the Republicans would use their advantage, painting any opposition to Barrett as anti-Catholic. But it was nonetheless true. As Lindsey Graham said candidly, "This is the first time in American history that we've nominated a woman who is unashamedly pro-life and embraces her faith without apology."[10] Josh Hawley of Missouri, an extreme conservative who had said he would only vote to confirm a pro-life justice, pronounced himself eminently satisfied with Barrett.[11]

McConnell was perfectly willing to have the confirmation hearings focus on Barrett's Catholicism and the abortion issue, since they energized the Republican base, reminding conservative voters of what was at stake in the election. He called the attacks on Barrett's faith "a disgrace," saying that the Democrats are "so disconnected from their own country that they treat religious Americans like strange animals in a menagerie."[12] McConnell was preparing to carry out his most audacious act yet; the danger for him was whether several Senate Republicans would rebel against his determination to confirm a Supreme Court justice days before a presidential election that Trump was likely to lose.

The press would blast McConnell for his hypocrisy in ramming through Barrett's nomination after he had refused to give Merrick Garland a hearing for nine months prior to the 2016 election. McConnell shrugged off the charge of hypocrisy as liberal whining. But he recognized that other members of his caucus had been outspoken on this point. Susan Collins and Lisa Murkowski, whose independence had long been a thorn in McConnell's side, quickly expressed their view that it was too late in an election year to consider a Supreme Court nominee.[13] But McConnell always recognized the possibility of losing their votes; Judge Barrett could still be confirmed if the other Republicans stayed in line.

Amy Coney Barrett's nomination quickly collided with the terrible realities of this extraordinary year.[14] On October 3, President Trump hosted a ceremony in the Rose Garden to announce her nomination, attended by the judge's family, Republican lawmakers, religious leaders, top Trump allies, and White House officials, in clear conflict with the District of Columbia's ban on gatherings of more than fifty people. Upon arrival, attendees were given a rapid coronavirus test, and if it was negative, they were told it was safe to remove their masks. Guests were seen shaking hands and hugging, in direct opposition to CDC guidelines. Alex Azar, the secretary of health and human services, fist-bumped without a mask on. Attorney General Bill Barr and Dr. Scott Atlas, a member of the White House coronavirus task force, were seen without masks, shaking hands. At least twelve people, including Senators Mike Lee and Thom Tillis, First Lady Melania Trump, former New Jersey governor Chris Christie, and University of Notre Dame president John Jenkins, contracted COVID-19. It is likely, although not certain, that President Trump himself contracted COVID-19 at this event. Other people in Trump's orbit tested positive as well.

Dr. Anthony Fauci called the Rose Garden ceremony a "superspreader event." Judge Barrett, perhaps immunized because she had already had COVID-19, was unaffected. Also unaffected was Mitch McConnell, who never criticized Trump's mishandling of the pandemic but always wore a mask and was wise enough to come nowhere near the White House, where masking and social distancing were widely disregarded.[15] McConnell's only concern was whether Senators Tillis and Lee would recover quickly enough to vote on Judge Barrett's nomination.[16]

On October 12, Lindsey Graham gaveled the beginning of the Judiciary Committee's confirmation hearings of Judge Barrett. The nominee's opening statement focused on her family, including her children and siblings. She reviewed her education and mentioned clerking for Justice Scalia, her mentor, whose judicial philosophy she shared: "A judge must apply the law as it is written, not as the judge wishes it were." She discussed her belief that courts should enforce the rule of law, but that policy decisions are not the responsibility of the courts. She assured the committee that in every case, she had "done my utmost to reach the result required by the law, whatever my own preferences might be."

After that, Judge Barrett skillfully fended off questions for almost twenty hours over two days. She readily acknowledged being a devout Catholic but said "my personal church affiliation or my religious belief would not bear in the discharge of my duties as a judge." She deflected questions about her involvement with the People of Praise, a tight-knit, charismatic religious community, although reporting by the *New York Times* and other media outlets revealed that she had served as a "handmaid" in the group and that her family's life had centered on the community. Her father served as a principal leader of the New Orleans branch and was on the board of governors, and her mother served as a handmaid.[17]

Judge Barrett conveyed little substantive information about her views, including the constitutionality of the Affordable Care Act and potential cases that might challenge the outcome of the 2020 presidential election. She relied on the "Ginsburg rule," stating that Justice Ginsburg, with her characteristic pithiness, used this to describe how a nominee should comport herself at a hearing: "No hints, no previews, no forecasts. This had been the practice of nominees before her but everybody called it the Ginsburg rule because she stated it so concisely." Judge Barrett was especially reticent, refusing to recognize even the most well-established Supreme Court precedents.[18] She defended her integrity against the charge that she might be a "political judge" with a feistiness that surprised many observers. The questions seemed reasonable, given the fact that Judge Barrett was little known and that her confirmation was being rushed through at a time when Trump was expressing his intention to contest the election results right up to the Supreme Court.[19] None of these issues would sidetrack Barrett's confirmation, and her strong legal credentials received a glowing endorsement from Noah Feldman, the liberal Harvard Law constitutional scholar, who had clerked alongside her at the Supreme Court.[20]

Everyone knew that the only issue that might affect the outcome was the outrageous process. The Democrats on the Judiciary Committee were livid about McConnell's decision to ram through the confirmation of a Supreme Court justice in what appeared to be the closing hours of the Trump presidency. Amy Klobuchar, who had run a strong campaign for the Democratic presidential nomination, posed the issue most eloquently. Speaking angrily to her Republican colleagues, she noted that they "had set out the precedent . . . that the people choose the President and the President chooses the nominee." She continued: "It has been said that the wheels of justice turn slowly. Injustice, however, can move with lightning speed, as we are seeing today. We cannot, and you at home should not, separate this hearing from the moment we are in, and the judge he is trying to rush through." Klobuchar, whose husband and father had both been stricken by COVID, excoriated Trump and the Senate Republicans for rushing forward with this nomination instead of legislation to provide needed COVID relief.[21]

With his characteristic flair, Lindsey Graham had already addressed the question of confirming a Supreme Court justice in an election year. In a 2016 interview, Graham had said, "If an opening comes in the last year of President Trump's term and the primary process is started, we'll wait for the next election." In a 2018 interview with Jeffrey Goldberg of *The Atlantic*, Graham doubled down on his previously stated position: "Now I'll tell you this. This may make you feel better but I really don't care. If an opening comes in the last year of President Trump's term and the primary process is started, we will wait to the next election. And I've got a pretty good chance of being the Judiciary Committee chairman."[22]

That seemed clear enough, but by now Graham's previous statements were utterly worthless. Graham loved being Trump's new best friend; equally important, Trump was much more popular in South Carolina than Graham, who was facing an unexpectedly tough election challenge from Democrat Jamie Harrison. On September 19, even before Judge Barrett was nominated, President Trump tweeted, "@GOP We were put in this position of power and importance to make decisions for the people who so proudly elected us, the most important of which has long been considered to be the selection of United States Supreme Court justices. We have the obligation, without delay."[23]

Graham responded immediately by tweeting, "I fully understand where @realDonaldTrump is coming from." Later that day, he issued a series of tweets that blamed the Democrats for the changes in the judicial confirmation process: "Harry Reid changed the rules to allow a simple majority vote for Circuit Court nominees, dealing out the minority. Chuck Schumer and his friends in the liberal media conspired to destroy the life of Brett Kavanaugh and hold that Supreme Court seat open. In light of those two events, I will support President @realDonaldTrump in any effort to move forward regarding the recent vacancy created by the passing of Justice Ginsburg."[24]

Mitt Romney had shown his integrity and independence by being the only Senate Republican to vote to remove Trump from office at his impeachment trial. Now Romney faced the decision of whether he would confirm a Supreme Court nominee put forth by a president whom he had labeled a threat to our democracy. But Trump was still president, and notwithstanding his escalating attacks on the integrity of the election, Romney had no problem focusing on Barrett's "distinguished legal and academic credentials" and confirming her eight days before Election Day, even as fifty-eight million votes had already been cast.[25]

Chuck Grassley, the longest-serving Republican senator, had chaired the Judiciary Committee until January 2019 and had a well-earned reputation for cantankerous independence. In July 2020, he expressed the view that if he were still chairman, he would not consider a Supreme Court nomination so close to a presidential election.[26] However, it quickly became clear that Grassley's principled position was limited to the hypothetical situation of his being chairman. If his successor as Judiciary Committee chairman chose to move the nomination forward, Grassley would support it.[27]

Lamar Alexander, age eighty, was perhaps the most respected Republican in the Senate. He had announced his retirement and was coming to the end of a storied career, having served as senator, governor, cabinet officer, presidential candidate, and university president. Even when the Senate seemed hopelessly gridlocked in 2016 after McConnell blocked consideration of Garland's nomination, Alexander still managed to work with a Democratic colleague, Patty Murray, to produce major education legislation revising the troubled No Child Left Behind Act and major health-care legislation, the Faster Cures Act.[28]

When Alexander spoke, other Republicans listened. During the impeachment trial, Alexander was always regarded as the potential deciding vote on whether witnesses would be called. But a longtime friend of Alexander noted, "Lamar's no Howard Baker. He's much more cautious." That assessment proved accurate. When Alexander announced his opposition to calling witnesses, he said that the divisions over impeachment mirrored the deep partisan divide in the country, and removing Trump in an election year would only fan the flames of partisanship. "Let the voters decide" was an appealing argument, although it was premised on the assumptions that Trump would learn some lesson from being impeached and there was a limit to how much more damage he could do in his final year in office.

But the nomination of Amy Coney Barrett showed that Alexander's willingness to leave important decisions to the voters only went so far. After meeting with Judge Barrett on October 21, Alexander said, "Having attended college in Tennessee and law school in Indiana, her background will strengthen the Supreme Court by diversifying it. . . . Senator McConnell is only doing what the Senate majority has a right to do and what Senate Democratic leaders have said they would do in similar circumstances. No one should be surprised that a Republican Senate majority would vote on a Republican President's Supreme Court nomination, even during a presidential election year."[29] It is not clear whether Alexander believed what he was saying. His protégé, Bill Hagerty, was running to succeed him in the Senate, and Alexander undoubtedly wanted to avoid taking any action that would anger Trump or alienate his supporters in Tennessee.

In addition to Alexander, six other Republican senators would never again face the voters: Mike Enzi, Richard Shelby, Pat Roberts, Richard Burr, Pat Toomey, and James Inhofe. They had all served multiple terms, they had been chairmen of major committees, they were big men in their states, and they had received the greatest privilege that a republic could bestow. Any of them could have stopped McConnell's train in its tracks. Instead, they chose to complete their careers without rocking the boat. Not one of them objected to a process that bore more resemblance to Russia or other authoritarian countries than to America.

The Republican senators would stay in line, following Trump and McConnell's dictates. (Collins was the exception; McConnell understood that she needed to show independence in the closing days of a tough race for reelection in Maine.)[30] Some undoubtedly believed that having one more extremely conservative Supreme Court justice was a moral imperative, overriding all other considerations. Others simply did not want the hassle of confronting aggressive Trump supporters in town hall meetings or restaurants. And, in a period of tribal politics, they were, and would remain, Republicans. And so Mitch McConnell had the votes to confirm Amy Coney Barrett, just as surely as he had had them for Neil Gorsuch, Brett Kavanaugh, and 228 Trump nominees for the district and circuit courts.

As the vote approached, McConnell treated the Senate to a long description of the judicial wars between the parties, which was his typical mix of fact, half-truths, and utter falsehoods. "It is a matter of fact—a matter of history—that it was the Senate Democrats who first began our contemporary difficulties with judicial nominations back in 1987, and who have initiated every meaningful escalation—every single one of them—from then up to the present day," McConnell claimed.[31] And indeed, the Democrats had plenty to regret in their approach to the judicial wars. Democrats had never matched the Republicans' laser focus on the importance of the courts or their long allegiance with the Federalist Society and the Heritage Foundation that had finally produced the result for which they had worked so hard. Dianne Feinstein provided one more painful reminder of Democrats' futility and fecklessness at the close of the Barrett hearings, when she inexplicably embraced Lindsey Graham and praised the quality of the proceedings.[32]

But McConnell's "history lesson" was incomplete and distorted. In truth, the Supreme Court confirmations after Bork had been relatively civilized, with the exception of the nomination of Clarence Thomas in 1991, until McConnell refused to consider the Garland nomination in 2016. There had been no precedent for refusing to consider a nomination in a presidential election year; many Supreme Court justices had been considered and confirmed in such circumstances. And there was certainly no precedent for ramming through Barrett's confirmation eight days before Election Day. Assessing his own work, McConnell concluded, "This confirmation process falls squarely within history and precedent. Neither falsehoods nor strong feelings change the facts."[33] This was an outright lie. But it is often said that history is written by the winners; McConnell had won and was determined to write the history.

In April 2020, when the Senate had joined the House in passing the $2.1 trillion CARES Act, a desperately needed response to the rampaging novel coronavirus, McConnell had proudly said, "The Senate stepped up."[34] Now, however, he claimed Barrett's confirmation as a personal triumph. It was, he judged, "the single most important accomplishment of my career. I'm proud of it, and I feel good about it. . . . At the risk of tooting my own horn, look at majority leaders since

L.B.J. and find another one who was able to do something as consequential as this." In case anyone was wondering, McConnell explained exactly why it was so consequential: "A lot of what we have done over the last four years will be undone sooner or later by the next election. They won't be able to do much about this for a long time to come."[35]

In truth, McConnell was completely justified in claiming his personal triumph; no one else would have had the shameless audacity to accomplish it. McConnell and the other Republican senators knew, as surely as night follows day, that it was fundamentally wrong to confirm a nominee to the Supreme Court so late in an election year. That would be true whoever was president, but they knew it was particularly outrageous to give that power to Donald Trump, who was conducting a continuing assault on the rule of law, threatening our democracy by working to undermine the election, and was about to be repudiated by the voters. Surely Trump should not get the opportunity to have another justice confirmed unless the American people chose to reelect him. And, on some level, the Republican senators probably understood that the last thing our crippled country needed, while struggling with disease, death, and fearsome economic damage from the coronavirus, in a moment of national soul-searching about systemic racism, was a bitter battle over the Supreme Court.

Criticism of McConnell's brazen action understandably focused on what the *Washington Post* editorial page would describe as the "poisonous, dishonorable hypocrisy" of ramming through Barrett's confirmation, given his refusal to consider President Obama's nomination of Judge Garland four years earlier.[36] But it was worse than that. Although McConnell's action in 2016 was unprecedented hardball, it retained some connection to our democratic process. In that election year, the voters still had the opportunity to decide on the president who would fill the seat. McConnell's action this time was intended to cut out the voters and to lock in a right-wing majority on the court, no matter what verdict the voters would render on Trump. It was a naked power grab of the sort that is more familiar in Russia, Turkey, or other authoritarian or banana republic countries. In their book *How Democracies Die*, Daniel Ziblatt and Steven Levitsky describe one of the essential elements of democracy: "forbearance," not pushing your power to the limit by doing anything and everything that is not illegal.[37] "Forbearance" had ceased to be a characteristic of Mitch McConnell years before, and it never had been one for Donald Trump. Nancy Pelosi's memorable observation that the founders had not anticipated the possibility of a rogue president and a rogue majority leader was right on the mark.[38]

McConnell had claimed his ultimate victory. He knew that Trump was likely to lose, and he was comfortable with it, having gotten everything out of Trump's dangerous and chaotic presidency that mattered to hm. Confirming Justice Barrett would be a boost for a number of the Senate Republicans facing tough races, but even if Joe Biden won the election and the Senate went Democratic, McConnell would still be the most powerful Republican in Washington, a roadblock or an ally to President Biden depending on what would help him return to the majority in two years.[39]

With eight days to go before the presidential election, McConnell, increasingly arrogant and self-satisfied, would have assessed his position as very strong. His 2016 memoir was titled *The Long Game*, and no one had matched his skill at it. Donald Trump dominated the political landscape as no previous president had. But we were living in Mitch McConnell's America before Trump arrived, and if McConnell had his way, that would continue long after Trump left Washington.

· 9 ·

The Big Lie

As election day approached, Mitch McConnell made his choices. He would model good behavior with respect to the coronavirus, wearing a mask and keeping the Senate safe without going anywhere near the White House or criticizing President Trump for his irresponsible and unhinged behavior. He would not permit the Senate to pass another coronavirus relief package, despite the soaring death toll and far-reaching economic damage. He would move quickly and ruthlessly to take advantage of the historic opportunity to confirm Amy Coney Barrett to the Supreme Court; it seemed that the only death in America that mattered to him was Ruth Bader Ginsburg's. And McConnell would do and say nothing to counter the increasingly visible and concerted campaign by Trump and his allies to undermine confidence in the presidential election.

Donald Trump's long record of seeking to undermine public confidence in America's presidential elections had begun in 2012. When President Obama defeated Mitt Romney to win reelection, Trump called the victory "a total sham," showing that the United States was "not a democracy." He tweeted, "We can't let this happen. We should march on Washington and stop this travesty. Our nation is totally divided."[1] Trump's rant got little attention because Romney quickly conceded and virtually everyone agreed the election had been conducted fairly.

In February 2016, when Trump lost the Iowa caucuses, he tweeted, "Ted Cruz didn't win Iowa, he stole it. That is why all of the polls were so wrong and why he got far more voters than anticipated. Bad!"[2] After winning the nomination, Trump and his political allies made wild claims of voter fraud, promoting conspiracy theories that ranged from "non-citizens" voting illegally in Virginia to a "huge, massive voter-fraud scheme" in Wisconsin to a fake document that supposedly revealed a Democratic plan to control Americans' minds with "pulsed ELF electro-magnetic emissions" and impose martial law. "Of course, there is large scale voter fraud happening on and before election day," Trump tweeted. "Why do Republican leaders deny what is going on. So naïve!" A follow-up tweet said, "This election is absolutely being rigged by the dishonest and distorted media pushing Crooked Hillary—but also at many polling places—SAD."[3]

Of course, none of these claims had any basis in fact, but even after Trump won the 2016 presidential election with a majority in the Electoral College, he asserted that he had won the popular vote as well, despite having no evidence to support the claim.[4] He ordered the formation of the Presidential Commission on Election Integrity to collect evidence of widespread voter fraud that would prove that he had indeed won the popular vote. The commission did make findings supporting Trump's claims, which Charles Stewart III, a political scientist at MIT, described as "a total dumpster fire" of sensational charges based on flawed data matching.[5] The commission disbanded quickly after its findings were widely discredited.

Trump's track record as a political arsonist was clear. Having attacked the integrity of presidential elections when he was not a candidate and of an election he won, he certainly would attempt to undermine confidence in the 2020 election, particularly as it looked increasingly likely that he would lose to Joe Biden. On the day of the Wisconsin presidential primary, Trump launched a false claim about the security of mail-in ballots: "Mail ballots are a very dangerous thing in this country because they're cheaters. They go and collect them. They're fraudulent in many cases."[6] In a July interview with Chris Wallace on *Fox News Sunday*, Trump again claimed that mail-in voting is "going to rig the election." When asked whether he would accept the election results, Trump responded, "No, I'm not going to say yes. I'm not going to say no, and I didn't last time either."[7]

In the summer and fall, as the polls showed him falling behind Biden, Trump's rhetoric grew shriller. "This is the most dangerous election we've ever had. The most dangerous because I don't think we can ever bring it back if they get in. . . . It will be another Venezuela," Trump said in an August 17 speech in Wisconsin. "I used to say that lightly. I now say it very strongly because it's a similar ideology. This will be a large scale, a very large-scale Venezuela, if they win."[8] Speaking at the Republican National Convention a week later, Trump tied his claims of election fraud to the medical agony that America was going through. "What they're doing is using COVID to steal an election. They're using COVID to defraud the American people, all of our people, of a fair and free election."[9]

Of course, the pandemic posed a profound challenge to election officials, Democrats and Republicans, who sought to ensure that Americans would have the opportunity to vote at a time when they were being urged not to leave their houses. Dedicated, experienced state and local officials were making maximum efforts to increase the opportunities to mail in ballots and vote early in polling places that were safe and uncrowded. McConnell and the Senate Republicans understood the scope of this challenge, and most of them understood that Trump was spouting dangerous lies. And yet none of them spoke out; instead, McConnell took the lead in actions that would make mail-in voting more difficult. The $2 trillion CARES Act included $400 million for elections, but Senate Republicans refused to release the money to help states count ballots or to aid the US Postal Service. Postmaster Louis DeJoy, a Trump appointee, implemented operational changes in the run-up to the election that led to a dramatic decline in the on-time delivery of first-class mail.[10] Senate Republicans blocked efforts to allocate funds for sorting equipment so that the states could count mail-in ballots more quickly. McConnell's long opposition to increased funds for election security morphed seamlessly into opposition to supplemental funds for the Postal Service.

Against great odds, heroic efforts by state and local election officials, combined with the fierce determination of Americans who wanted to vote, produced a presidential election with record turnout. More than 158 million Americans voted, nearly 20 million more than in 2016. The turnout rate was nearly 67 percent, the highest in 120 years (improving on the already high turnout of 61 percent in 2012 and 2016).[11]

But these numbers carried little weight for Trump. The president had signaled clearly that he would only accept the result of an election that he won, and the "Stop the Steal" movement sprang into immediate action. Even as the votes were still being counted, Republican political operatives Steve Bannon and Roger Stone spread wild conspiracy theories on Facebook and traditional media that Trump had won the election. Aided by right-wing activists like Ali Alexander and high-profile conservatives such as Donald Trump Jr. and Ann Coulter, the "Stop the Steal" hashtag went viral as early as election day, and ten days later had been tweeted 1.7 million times.[12]

Because of the huge turnout, the large number of mail-in votes, and close races in key states, it was understood that the major national media outlets would probably not be able to call the race for several days. But on Saturday, November 7, with the posting of definitive results from Pennsylvania, all the major networks and the Associated Press projected that Joe Biden had won enough states to give him more than the 270 electoral votes needed to gain a majority, and thus proclaimed him the winner. Traditionally, the "call" by the networks and the AP marked the end of the presidential election, with everything that followed just a formality. Trump, of course, did not accept this determination; it was the pivotal moment when McConnell and other Senate Republicans could have healed the nation, without criticizing Trump, by simply recognizing that Joe Biden was the president-elect.

It was not to be. With the notable exceptions of Susan Collins (who had defied the pundits' predictions by winning reelection in Maine by a comfortable margin), Lisa Murkowski, Mitt Romney, and Ben Sasse, the abdication of responsibility by Senate Republicans, led by McConnell, would continue. On November 9, McConnell went to the Senate floor and gave Trump cover to pursue endless challenges to the election result.

"The core principle here is not complicated. In the United States of America, all legal ballots must be counted; any illegal ballots must not be; the process should be transparent or observable by all sides, and the courts are here to work through concerns," McConnell lectured. "Our institutions are built for this. We have a system in place to consider concerns. And President Trump is 100 percent within his rights to look into allegations of irregularities and weigh his legal options."

It was an anodyne, ostensibly neutral statement with a profoundly non-neutral effect. There was no precedent for a Senate majority leader to refuse to accept the outcome of a presidential election, when the outcome had been determined in the traditional way. By withholding acknowledgment of Biden's victory, McConnell was clearly giving support to Trump's claims of grave irregularities that required investigating, and possibly reversing, the election results. And while "the courts are here to work through concerns," the courts should not have to wade through frivolous lawsuits all over the country only to find their verdicts would not be accepted by Trump and his supporters. "Our institutions" are in fact not "built for this." They needed reinforcement and defending by Republican senators.

Reaching for his usual sardonic humor, McConnell concluded with a statement he would later regret: "Suffice it to say that a few legal inquiries by the President do not exactly spell the end of the Republic."[13]

Lindsey Graham went even further. After Donald Trump Jr. criticized Graham for not immediately taking Trump's side hours after the polls closed, Graham appeared on Sean Hannity's Fox News show two days later to make amends. "Philadelphia elections are crooked as a snake," Graham claimed, "and allegations of wrongdoing are shattering."[14] Graham later told Fox News, "If Republicans don't challenge and change the U.S. election system, there will never be another Republican president elected again. President Trump should not concede. We're down to less than 10,000 votes in Georgia. He's going to win North Carolina. We've gone from 93,000 votes to less than

20,000 votes in Arizona, where more votes to be counted."[15] Graham also pledged a $500,000 donation to the president's "legal defense fund" and urged others to donate via Trump's website.[16]

When Mitt Romney voted to convict Trump at his impeachment trial in February 2020, he became the first senator in history to vote to remove a president of his party. Romney had faced severe criticism and significant harassment from angry Trump supporters since that vote. On Friday, November 6, he spoke out strongly again: "The President is within his rights to request recounts, to call for investigation of alleged voting irregularities where evidence exists and to exhaust legal remedies—doing these things is consistent with our election process. He is wrong to say that the election was rigged, corrupt and stolen—doing so weakens the cause of freedom here and around the world, weakens the institutions that lie at the foundation of the republic, and recklessly inflames destructive and dangerous passions."[17] After the national media confirmed Biden's victory the following day, Romney immediately tweeted his congratulations to Biden and Vice President Elect Kamala Harris: "We know both of them as people of good will and admirable character. We pray that God may bless them in the days and years ahead."[18]

Ben Sasse, a rising star among Senate Republicans, won a comfortable reelection in Nebraska. On Friday, he, too, spoke out sharply: "Fraud is poison to self-government, so these are major allegations. If the President's legal team has real evidence, they need to present it immediately to the public and the courts. In the meantime, all legal votes need to be counted according to relevant state laws. This is our American system, and it works."[19] Two days later, after the results showed Biden to be the winner, Sasse immediately congratulated Biden and Harris on their victory.[20] Susan Collins and Lisa Murkowski also quickly congratulated Biden.

But McConnell and Graham carried the most weight, and other Republicans chose to say as little as possible. Crucial days and then weeks passed, without Senate Republican acceptance of Biden's victory. "Stop the Steal" lit up social media, with the Trump campaign and the Republican National Committee raising $207 million using

"Stop the Steal" messaging in the three weeks after the November election, sending out more than six hundred emails asking for donations for an "Election Defense Fund" and claiming that the election had been stolen.[21]

Trump ratcheted up his frenzied attack. Because Biden won Georgia narrowly and unexpectedly, the state was ground zero for Trump's efforts to overturn the election. On November 13, Trump and Graham joined a call to Georgia's secretary of state, Brad Raffensperger, who had been in the public spotlight during Georgia's attempt to deal with a massive wave of newly registered voters. According to Raffensperger, Graham asked him "whether he had the power to toss out all mail ballots in certain counties." Although Graham denied the claim, it was widely believed, given the fact that Raffensperger, a Republican, had no incentive to lie or exaggerate about the pressure to which he was subjected.[22]

Christopher Krebs, the administration's most senior cybersecurity official responsible for securing the presidential election, had also joined the ever-expanding group of dedicated public servants who committed the unpardonable offense of refusing to go along with Trump's lies and irrationality about the integrity of the election. Four days after the call to Raffensperger, Trump fired him, tweeting, "The recent statement by Chris Krebs on the security of the 2020 Election was highly inaccurate in that there were massive improprieties and fraud—including dead people voting, Poll Watchers not allowed into polling locations, 'glitches' in the voting machines which changed votes from Trump to Biden, late voting, and many more."[23]

Rudy Giuliani, Trump's personal attorney and a principal adviser, joined the attack. At one time, many years earlier, Giuliani had been one of the nation's most respected lawyers, but now he was a tool in Trump's scorched-earth offensive, following a pattern of aggressive litigation that had long characterized Trump's business career. In a press conference on November 19, Giuliani called the election a "massive fraud." Sidney Powell, who had risen rapidly in the ranks of Trump advisers by being even more extreme than Giuliani or Trump, alleged that the election had been corrupted by a "massive influence of communist money." Powell also suggested a revolution, calling this moment "the 1775 of our generation and beyond."[24] The Trump campaign launched a nationwide litigation blitz, bringing more than sixty lawsuits challenging the election results in seven swing states.

Neither the lawsuits nor the lawyers who filed them were subjected to quality control. The lawsuits ranged from weak to utterly laughable. Most of the suits contained allegations of incidents of fraud affecting a tiny number of votes at most. None was compelling enough to convince a court to overturn the ruling of a state election official. In the first two weeks of December, the Trump team took one loss in court after another, almost daily.

Angered that the courts were ruling against him, Trump intensified his efforts to pressure state officials to overturn the election results. On November 20, he invited the Republican leaders of the Michigan legislature to the White House and was rebuffed; the lawmakers said they found nothing that would change the outcome. (Biden's margin in Michigan was 155,000 votes.)[25] On December 5, Trump called Georgia's Republican governor, Brian Kemp, and asked him to call a special session of the state legislature to overturn Biden's win in Georgia. "If we win Georgia, everything else falls into place," the president tweeted. Kemp responded that he had already implemented a signature audit three times, politely rejecting Trump's demand for further action.[26] On December 8, the US Supreme Court rejected a petition from Republicans in Pennsylvania who sought to overturn Biden's victory there.[27] Undaunted but increasingly desperate, that same day Trump called the Republican speaker of the Pennsylvania House of Representatives to encourage challenges to the official results of the presidential election.[28] Each of Trump's calls might have been a criminal violation of state law, and it was not unreasonable to consider that a president pressuring state officials to change the results of an election in which he was a candidate was grounds for impeachment. But still the Senate Republicans under Mitch McConnell refused to criticize or condemn Trump's behavior.

The Trump legal team had one more "Hail Mary" pass in its arsenal. Trump frequently indicated that he was counting on the Supreme

Court to throw out the election results.[29] Toward that end, Texas attorney general Ken Paxton, a Republican facing criminal charges for securities fraud, filed an extraordinary petition with the court, seeking to overturn Biden's victories in four states: Pennsylvania, Michigan, Wisconsin, and Georgia. Paxton based his suit on the fact that the Supreme Court had original jurisdiction over disputes between states, but, historically, that jurisdiction was used for boundary disputes and other routine matters of interstate commerce. On December 11, the Supreme Court quickly rejected Paxton's claim in an unsigned ruling, stating, "Texas has not demonstrated a judicially cognizable interest in the manner in which another State conducts its elections."[30] But 17 of his fellow Republican state attorneys general and 126 Republican members of the House of Representatives backed the bizarre lawsuit, a stark measure of a nation on the verge of disunion.

Clearly, the election of Joe Biden had not broken the political fever raging in the country, but it did have a significant impact on the Senate. America desperately needed a second major coronavirus relief package; under current law, as many as twelve million Americans could lose their eligibility for unemployment benefits at year's end. Millions of people could be evicted from their homes, and thousands more businesses might close during the winter before vaccines could be available. Congress had been hopelessly deadlocked for six months on how to pass a supplemental relief package. *New York Times* columnist David Brooks succinctly described the danger of the moment: "The core problem is that Republicans have applied a dogmatically ideological approach to a situation in which it is not germane and is in fact ruthlessly destructive. . . . This is not a normal recession. It is a natural disaster. The proposals on offer are not conventional stimulus. They are measures to defend our national economic infrastructure from that disaster over the next five brutal months." His column was titled "The Winter Mitch McConnell Created."[31]

A determined group of senators was no longer willing to wait for their leaders. Joe Manchin's hatred for the polarized Senate was well known. "This place sucks," the West Virginia Democrat reportedly said, fuming over the dysfunction and seriously considering leaving after one term to seek to reclaim his old job as governor.[32] But Manchin decided to seek one more term in the Senate in 2018, winning reelection by three points in a state that Trump would carry in 2020 by nearly forty points. Manchin's independence had led him to become the only Senate Democrat to endorse Susan Collins in her tough reelection race in 2020, and Collins now joined Manchin to bring together several other moderate and independent senators—Mark Warner, Mitt Romney, Angus King, Bill Cassidy, and Jeanne Shaheen—to meet in Lisa Murkowski's Capitol Hill living room the week before Thanksgiving. Over dinner, maintaining social distance and keeping the windows open, they hammered out the initial parameters of an immediate relief package to tide the country over until Joe Biden took office in January.

Dick Durbin, the number two Senate Democrat, was an unexpected arrival at the meeting. But he made a pivotal contribution. "Forget about a sweeping stimulus initiative," Durbin said. "What we need is a limited emergency plan to get the country through March." Romney later recalled, "That was what really opened the eyes of all of us."[33]

In Wilmington, Delaware, President-Elect Biden had reached the same conclusion. Three days after the dinner at Senator Murkowski's house, Speaker Pelosi and Minority Leader Schumer drove to Wilmington to meet with Biden, who delivered a clear message. "He knew that we could not get everything now, but anything we could get would make his job easier when he became president," Schumer said. "We agreed."

The limited emergency package would still be nearly a trillion dollars. It involved sensitive issues and would require painful compromises. But in an extraordinary departure from their usual approach, the Democratic leaders essentially allowed the Senate moderates to hammer out the outlines of the package. The senators worked over Thanksgiving, on weekends, and late at night, forming subgroups to tackle the key issues that had blocked agreement for months, including the size and duration of unemployment benefits, aid to states and cities, funds for school reopening, and whether to give businesses protection from liability in lawsuits by their employees who contracted COVID. Drawing on a $1.8 trillion stimulus package offered by the House Problem Solvers Caucus, a group of centrist members, the senators essentially split the differences between the Democrats and Republicans, including items that both sides agreed on but also two competing priorities that had frustrated the leaders: the liability shield for businesses that Republicans wanted and the money that Democrats sought for state and local governments.

The negotiations continued round the clock, with the senators deeply engaged. "This was not an instance where members started it off and turned it over to staff," Collins later observed. Two weeks after the dinner at Murkowski's house, the senators held a press conference unveiling a $908 billion framework. "None of us thought in good conscience we could go home for Christmas with all these people thrown out of their apartments, closing their businesses, getting into food lines," said Warner. "It would be the ultimate Scrooge-like activity."[34] Schumer and Pelosi endorsed the moderates' package as the path forward, even though they would have preferred a larger package.

The moderates faced the ultimate challenge: getting Mitch McConnell to sign on. The Senate majority leader had been implacably opposed to further coronavirus relief and seemed unmoved by the suffering in the country. What did concern him were the two runoff elections in Georgia, scheduled for January 5, on which his majority depended. Two Senate seats were still undecided in Georgia—one for a full six-year term and one to complete the last two years of an unexpired term—because state law required a majority vote, and no candidate had reached 50 percent in the November election (because of the presence of third parties). Incumbent Republican senators David Perdue and Kelly Loeffler faced strong opposition from Jon Ossoff and Raphael Warnock, respectively, and Democrats around the nation were pouring money into these races in the hope of winning both seats and, with them, a Senate majority once Kamala Harris became vice president and could wield a tiebreaking vote. Among the issues in Georgia was Congress's failure to deliver more pandemic relief, for which Perdue and Loeffler were receiving intense criticism.

McConnell met with the Republican moderates Collins, Murkowski, Romney, and Cassidy and congratulated them on getting the Democrats to agree to a lower dollar figure for the emerging package. A week later, McConnell made what would prove to be a crucial offer: the Republicans would drop their demand for liability protections for businesses if the Democrats would not seek billions of dollars in federal grants to state and local governments. McConnell had previously said that liability protection was a "red line" issue for Republicans, but now he used it as leverage to force the Democrats to give up one of their priorities. Privately, he assured Perdue and Loeffler that the Senate would reach a deal before leaving for Christmas. Lindsey Graham sat down with the president to sell him on the package. "This bipartisan working group is your best way forward," Graham told Trump. The president seemed to agree, and Graham went back to Capitol Hill and told reporters that Trump had agreed. The Republicans later bowed to Democratic demands for additional monthly cash payments, which had provided extraordinary lifelines for millions of Americans but were set to expire.

The $900 billion stimulus agreed to on December 20 became the first significant infusion of federal funds since April for the American people. It also became the centerpiece for the longest piece of legislation in history (5,872 pages), as Congress merged it with a catchall spending measure to fund the government for the remainder of the fiscal year. The legislation included an unexpected set of progressive accomplishments. It contained a ban on surprise medical bills that occur when patients unexpectedly must receive care from an out-of-network health provider; it expanded the federal Pell Grant program for low-income students and eliminated a long-standing ban on extending the grants to prisoners pursuing degrees; it forgave more than $1 billion in federal loans for historically black colleges and universities; and it included funding to counter climate change and promote clean energy, the first legislation of this type in nearly ten years.[35]

"We can finally report what our nation has needed to hear for a very long time," McConnell said on the Senate floor. "More help is on the way."

Many people could take pride in the legislation, none more so than the Senate moderates led by Collins, Manchin, Romney, and Warner. They broke the months-long stalemate by showing that a bipartisan group could leverage its influence in a closely balanced Senate, particularly when working with an incoming president who had unmatched experience in dealing with Congress. The senators proved again what the partisan gridlock usually obscured; many of them were capable, creative legislators and committed public servants. They could understand the country's needs, articulate principles, negotiate compromises, and deliver for America—in those rare situations when McConnell allowed them to do so.

The legislative triumph came together at a moment that was politically fraught. Nearly seven weeks had passed since election day. The Supreme Court had ended Trump's hope that "my judges" would save him.[36] Six days earlier, on December 14, the Electoral College had certified the results of the presidential election. Biden received 306 electoral votes to Trump's 232, precisely the outcome that the networks and the AP had announced on November 7. The next day, McConnell went to the Senate floor and finally acknowledged Biden as president-elect. Most of his brief remarks were devoted to praising Trump's "endless" accomplishments. He expressed regret that Trump had lost but said, "The Electoral College has spoken. So today I want to congratulate President-Elect Joe Biden." He also congratulated Vice President Elect Harris.[37] Even then, he would not call Biden himself; rather, he accepted a call from the president-elect.

McConnell started immediately on an effort to unify the Senate Republicans in accepting Biden's victory. The Electoral College vote was always certified in a routine ceremony on January 6, two weeks before the inauguration, but an individual state's certification would require a separate debate and vote if one member of the House and one member of the Senate objected to that state's electoral vote. Representative Mo Brooks, an Alabama Republican, had already indicated his intention to object; there was no doubt that many other House Republicans, fresh from their recent support of the Texas lawsuit in the Supreme Court, would join him. Privately, McConnell told his caucus that challenging the certification would force them to take a "terrible vote" because they would need to vote it down, going against Trump.[38] John Thune, the number three Senate Republican, reinforced McConnell's message. "The thing they've got to remember is [the challenge] is not going to go anywhere. I mean, in the Senate, it would go down like a shot dog," Thune told reporters. "I don't think it makes a lot of sense to put everyone through this when you know what the ultimate outcome is going to be."[39]

Although none of the Republican senators had joined Paxton's absurd lawsuit, some were not ready to fall in line with McConnell's request. James Inhofe, John Kennedy, Marsha Blackburn, and Steve Daines still refused to acknowledge Biden's victory. Others, newly elected but not yet sworn in, had not expressed their views.[40]

McConnell was the most powerful Senate leader in history. His members respected his political judgment and his commitment to keeping them in power; his control over the caucus in important moments almost never failed. But for the past four years, McConnell's iron grip on his caucus had also reflected his alignment with Trump. Now he and the president were no longer aligned; Trump saw the Electoral College vote as one more outrage, rather than the end of his effort to overturn the election results. Even as McConnell spoke on December 15, Trump was asking the acting attorney general, Jeffrey Rosen, to enlist the Justice Department in support of lawsuits to reverse the election, and he urged Rosen to appoint a special counsel to investigate Dominion Voting Systems, a company that had supplied voting machines and software to several states.[41] On December 12, two days before the Electoral College met in their state capitals, Trump tweeted about "Stop the Steal" rallies across the country: "Wow! Thousands of people forming in Washington (D.C.) to Stop the Steal. Didn't know about this, but I'll be seeing them! @MAGA." On December 19, Trump again tweeted, "Big protest on January 6th. Be there, will be wild!"[42]

McConnell understandably prided himself on his mastery of American politics and his knowledge of American history. However, he was about to learn the wisdom of George Ball's observation that "he who rides the tiger cannot choose where he dismounts." As long as Trump did not concede, some Senate Republicans—those who were afraid to break with him, and those seeking to cultivate his followers for their own future political plans—would not.

Josh Hawley, one of the Republicans' brightest right-wing rising stars, had won election to the Senate from Missouri. A graduate of Stanford University and Yale Law School and a former Supreme Court clerk, Hawley was by all reports a brilliant man, and at forty-one he had a bright future. Former senator John Danforth, his mentor, predicted that Hawley would become the Senate's intellectual leader, following in the footsteps of the legendary Daniel Patrick Moynihan.[43] And Hawley did promote some interesting ideas, writing a book criticizing big tech companies and urging larger cash payments during COVID. Now, however, Hawley vaulted into the public eye on December 30, becoming the first senator to answer Trump's call to challenge the election at the pro forma tallying of electoral votes the following week. Hawley framed his objection as "an effort to highlight the failure" of states "to follow their own election laws as well as the unprecedented interference of Big Tech monopolies in the election." While he did not echo Trump's false claim of widespread voter fraud, "millions of voters concerned about election integrity deserve to be heard," Hawley said. "I will object on January 6 on their behalf."[44]

Of course, the concerns of voters worried about election integrity had been heard and rejected in sixty courts, including the Supreme Court, but given Hawley's intense ambition, those details were overlooked. Ben Sasse, probably the brightest and among the few principled Republican senators, tore into Hawley and the House Republicans who had taken the same course. "Let's be clear what is happening here: We have a bunch of ambitious politicians who think there is a quick way to tap into the president's populist base without doing any real, long-term damage," Sasse wrote just hours after Hawley's announcement. "But they're wrong—and this issue is bigger than anyone's personal ambitions. Adults don't point a loaded gun at the heart of legitimate self-government."[45]

But despite McConnell's increasingly urgent efforts and Sasse's fierce eloquence, Hawley would not be a lone ranger for long. Having already sought the Republican presidential nomination in 2016, Ted Cruz was not conceding the extreme right-wing lane to the new-comer Hawley. On January 2, Cruz announced that he and ten other sitting and newly elected Republican senators would join Hawley in objecting to the certification. The current senators were Ron Johnson, James Lankford, Steve Daines, John Kennedy, and Michael Braun. The newly elected senators, not yet even sworn in, were Cynthia Lummis, Roger Marshall, Tommy Tuberville, and Bill Hagerty.[46] The big surprises were Lankford, respected for his intelligence and occasional independence, and Hagerty, Lamar Alexander's protégé, who had been ambassador to Japan and was supposedly a pro-business, moderate conservative. Trump now had important cover for his wild claims, and McConnell had lost control over his caucus.

McConnell could live with Biden's election, but as the new year began he faced the disaster he most feared: the incoming Democratic president might also have a Democratic Senate as well as the Democratic House. The Republicans had fifty senators; the Democrats, forty-eight. Despite Biden's narrow victory in Georgia, few people believed that the Democrats could win the two runoff elections on January 5, which they needed to do in order to deadlock the Senate and allow Vice President Harris to cast the deciding vote to create a Democratic majority. But Georgia Democrats, led by the brilliant and tireless Stacey Abrams, had been organizing nonstop since Abrams's narrow defeat in the 2018 race for governor.

The Republicans furiously attacked the Democratic "odd couple"[47] candidates: Raphael Warnock, the African American reverend who held Martin Luther King's pulpit in Atlanta's Ebenezer Baptist Church, and Jon Ossoff, a thirty-three-year-old Jewish filmmaker who had lost a congressional special election in the Atlanta suburbs in 2017 despite raising a record amount of money. But Warnock and Ossoff proved to be terrific candidates: energetic and eloquent, running as a team, riding the tide of Democratic aspirations and donations in Georgia and nationally. "The fact that we're even talking about a competitive race in Georgia tells you the impact of demographic change on American politics," noted the Republican pollster Whit Ayres.[48] McConnell was by now the leading bogeyman for Democrats, next to Trump. No one doubted what was at stake in the Georgia Senate races. January runoff elections usually saw a light voter turnout, but not this time.

McConnell was enraged at Trump, who was making it virtually impossible for Senators Perdue and Loeffler to deliver a coherent message. Trump's constant attacks on the integrity of the election might bring his hard-core supporters into the streets, but they seemed likely to convince many Republicans and independents that voting was not worth their time. But McConnell himself became one more major obstacle in the path of his Senate candidates. Just days after Congress agreed to the coronavirus relief package, Trump, in a surprise video address, attacked the proposed $600 stimulus checks as "ridiculously low" and called for them to be increased to $2,000, which Schumer and Pelosi quickly applauded.[49] Perdue and Loeffler, fighting for their political lives in Georgia, jumped on the bandwagon almost immediately.[50]

McConnell had resisted additional coronavirus relief for eight months before stepping forward to take credit for the $900 billion relief package. Now he refused to increase the package despite the pressure from Trump, the Democrats, and the Perdue and Loeffler races. He declared that he would not separate the $2,000 checks from other matters demanded by Trump, such as stripping legal protections from tech companies and establishing an election fraud commission. McConnell described the House proposal as too generous and said that the Senate would consider only "smart targeted aid, not another fire hose of borrowed money that encompasses other people who are doing just fine."[51] He had effectively sawed off the last limb to which Perdue and Loeffler were clinging. Those who thought McConnell would do anything to keep the Senate majority proved to be wrong; there was at least one thing that was a bridge too far. On January 5, the voters of Georgia gave Raphael Warnock and Jon Ossoff narrow victories, which would make Chuck Schumer the majority leader once the presidential inauguration took place two weeks hence.

As Trump and his key operatives blasted out their claims of election fraud, and Congress struggled to resuscitate the COVID relief package, there was increasing chatter about potential violence on January 6. Trump supporters had signaled on various online forums and websites that they were planning to go to Washington to protest the certification of the electoral vote, with many stating that they had violent intentions. On encrypted apps and on mainstream media and smaller social media sites, they discussed logistics, including what type of weapons to bring to the capital. Steven Sund, the chief of the Capitol Police, later said that these Trump supporters brought "helmets, gas masks, shields, pepper spray, fireworks, climbing gear—climbing gear!—explosives, metal pipes, and baseball bats."[52]

As early as December 31, the police were bracing for pro-Trump rallies on January 6.[53] The New York Police Department shared intelligence with the Capitol Police and the FBI indicating that there would likely be violence during the electoral vote certification. Inexplicably, the Department of Homeland Security and the FBI did not create an intelligence report for the upcoming "Save America Rally," as is usually the case in such situations. But Homeland Security did release a threat assessment, with an emphasis on "heightened threat environment during the 2020–2021 election season, including the extent to which the political transition and political polarization are contributing to the mobilization of individuals to commit violence."[54]

Washington's mayor, Muriel Bowser, and Chris Rodriguez, the director of the District of Columbia's Homeland Security and Emergency Management Agency, requested assistance from the National Guard for the day of the congressional certification. On January 2, Christopher Miller, the acting secretary of defense, met with General Mark Milley (chairman of the Joint Chiefs of Staff) and Ryan McCarthy (secretary of the army) regarding Mayor Bowser's request.[55] The next day, the mayor issued a press release warning the public to avoid downtown on January 6 and reminding those planning to attend rallies that it is illegal to carry a firearm on US Capitol grounds and in National Park Service areas.[56]

On January 4, a twelve-page internal Capitol Police intelligence report warned of a "violent scenario" in which "Congress itself" could be the target of angry supporters of President Trump and that thousands of protestors could descend upon Washington, D.C., calling the "Stop the Steal" protest a potential "significantly dangerous situation for law enforcement and the general public alike."[57] That same day, Chief Sund asked the Capitol Police Board to declare a state of emergency and authorize a request to secure National Guard support, which was declined by the House and Senate sergeants-at-arms.[58]

And on January 5, the FBI field office in Norfolk, Virginia, issued an explicit warning that extremists had plans for violence on January 6, the bureau's analysts having found "specific threats against members of Congress, an exchange of maps of the tunnel system under the Capitol complex and organizational plans like setting up gathering places in Kentucky, Pennsylvania and South Carolina so extremists can meet to convoy to Washington."[59] How and why so much evidence of impending violence produced so little response would be studied for many months, and years, to come.

On the fateful morning of January 6, members of the House and Senate gathered in their respective chambers to certify the election of Joe Biden and Kamala Harris, which the Electoral College had confirmed three weeks earlier. McConnell was in an angry mood. Not only had Biden won and Trump lost, but the Senate Republican majority was gone as well; Ossoff and Warnock had defeated Perdue and Loeffler in Georgia the day before. McConnell was long past ready to be rid of Trump and saw no need to hide his true feelings anymore. Given the perilous condition of the country at this fraught moment, McConnell might well have been thinking about his place in history as well, as he rose to speak:

> President Trump claims this election was stolen. The assertions range from specific local allegations to constitutional arguments to sweeping conspiracy theories. *But nothing before us proves illegality anywhere near the massive scale that would have tipped the entire election. Nor can public doubt alone justify a radical break when that doubt was incited without evidence.* The Constitution gives Congress a limited role. We cannot simply declare ourselves a national Board of Elections on steroids. The voters, the courts, and the states have all spoken. If we overrule them all, it would damage our republic forever.

The election was not unusually close. Just in recent history, 1976, 2000, and 2004 were all closer. This Electoral College margin is identical to 2016. *If this election were overturned by mere allegations by the losing side, our democracy would enter a death spiral. We'd never see the whole nation accept an election again. Every four years would be a scramble for power at any cost.* The Electoral College would soon cease to exist, leaving the citizens of entire states with no real say in choosing presidents.

The effects would go even beyond elections themselves. Self-government requires a shared commitment to truth and a shared respect for the ground rules of our system. We cannot keep drifting apart into two separate tribes; with separate facts, and separate realities; with nothing in common except hostility toward each another and mistrust the few national institutions that we still share. . . .

The framers built the Senate to stop short-term passions from boiling over and melting the foundations of our Republic. I believe protecting our constitutional order requires respecting limits on our own power. It would be unfair and wrong to disenfranchise American voters and overrule the courts and the states on this thin basis. And I will not pretend that such a vote would be a harmless protest gesture while relying on others to do the right thing. I will vote to respect the people's decision and defend our system of government as we know it.[60] (Emphasis added)

It was a fine speech, worthy of a true Senate leader. But it came two months too late. If McConnell had spoken like this on or shortly after November 7, he could have played a large role in stopping the "big lie" in its tracks. Once he chose to stay silent until the flood of baseless lawsuits was rejected, McConnell might still have made a useful speech on December 14, after the Electoral College voted. Instead, he heaped praise on Trump and gave a grudging, minimalist acknowledgment that Biden was the president-elect. McConnell had the power to help steer the nation to a better place, but he had done nothing. By January 6, a series of polls showed that 70 percent of the seventy-four million people who had voted for Trump thought the election had been stolen: fifty million Americans.[61]

Shortly after McConnell's speech, President Trump spoke to his supporters at the rally on the Ellipse, inciting them to march on the Capitol, to engage, as Rudy Giuliani put it, in "trial by combat." Soon afterward, the small Capitol Police presence was overrun by a huge swarm of protestors, numbering around eight thousand on both the east and the west sides of the Capitol. The protest quickly escalated to violence, with rioters clashing with police and using any available weapons they had to break into the Capitol and battle through police officers' attempts to hold them back. Once the rioters breached the Capitol's barricades, they moved through the halls inflicting destruction. Some of the insurrectionists tried to hunt down and kill Vice President Mike Pence, Speaker Nancy Pelosi, and Congresswoman Alexandria Ocasio-Cortez.[62] Images soon surfaced of rioters stealing items from members' offices and scaling the walls of the Senate chamber as senators, representatives, and their staff hid in various locations in the Capitol.

Donald Trump was not visible the whole day, other than through a few tweets, even when members of his own party pleaded with him to call off the rioters. When House Republican Leader Kevin McCarthy urged Trump to act, Trump snarled, "Well, Kevin, I guess these people are more upset about the election than you are." A furious McCarthy told Trump that the rioters were breaking into his office through the windows and said, "Who the f—k do you think you're talking to?" Republican members who spoke to McCarthy said that the exchange showed that Trump had no intention of calling off the rioters even when lawmakers of his own party were pleading with him to do so.[63]

Finally, after a considerable delay, the National Guard was deployed. It took nearly seven hours for the Capitol to be declared secure and for the shaken members of the House and Senate to return to their task of certifying the electoral vote.

"The United States Senate will not be intimidated. We will not be kept out of this chamber by thugs, mobs or threats. We will not bow to lawlessness or intimidation," McConnell said on the Senate floor. "We are back at our posts. We will discharge our duty under

the Constitution for our nation. And we are going to do it tonight.
. . . Criminal behavior will never dominate the United States Congress. This institution is resilient. Our democratic republic is strong. The American people deserve nothing less."[64]

At the end of one of the worst days in American history, Congress certified the election of Joseph R. Biden Jr. as the forty-sixth president of the United States and Kamala Harris as vice president. McConnell and other leaders spoke the words appropriate to calm a shocked nation. But the strength of our democratic republic after the insurrection at the Capitol remained very much an open question.

· 10 ·

Acquitting the Insurrectionist

$\mathcal{T}$he United States Capitol, the most iconic symbol of our democracy, had been breached for the first time since the War of 1812, and by Americans, for the first time in our history. But of course this was not the worst of it. The president of the United States had incited an insurrection to prevent Congress from certifying the results of an election that he had lost. The peaceful transfer of power, the hallmark of our democracy for 230 years, would not occur. Donald Trump had committed the most heinous act ever by an American president.

Representative Liz Cheney of Wyoming, the third-ranking House Republican leader and the daughter of former vice president Dick Cheney, expressed the outrage felt by most Americans in a speech on the House floor on January 12: "Much more will become clear in the coming days and weeks, but what know now is enough. The President of the United States summoned this mob, assembled the mob, and lit the flame of this attack. Everything that followed was his doing. None of this would have happened without the President. The President could have immediately and forcefully intervened to stop the violence. He did not. There has never been a great betrayal by a President of the United States of his office and his oath to the Constitution."[1]

Given Cheney's stature in the Republican party, her statement seemed to mark the moment when Trump would no longer be protected by his party, and that he would be condemned on a broad, bipartisan basis. Speaker Pelosi moved quickly to advance a single article of impeachment against Trump, charging the president with having "repeatedly issued false statements asserting that the Presidential election results were the product of widespread fraud and should not be accepted by the American people or certified by State or Federal officials" and that he had "willfully made statements that, in context, encouraged—and foreseeably resulted in—lawless action at the Capitol, such as 'if you don't fight like hell you're not going to have a country anymore.'"

The article of impeachment concluded that Trump had incited the crowd at his rally, whereupon they "unlawfully breached and vandalized the Capitol, injured and killed law enforcement personnel, menaced Members of Congress, the Vice President, and Congressional personnel, and engaged in other violent, deadly, destructive and seditious acts." The article also noted that President Trump had engaged in "prior efforts" to subvert and obstruct the certification of the election results, including a phone call on January 2 urging Georgia secretary of state Brad Raffensperger to "find" enough votes to overturn Biden's victory in that state and threatening Raffensperger if he did not comply.

On January 13, one week after the attack on the Capitol, the House of Representatives voted to impeach Donald Trump for the second time. Only 10 Republicans joined the 222 Democrats. Even after Trump had incited an insurrection at the Capitol that put their lives in danger, the House Republicans chose to stand by Trump and sought to ostracize Cheney and the nine other courageous Republicans who did not stay obedient to him.[2]

A year had passed since Trump's first impeachment—undoubtedly one of the worst years in our country's history, culminating in the attack at the Capitol. Yet the catastrophic events had not changed the basic political dynamic. The question once again was whether the Senate Republicans could overcome their slavish partisan allegiance to Trump and vote to convict the president on this grave impeachment charge. In January 2016, Trump memorably had said that he could shoot someone on Fifth Avenue and not lose voters.[3] That assertion would be put to the test. All eyes inevitably focused on the senator whose influence would decide the verdict.

Mitch McConnell was plainly seething at Trump. He had not spoken to Trump after December 14, when the president refused to accept the Electoral College vote and the indisputable fact that Biden had won. On the morning of January 6, before the attack on the Capitol, McConnell called for the electoral vote to be certified and decried the baseless claims of election fraud by Trump and his allies. On January 12, the *New York Times* reported that McConnell had told associates his view that Trump had committed impeachable offenses. He made it clear in private conversations that it was time for the Republican Party to move on from the weakened, lame duck president.[4] McConnell's circle of advisers was legendarily loyal and said nothing without the leader's permission. An account like this could not have made its way into the pages of the *New York Times* without McConnell's tacit approval.

But despite his outrage and his desire to be rid of Trump, McConnell's political calculus was complex. He knew that many members of his caucus would not vote to condemn Trump. He had to consider the timing of an impeachment trial and what would help or hurt Biden, who would be sworn in as president on January 20. McConnell may have resented Pelosi's jamming him with an impeachment vote in the closing days of Trump's presidency, but he probably thought she had given him some higher ground. "There is simply no way that a fair or serious trial could conclude before President-Elect Biden is sworn in next week," McConnell said immediately after the House vote.[5] He promptly recessed the Senate until January 19, the day before the inauguration. With Biden taking the oath of office in a peaceful inaugural with unprecedented security ringing the Capitol, McConnell sent Chuck Schumer a suggested pretrial schedule.[6]

On January 22, McConnell spoke on the Senate floor. "This impeachment began with an unprecedently fast and minimal process in the House," he said. "The sequel cannot be an insufficient process that denies former President Trump his due process or damages the Senate or the presidency itself."[7] Later that day, Schumer, now the majority leader, announced a schedule in which the House would deliver the articles of impeachment on January 25, the senators would be sworn in as jurors on January 26, and the trial would commence on February 8, after briefs were filed by the House managers and Trump's defense team.[8] It was a fair schedule; the Senate would avoid a rush to judgment, and President Biden would have some time to get his key cabinet appointments approved.

McConnell's caucus displayed significant divisions. Lindsey Graham was on a nonstop rant. On January 8, he tweeted that "any attempt to impeach President Trump would not only be unsuccessful in the Senate, but would be a dangerous precedent for the future of the presidency."[9] Five days later, he added, "The House impeachment process seeks to legitimize a snap impeachment totally void of due process. . . . Democrats have already impeached the President once over a matter that was not worthy of that process. Now they seek to do it again, believing that this effort will wash for history the fact that the first impeachment was based on the thinnest of pretenses: a phone call with the leader of Ukraine. Impeachment should never be a 'do over' but that is what Democrats are seeking here." Graham warned that an impeachment "could invite further violence at a time when the President is calling for calm."

Graham also had pointed words for McConnell: "As to Senate leadership, I fear they are making the problem worse, not better. . . . To my Republican colleagues who legitimize this process, you are doing great damage not only to the country, the future of the presidency but also to the party. The millions who supported President Trump and his agenda should not be demonized because of the seditious actions of a despicable mob."[10]

Marco Rubio had briefly been Trump's strongest opponent for the Republican nomination in 2016 and among his harshest critics. He was also a senior Republican on the Intelligence Committee, whose members had been particularly sensitized to the connections between Trump and Russia. But Rubio was vehemently against impeachment. "I think the trial is stupid," he told Chris Wallace on Fox News. "I think it is counterproductive. We already have a flaming fire in this country, and it's like taking a bunch of gasoline and pouring it on top of the fire."[11] Two days later, he tweeted, "Waste of time, impeachment isn't about accountability. It's about demands for vengeance from the radical left." Even so, Rubio did acknowledge that "the president bears some responsibility for some of what happened, it was certainly a foreseeable consequence of everything that was going on, and I think that is widely understood."[12]

In stark contrast to Graham and Rubio, Lisa Murkowski was unsparing toward Trump. "I want him to resign. I want him out. He has caused enough damage," she said. "He's not going to appear at the inauguration. He hasn't been focused on what is going on with Covid. He's either been golfing or he's been inside the Oval Office fuming and throwing every single person who has been loyal and faithful to him under the bus, starting with the Vice President. . . . He needs to get out, but I don't think he's capable of doing a good thing."[13]

When asked whether the House impeachment was appropriate, Mitt Romney responded, "I believe that what is being alleged, and what we saw, which is incitement to insurrection, is an impeachable offense. If not, what is?"[14] And Ben Sasse told *CBS This Morning*, "I will definitely consider whatever articles [the House] might move, because as I told you, I believe the president has disregarded his oath of office. He swore an oath to the American people to preserve, protect and defend the Constitution. He acted against that. What he did was wicked."[15]

The Senate convened on January 26 for the senators to take the oath to be jurors in the impeachment trial, which was to begin on February 8, following Schumer's schedule. Rand Paul raised a point of order, challenging the trial on the grounds that the Constitution did not permit the former president to be impeached once he was out of office. Although Paul's point of order was unexpected, the issue, obviously of fundamental importance, had generated serious debate for several weeks. The nonpartisan Congressional Research Service had concluded, "Though the text is open to debate, it appears that most scholars who have closely examined the question have concluded that Congress has authority to extend the impeachment process to officials who are no longer in office."[16] One hundred fifty legal scholars, including the cofounder of the Federalist Society, joined a letter saying that they believed a Senate trial on President Trump's impeachment was constitutional, even though he was no longer in office.[17] The Senate tabled Paul's point of order, with five Republicans—Collins, Murkowski, Sasse, Romney, and Toomey—joining all the Democrats.[18]

In Trump's first impeachment trial, the House managers, led by Adam Schiff, had done an impressive job laying out the facts of Trump's attempt to shake down Ukrainian president Zelensky by holding back military aid unless his government investigated the Bidens, at a time when Joe Biden looked to be Trump's most formidable opponent. For this trial, Pelosi selected a different team of managers to present the case, led by Jamie Raskin of Maryland, a superb debater and a professor of constitutional law. Raskin's selection came only days after the tragic news that his son, Tommy, a brilliant law student and from all reports a wonderful young man, had committed suicide. Raskin threw himself into the intense work, the only thing that could have taken his mind off the grief that he and his family were going through.

For the defense, the situation was murkier. Ordinarily there would be countless capable lawyers eager to participate in a case guaranteed to produce national publicity. But Trump's conduct on January 6 was so repellant that he was having trouble finding legal representation. Almost two weeks passed before Trump was able to announce that Butch Bowers, a prominent South Carolina trial lawyer recommended by Lindsey Graham, would head his defense team. But on January 30, only a week before the trial was scheduled to begin, Bowers and Deborah Barbier, Trump's two lead lawyers, resigned. The three other lawyers on the team also quickly exited, reportedly because of Trump's insistence that they argue that he had actually won the election.[19] The next day, Trump announced that David Schoen and Bruce L. Castor Jr. would head his legal defense team. Schoen was best known for having represented Roger Stone and for meeting with Jeffrey Epstein in 2019. Castor had been denounced by victims of sexual abuse for his failure to prosecute Bill Cosby in 2005 and his stance against helping victims.[20]

In the immediate aftermath of the shocking events of January 6, it seemed possible that Republican senators, who had lived through the horrific attack, might condemn Trump. In contrast to the first impeachment trial, McConnell refrained from whipping the vote, raising the question of whether he might actually break with Trump and giving his senators space and time to follow their consciences. Waiting several weeks before starting the trial could be justified as a way to give Trump a fair trial, but it chiefly served to give Senate Republicans time to gauge their politics, rather than search their consciences. Trump sent a clear message that he would not start a third party; his political future was in the Republican Party, and he would not hesitate to plunge into primaries against any senator who opposed him. "A lot of people made strong statements [after January 6], and I put myself in that category," West Virginia's Shelley Moore Capito noted. "And I suppose as time goes [on], political considerations begin to weigh in." As Kent Cramer of North Dakota put it, "The Republican Party is still overwhelmingly supportive of this president."[21] Sadly, with a handful of exceptions, the Senate Republicans would show less conscience than Butch Bowers and his team of trial lawyers, who could not stomach Trump's insistence on promoting falsehoods.

On February 2, the House managers filed an eighty-page trial brief, in which they called President Trump "singularly responsible" for the Capitol insurrection.[22] Trump's legal team filed a fourteen-page response contending that the Senate "lacks jurisdiction" to try a former president.[23] On February 4, the House managers issued a request for President Trump to testify in the Senate trial; his lawyers rejected the request, calling it a "public relations stunt," which was probably the most accurate statement they would make during the proceedings.[24] During the Mueller investigation, Trump repeatedly had expressed his willingness to be questioned under oath, but somehow it never came about.[25] The chances that he would agree to testify before the Senate were absolutely zero.

Trump's lawyers also argued that Trump's speech at the Ellipse on January 6 was constitutionally protected free speech. On February 5, 144 constitutional scholars and First Amendment lawyers, including prominent Republicans as well as Democrats, joined in a letter calling that argument "legally frivolous." Taking aim at one of the central claims in Trump's defense, the lawyers argued that constitutional protections do not apply in an impeachment proceeding. "Asking whether President Trump was engaged in lawful First Amendment activity misses the point entirely," they wrote. "Regardless of whether President Trump's conduct on and around January 6 was lawful, he may be constitutionally convicted in an impeachment trial if the Senate determined that his behavior was a sufficiently egregious violation of his oath of office to constitute a 'high crime or misdemeanor' under the Constitution." If that essential point were not enough, the letter continued: "No reasonable scholar or jurist could conclude that President Trump had a First Amendment right to incite a violent attack on the seat of the legislative branch, or then to sit back and watch on television as Congress was terrorized and the Capitol sacked."[26]

After the publication of the letter, Trump's defense lawyers focused their argument on the claims that Trump had not encouraged violence and that the trial of a former president was unconstitutional. And on February 8, Raffensperger opened an investigation into whether Trump had tried to overturn the election by asking him to "find 11,780 votes," underscoring the final part of the article of impeachment.[27]

On February 9, the Senate passed, by a vote of 80–11, the procedures worked out by Schumer and McConnell to govern the trial. The first issue for the Senate would be to resolve whether it was constitutional to try the former president. By a 56–44 vote, the Senate voted to proceed with the trial. Collins, Murkowski, Romney, Toomey, and Sasse were joined this time by Bill Cassidy of Louisiana, who said he had changed his vote based on the persuasive arguments of the impeachment managers. An impeachment trial of unmatched drama would now begin.

The House managers opened the prosecution with a meticulous account of President Trump's campaign to overturn the election and goad his supporters to join him in this effort. They brought the most violent spasms of the attack to life with footage from the Capitol riot that had not been seen in public before.[28] Filling the Senate chamber with the profane screams of the attackers, images of police officers being brutalized, and near-miss moments in which Vice President Mike Pence and various lawmakers came steps away from confronting the mob hunting them down, the prosecutors made an emotional case that Trump's election lie had directly endangered the heart of American democracy.

They played frantic police radio calls warning that "we've lost the line"; body camera footage showing an officer being pummeled with poles and fists on the West Front of the Capitol; and silent security footage showing Pence, his family, and members of the House and Senate racing to evacuate as the mob closed in, chanting, "Hang Mike Pence! Hang Mike Pence!"

All of it, the Democratic managers said, was the foreseeable and intended outcome of Trump's desperate attempts to cling to the presidency. Reaching back as far as the previous summer, they traced how he had spent months not only cultivating the "big lie" that the election was "rigged" against him but also stoking the rage of a throng of supporters who made it clear that they would do anything—including resorting to violence—to help him.

"Donald Trump surrendered his role as commander in chief and became the inciter in chief of a dangerous insurrection," Raskin argued. "He told them to 'fight like hell,'" he added, quoting the speech that Trump gave supporters as the onslaught was unfolding, "and they brought us hell on that day."

Though the House managers used extensive video evidence of the January 6 riot to drive home their case, they spent just as much time placing the event in the context of Trump's broader effort to falsely claim that the election had been stolen from him, portraying him as a president increasingly desperate to invalidate the election. "With his back against the wall, when all else failed, he turns back to his supporters—who he'd already spent months telling that the election was stolen—and he amplified it further," said another House manager, Joe Neguse of Colorado.

After dozens of frivolous lawsuits had failed, the managers said, Trump began pressuring officials in key battleground states like

Michigan, Pennsylvania, and Georgia to overturn his losses there. When that failed, he tried to enlist the Justice Department and then publicly attempted to shame Republican members of Congress into helping him. Finally, he insisted that Mike Pence assume nonexistent powers to unilaterally overturn their loss on January 6, when the vice president would oversee the counting of the electoral votes in Congress.

Another House manager, Stacey Plaskett of the Virgin Islands, guided the senators through much of the video, including scenes of rioters inside the Capitol tauntingly calling for Speaker Pelosi and flooding into her office just after aides had raced to barricade themselves in a conference room and had hidden under a table. "Nancy! Oh, Nancy! Where are you, Nancy?" one of the invaders could be heard shouting in a sing-song voice.

"This was a mob sent by the president of the United States to stop the certification of an election," Plaskett said. "President Trump put a target on their backs, and his mob broke into the Capitol to hunt them down."

Mindful that individual lawmakers still had only a limited view of the day, the House managers used a computer-generated model of the Capitol to show in precise detail the mob's movements relative to the location of members of Congress.[29] In one jarring scene, Schumer was shown literally running with a security detail through the basement of the Senate in search of safety. Eric Swalwell of California, another impeachment manager, told the senators that he had counted fifty-eight steps between where senators could be seen scurrying toward a secure location and where armed extremists were massing.

The managers asserted that instead of intervening to help as the Capitol fell, President Trump simply stood back and watched in a "dereliction of duty" as the vice president and the speaker of the House, the first and second in line of succession to the presidency, were put in peril. Citing news reports and accounts from Republican senators themselves who had contacted the White House desperate for the president to call off the attack or send in security reinforcements, the managers said the evidence suggested Trump refused because he was "delighted" with what he saw unfolding. "When the violence started, he never once said the one thing everyone around him was begging him to say," said Joaquin Castro of Texas. "Stop the attack."

Glued to their desks, some senators averted their eyes from the hours of footage, including their own evacuation as the mob closed in just down a corridor. "It tears at your heart and brings tears to your eyes," said Mitt Romney, who could be seen in one of the videos being directed by a Capitol policeman to seek safety. "That was over-whelmingly distressing and emotional." Other Republicans acknowl-edged the power of the presentation. John Thune conceded that the managers had "done a good job connecting the dots" and re-creating "a harsh reminder of what happens when you let something like that get out of hand." Ted Cruz, who had played an ignoble role on Janu-ary 6, said, "Today's presentation was powerful and emotional, reliving a terrorist attack on our nation's capital." Even so, Cruz continued to echo a major line of Trump's defense: "But there was very little said about how specific conduct of the president satisfies the legal standard."

Over the next two days, the House managers would use most of their remaining time, and the Trump legal team would spend only three hours on opening and closing statements focusing on Trump's calling for "peaceful action"; the fact that other politicians sometimes exhorted audiences to "fight"; and the general claim that the House managers and the media misrepresented Trump's tweets, words, and meaning.[30] But the outcome of the trial was never in doubt. As Lind-sey Graham told Fox News before the House managers' presentation, "It's not a question of how the trial ends; it's a question of when it ends. Republicans are going to view this as an unconstitutional exer-cise, and the only question is, will they call witnesses, how long does the trial take?"

That much was a matter-of-fact statement of the political realities. But, characteristically, Graham went on: "The Constitution has been flagrantly violated when it comes to Trump, there seems to be no end to all of this." For the first time, however, Graham did acknowledge that "January 6th was a very bad day for America, and he [President Trump] will get his share of blame in history."[31]

The trial moved to completion at a blistering speed. The fastest presidential impeachment over the vilest act by an American president produced the shortest trial, which was also the most shocking and compelling. Saturday, February 13, was a snowy day in Washington, D.C., the start of a holiday weekend during a pandemic—an unlikely day to be working. But on that day the demands of history were weighty, and so all one hundred members of the Senate were in the chamber, somber and masked, prepared to vote on the conviction or acquittal of former president Donald Trump in his second impeachment trial. Exactly one month had passed since the House had adopted the article of impeachment.

As the senators assembled in anticipation of hearing closing arguments and then voting, nothing could better illustrate the deep partisan divide in the country than the fact that the outcome appeared preordained. Although Trump had committed the most heinous act in the history of the American presidency, no one doubted that nearly all the Senate Republicans would vote to acquit him. He retained an iron grip on the support of a large majority of the seventy-four million Americans who had voted for him, largely because 70 percent of them believed the months of Trump's lies about the election being "rigged" and stolen. The lies had brought the attackers to the Capitol, the lies had been discredited by more than sixty courts, and the same lies created the reason that the Senate Republicans could not vote to convict Trump.

With the die cast and the script written, there was an unexpected flurry of activity; it suddenly appeared that the House managers would seek to call at least one witness. In the final day of their presentation, the managers increasingly focused on Trump's refusal to act after the attackers entered the Capitol. Overnight, CNN reported a description by Representative Jaime Herrera Beutler of Washington of the angry exchange on January 6 between House Republican leader Kevin McCarthy and President Trump, in which Trump said, "Well, Kevin, it looks like these people are more concerned about the election than you are." CNN also reported that Trump had called Alabama's newly elected Republican senator, Tommy Tuberville, to ask him to slow down the Senate's consideration of the electoral vote even as the attack was going on.

Angered by these new revelations, the Senate voted 55–45 in favor of the House managers' motion to hear witnesses. But after a ninety-minute break during which the Senate leaders and the House managers assessed the situation, both sides decided against calling witnesses, in favor of bringing the trial to a conclusion. The Republicans did not want Trump to look any more despicable than he already did; the Democrats feared that a protracted trial would prevent Biden from making a strong start on his agenda, including the confirmation of his cabinet. Besides, as Jamie Raskin said later, "We could have called five hundred witnesses" and it would not have changed any votes.[32]

In ordinary Senate debates, the senators would offer their own closing statements before the final vote was taken. In an impeachment trial, however, the senators would vote first and make statements afterward. Patrick Leahy, presiding over the trial as president pro tempore of the Senate, asked the clerk to call the roll. The tally was fifty-seven guilty and forty-three not guilty, which fell ten votes short of the two-thirds—sixty-seven—needed to convict Trump. Seven Republicans, two more than anticipated, joined all fifty Democrats in voting for conviction. Trump was, of course, no longer president, but a conviction could have disqualified him from ever holding federal office again.

Majority Leader Schumer was recognized to speak first, as is customary. Schumer faced a difficult task, following the eloquence of the House managers, particularly Raskin, Neguse, and Plaskett. His speech was partisan and pedestrian.

"January 6 will live as a day of infamy in the history of the United States of America," Schumer declared. "The failure to convict Donald Trump will live as a vote of infamy in the history of the United States Senate. The former president tried to overturn the results of a legitimate election and provoked an assault on our own government, and well over half the Senate Republican Conference decided to condone it." It seemed odd to describe forty-three out of fifty Republicans so mildly as "well over half."

McConnell rose to speak next. He had just voted to acquit Trump, ending the small amount of suspense created by the possibility that the veteran leader—once again the most powerful Republican in Washington—might vote to convict Trump. McConnell had not spoken to Trump in two months; now it was clear that he remained outraged.

"President Trump's actions preceding the riot were a disgraceful dereliction of duty. . . . There is no question that [former] President Trump is practically and morally responsible for provoking the events of that day," McConnell declared. "The people who stormed this building believed they were acting on the wishes and instructions of their president. And having that belief was the foreseeable consequence of the growing crescendo of false statements, conspiracy theories, and reckless hyperbole which the defeated president kept shouting into the largest megaphone on planet earth."

McConnell went on to say, "The issue is not only the President's intemperate language on January 6th. It is not just the endorsement of remarks in which an associate [Rudy Giuliani] urged 'trial by combat.' It was the entire manufactured atmosphere of looming catastrophe, the increasingly wild myths about a reverse landslide election that was being stolen in some secret coup by our now-President."

Although McConnell is not an eloquent speaker, the force of his denunciation of Trump left the Senate and the television audience rapt.

"The leader of the free world cannot spend weeks thundering that shadowy forces are stealing our country and then feign surprise when people believe him and do reckless things," McConnell said scornfully. "Sadly, many politicians sometimes make overheated comments or use metaphors that unhinged listeners might take literally. This was different. This was an intensifying crescendo of conspiracy theories, orchestrated *by an outgoing president who seemed determined to either overturn the voters' decision or else torch our institutions on the way out*" (emphasis added).

No one could have stated the damage that Trump inflicted on our democracy more clearly than that. It was a powerful speech that any Democrat would have been proud to make. In this speech, as in those he made on January 6, McConnell sounded like a great Senate leader, rising to the moment, condemning a president of his own party, speaking to the nation as well as the Senate. But then McConnell pivoted abruptly to embrace the argument that the Senate did not have the power to hold an impeachment trial of Trump because he was out of office.

"After intense reflection, I believe the best Constitutional reading shows that Article II, Section 4 exhausts the set of persons who can legitimately be impeached, tried, or convicted: the President, Vice President, and civil officers," McConnell stated. "We have no power to convict and disqualify a former officeholder who is now a private citizen." He expressed the fear that "if the provision does not limit the impeachment and conviction powers, then it has no limits at all." He raised the specter of private citizens being pursued years after they had left office.[33]

McConnell reached this conclusion although numerous constitutional scholars, including some of the most distinguished Republican lawyers, had expressed their opinion that the Senate had the authority to hold a trial of and convict and disqualify a former president. McConnell ignored the fact that Trump had been impeached for actions taken as president and that the House had impeached him while he was still president. McConnell's argument was particularly brazen given the fact that after the House had impeached Trump, McConnell had adjourned the Senate until January 19, making it virtually impossible for the House to deliver the article of impeachment while Trump was still president. Speaker Pelosi responded by calling his speech "pathetic" and labeling the Senate Republican leader "cowardly."[34]

In fact, McConnell did not seem comfortable with his own argument. While saying that he was persuaded that "impeachments are primarily a tool for removal and therefore [the Senate] lacks jurisdiction," McConnell admitted that in this instance, it was "a close call." That was a significant "tell" for McConnell, who never acknowledges a trace of doubt.

McConnell had stated his true feelings about Trump, about his lies, and about the insurrection he had incited. McConnell is probably the most partisan person in public life, and yet this time he had spoken to, and for, the nation. After venting his anger, McConnell returned to his real work: protecting and advancing his own political interests and those of the Republican Party. He had made the calculation that the political price of breaking with Trump was too high for the Senate Republicans to bear. Mitch McConnell wanted Donald Trump gone, but the moment was not yet ripe.

But there were Republican senators who chose conscience over calculation, summoning the independence and character to vote for Trump's conviction. Richard Burr said that he believed that an impeachment trial of a former president was unconstitutional, but once the Senate had decided otherwise, Burr accepted that precedent. He voted to convict. "The President promoted unfounded conspiracy theories to cast doubt on the integrity of a free and fair election because he did not like the result," Burr said. "The evidence is compelling that President Trump is guilty of inciting an insurrection against a coequal branch of government and the charge rises to the level of high crimes and misdemeanors."[35]

The impeachment trial had only hardened Lisa Murkowski's anger toward Trump. "If months of lies, organizing a rally of supporters in an effort to thwart the work of Congress, encouraging a crowd to march on the Capitol, and then taking no meaningful action to stop the violence once it began is not worthy of impeachment, conviction, and disqualification from holding office in the United States, I cannot imagine what is," she said.[36] Bill Cassidy posted a video in which he stated, "Our Constitution and our country are more important than any one person. I voted to convict President Trump because he is guilty."[37]

Susan Collins said, "President Trump had stoked discontent with a steady barrage of false claims that the election had been stolen from him. The allegedly responsible officials were denigrated, scorned and ridiculed by the President, with the predictable result that his supporters viewed any official that they perceived to be an obstacle to President Trump's reelection as an enemy of their cause. That set the stage for the storming of the Capitol for the first time in more than 200 years."[38]

Ben Sasse voted to convict based on the same abuses of power by Trump, but he also homed in on the checks and balances in our system. "Congress is a weaker institution than the Founders intended, and it is likely to shrivel smaller," he observed. "Conservatives regularly denounce executive overreach—but we ought primarily to denounce legislative impotence. . . . If Congress cannot forcefully respond to an intimidation attack on Article I instigated by the head of Article II, our constitutional balance will be permanently tilted. . . . This institution needs to respect itself enough to tell the executive that some lines cannot be crossed."[39]

Some lines cannot be crossed. That fundamental belief separated the seven Republicans who voted to convict Trump from the forty-three who acquitted him. For McConnell, Graham, and the others, political calculation dictated the decision: not principle, not their responsibility, not the rule of law, not even the Constitution. McConnell's political calculation was undoubtedly right. Even after defeat by Joe Biden, the insurrection he incited, and his second impeachment trial, Trump remained the dominant figure in the Republican Party. The Republicans who stood against Trump were censured or harshly criticized by their state party officials.[40] "Republicans don't have a snowball's in hell chance of regaining the Senate majority without Trump," Graham stated after the trial's conclusion. "I think Senator McConnell's speech, he got a load off his chest obviously, but unfortunately he put a load on the back of Republicans. That speech you will see in 2022 campaigns."[41] Graham called for the party to unify behind Trump. However, peace in the valley was never Trump's style. The former president unleashed a caustic statement calling McConnell "a dour, sullen, unsmiling political hack, and if Republican senators are going to stay with him, they will not win again."[42]

What Trump's vituperation failed to recognize was that McConnell was no "political hack"; he was a superb political strategist and tactician who had never lost an election. He successfully surfed the madness that had engulfed the Republican Party since the rise of Newt Gingrich thirty years earlier to become the most powerful Senate leader in history. More than any other person, he had diminished Obama's presidency and had helped Trump defeat Hillary Clinton in 2016. With Trump in the White House, McConnell engineered the radical transformation of the Supreme Court and stacked the lower federal courts with right-wing judges; his legacy was secure. Very few people, including presidents, have ever put more of a stamp on our country. What McConnell lacked was a moral compass that would cause him to rise above political calculation. Mark Twain once wrote, "Just do the right thing. It will gratify some people and astonish the rest." McConnell never just did the right thing.

As in the first impeachment trial, Trump would be acquitted without censure. Predictably, he reacted the same way as he had a year earlier, claiming exoneration and victory. "This is another phase in the greatest witch hunt in the history of our Country, no president has ever gone through anything like it," he said. "Our historic, patriotic and beautiful movement to Make America Great Again has only just begun."[43]

It was fair to say that Democrats and the media often suffered from what some have called "Trump derangement syndrome." Evidently, though, so did McConnell. In the two months between Election Day and the insurrection, McConnell made a lifetime's worth of mistakes, miscalculating repeatedly. Against all evidence, McConnell believed that Trump would, after losing his legal challenges, acknowledge defeat and accept Biden's victory after the electors voted on December 14, as McConnell himself had done. When Trump, having lost sixty court decisions in every corner of the country, shifted to exerting lawless pressure on state officials and the Justice Department, McConnell, laser-focused on the Georgia Senate races, said nothing. He did not want to divide the Republicans. He also assumed that Trump would understand the importance of the races, which, of course, meant nothing to Trump. When Trump created confusion among Georgia Republicans with his ranting allegations about election fraud, McConnell damaged his party's candidates, Senators Perdue and Loeffler, by inexplicably blocking legislation that would have sent $2,000 relief checks, a policy that they, the Democrats, and Trump all supported.

Even as Trump raged on about a "rigged" election, McConnell thought that he could control the Senate Republicans, assuming that no one would step forward to challenge any state's electors, ensuring that the January 6 certification of the electoral vote would be ceremonial. He gravely misjudged the unbridled ambition of Josh Hawley and Ted Cruz and the radicalization of the ten other "conservative" senators who joined them. For the first time in his fourteen years as Republican leader, McConnell had lost control of his troops.

Ultimately, McConnell did not understand the breadth of Trump's narcissism, the depth of his depravity, and his desperation to avoid giving up the protection of the presidency. Trump's biographers, including his niece Mary Trump, had said it very clearly: Donald Trump will stop at nothing in order to stay in power.

McConnell never admitted mistakes, and he was too old to change now. He would certainly never acknowledge his role in causing the January 6 insurrection. If McConnell, the most powerful Republican in the country other than Trump, had said that the election had been conducted fairly and had acknowledged Biden's victory on November 7, many elected Republicans, business leaders, and other influential figures would have followed. It is impossible to be certain, but it is likely that millions of Trump voters would have reluctantly accepted that Trump had lost. Instead, McConnell's passive approach allowed Trump's wild lies and conspiracy theories to go uncontested for five long weeks. And when McConnell had the chance to rectify his earlier mistakes by voting to convict Trump, he failed once more.

Only a few thousand people joined the attack on the Capitol to "stop the steal." But millions of other Americans shared their views about the election, posing a continuing threat to our democracy that would have to be countered, and overcome to the extent possible, by President Joe Biden and a Democratic Congress. It seemed unlikely that Mitch McConnell would be of much help, based on his long track record of cynical actions and failures to act.

Good Faith, Bad Faith

*H*aving orchestrated President Donald Trump's second acquittal, this time with a lighter touch, Mitch McConnell returned to his day job. He would be the Republican leader holding the fort against President Joe Biden and the congressional Democrats.

McConnell had known Biden for more than thirty-five years and liked him. As Barack Obama's vice president from 2009 to 2017, Biden didn't waste time repeating talking points or trying to convince McConnell that he was wrong about things; he just cut the best deals possible.[1] McConnell would occasionally observe that he was the only Republican senator who had attended the funeral of Biden's son Beau in 2015, which was a credit to him and an embarrassment to the other Senate Republicans, many of whom should have been there.[2]

But for McConnell these personal considerations didn't matter in the end. Biden was a Democratic president, and the 2022 midterm elections were just around the corner. Biden could not be allowed to succeed, irrespective of America's needs. In that fundamental sense, McConnell viewed President Biden in 2021 exactly the way he had viewed President Obama in 2009.

Despite knowing Biden well, McConnell may have underestimated him. Biden's ascent to the presidency had been nothing short of remarkable. He was gaffe prone and seemingly handicapped by his mishandling of Anita Hill's sexual harassment allegations against

Clarence Thomas in 1991, and he had failed miserably in two previous bids for the presidency. Biden had stumbled badly for months in the 2020 campaign, running fourth in the Iowa caucuses and fifth in the New Hampshire primary, inspiring most observers to prepare his political obituary. But his decades of experience and his extraordinary decency made him broadly acceptable to the Democratic electorate, and he virtually clinched the nomination after winning the South Carolina primary (with the crucial endorsement of Representative James Clyburn). Democrats across the country, who rarely agreed on anything, generally grasped the fact that Biden was the best bet to defeat Donald Trump and lined up to support him. He led Trump in the polls from the beginning, and despite the turbulence in the country, that never changed. At seventy-eight, Biden was eight years older than any other newly elected president in American history.

Of course, McConnell knew all that. But he may have underestimated Joe Biden's continuous and remarkable growth, professional and personal. Biden had gone from being a flashy junior senator who talked too much to an experienced Senate dealmaker to one of the most engaged and impactful vice presidents, and now the president. At the personal level, the tragedies that bookended his life—the death of his first wife and daughter in 1972 and the death of his son in 2015— gave Biden a capacity for empathy that few people ever acquire. Biden was not just a political contrast to Donald Trump; he was a personal contrast to him as well. And in the same way, President Biden contrasted profoundly with Mitch McConnell.

Even his opponents regarded Biden as a person of uncommon goodwill who sought to bridge differences where possible; he was a practical politician who would work with anyone and everyone to get things done. But Biden understood the damage that McConnell had inflicted on Obama's presidency and bore no illusions that McConnell was a good-faith player. And Biden came to the presidency with another powerful asset: a clear-eyed and deeply felt understanding of the magnitude of America's problems.

Biden had initially decided to run for president in response to Trump's reaction to the neo-Nazi rally in Charlottesville, Virginia, in

August 2017—particularly his comment that "there were good people on both sides."[3] Biden would wage his campaign for "the soul of America" as the anti-Trump, seeking to bring decency back to the White House and to restore American values. But as COVID-19 brought death, disease, and economic harm to millions of Americans, exposing the magnitude of the country's problems, Biden's conception of himself and his candidacy broadened. He now recognized that America needed him to be a transformational president.[4] He would seek to do more than roll back the detrimental impact of the Trump presidency, as large a task as that would be. He saw that the time had arrived for a period of activist, progressive government, responding to challenges similar in magnitude to those that had faced Franklin D. Roosevelt in 1933 and Lyndon B. Johnson in 1964–1965.

McConnell's task was simpler. He would do everything he could to make Biden fail in enacting his ambitious agenda, or alternatively make sure that Biden was solely responsible for anything he passed. McConnell seemed very much like Woody Hayes, the Ohio State football coach in the 1950s and 1960s and an influential thinker for boys growing up in the Midwest. Hayes would run the same play until someone stopped it, and so would McConnell. The needs of the country did not matter in 2021 any more than they had mattered in 2009, when he had made exhaustive efforts to block Obama's economic stimulus bill. And having just won another six-year term, he did not care about his national approval (or disapproval) rating. Showing that he was undaunted by the criticism of his scorched-earth opposition to Obama, McConnell announced that "100 percent of his focus was on stopping Biden's agenda."[5] The only change that McConnell would make, in light of COVID, was to downplay his self-proclaimed title as "the grim reaper."

McConnell, of course, faced the special challenge of how to deal with former president Trump. Although McConnell's political calculus at the end of the impeachment trial probably had brought him to the best position he could reach, he had enraged Trump without bringing him down. Now Trump would be taking repeated shots at McConnell, calling for the Senate Republicans to replace him. He would also be endorsing Trumpist nominees in Senate primaries,[6] bringing back McConnell's nightmare of 2012, when the presence of extreme Republican candidates in several races prevented the Republicans from winning the Senate majority. McConnell would be walking a treacherous path; there was no precedent for a Senate leader under continuous fire from a former president of his party.

It was fitting, and in fact inevitable, that the Senate would determine the scope of the Biden agenda and the success of his presidency, as the longest-serving senator ever to become president clashed with the oldest Senate leader in history. The Senate had been the focus of America's political dysfunction since the 1990s, culminating in a broken Senate even before Donald Trump became president. Then the Senate failed catastrophically in meeting its fundamental responsibility to check Trump's assault on American democracy. The debate over the Biden agenda would be intertwined with the arcane rules of how the world's once greatest deliberative body functioned, or failed to function. Every day would be an argument about both substance and process.

The only thing that might derail McConnell's strategy of obstruction would be if a significant part of his caucus threatened to go in a different direction, either by following Trump or by seeking accommodation with Biden. One key indicator of whether McConnell's caucus would show independence was the behavior of Ohio senator Rob Portman. He was a gifted and experienced public servant who had been elected to six terms in the House and had served as George W. Bush's trade representative and budget director before being elected to the Senate in 2010. Portman had been admirably bipartisan even in the intensely partisan House, working closely with Democrat Ben Cardin on pension reform, and was the epitome of the moderate conservative, business-oriented wing of the Republican Party, reflective of his home city, Cincinnati. Portman had a gay son and a deep commitment to fighting the opioid epidemic, which left him uncomfortable with a harsh social agenda and uncomfortable opposing strong federal government action where the need was clear. But he had been virtually silent throughout Trump's multiple outrages. His Washington admirers frequently asked themselves, "When would Rob Portman become Rob Portman again?"[7]

On January 25, just five days after Biden's inauguration, Portman announced that he would not seek another Senate term. "It's gotten harder and harder to break through the partisan gridlock and make progress on substantive policy," he said. But Portman had been a loyal supporter of McConnell, the architect of gridlock.[8] Perhaps now that he was retiring, he would seek to finish his Senate career with accomplishments rather than silent complicity. Richard Burr and Pat Toomey were also finishing their Senate careers and might be thinking about their legacies, too, although they at least had mustered the courage to vote to convict Trump, whereas Portman had voted for acquittal.

In a 50–50 Senate, where the Democrats held the majority only because Vice President Kamala Harris had the deciding vote, President Biden and Majority Leader Chuck Schumer faced their own challenges. The Democratic caucus had a wide range of views, given the ideological distance between Bernie Sanders and Elizabeth Warren, on the liberal side, and Joe Manchin, Jon Tester, and Kyrsten Sinema in the more conservative wing. But Schumer, elated to be majority leader working with a Democratic president who was a longtime friend, at a time of enormous opportunity, undoubtedly welcomed the challenge. Although neither a great public speaker nor a telegenic presence, Schumer was a superb political strategist and tactician, much like McConnell in skills, but a man with a good heart and a commitment to progressive policies and a desire to use government to address the nation's problems.

Schumer also benefited from the presence of a large group of experienced Democratic senators eager to fashion legislation to address the nation's needs. The chairs of the Senate's major committees— Ron Wyden of Oregon at Finance; Dick Durbin of Illinois at Judiciary; Patty Murray of Washington at Health, Education, Labor and Pensions; and Jack Reed of Rhode Island at Armed Services—were all strong legislators. Bernie Sanders, who had become a liberal icon in his two strong presidential campaigns, was prepared to battle for a historic agenda as Budget Committee chairman. Elizabeth Warren,

Amy Klobuchar, and Michael Bennet had fallen short in their presidential campaigns but were first-rate legislators as well. Schumer was a team builder; as minority leader, he had quickly established a leadership group with ten Democratic senators on it.[9] Now he enlarged it further, to include twelve senators. Joe Manchin expressed the general sentiment of the caucus: "There's no one who works harder than Chuck, there's no one who tries to listen to more people than Chuck."[10]

Schumer had one more advantage. Although the polarized environment had virtually destroyed the Senate's ability to function in a bipartisan manner, it certainly strengthened the hand of the majority leader. The more conservative Democrats would need to be handled carefully, but at the end of the day, if they faced a choice between Biden and McConnell, Schumer believed that he knew where they would come out.

Schumer faced this choice: Would he seek to rebuild a Senate that functioned on a bipartisan basis, or would he recognize that in a bitterly partisan period, his Senate would have to be a majoritarian institution, much as McConnell's had been? Unsurprisingly, the answer from the majority leader—and from the president—was both. They would welcome the chance to work with Senate Republicans on a bipartisan basis when possible, but they would be prepared to go it alone, with fifty Democratic senators plus Vice President Harris, wherever necessary.

During the transition, Biden had made it clear that the December coronavirus package was a down payment on a larger rescue plan that he would drive through Congress in the first weeks of his term, using the budget reconciliation process to enact it by a majority vote in both houses. On January 14, the day after Trump was impeached, Biden outlined a $1.9 trillion rescue package to combat the economic downturn and the COVID-19 crisis, signaling a shift in the federal government's pandemic response. The proposed package included more than $400 billion to combat the pandemic directly, including money to accelerate vaccine deployment and to safely reopen most schools within one hundred days. Another $350 billion would help state and local governments bridge their budget shortfalls. The plan also included

$1,400 direct payments to individuals (to bridge the gap between the $600 that had already been appropriated and the $2,000 that McConnell had blocked), increased unemployment benefits, federally mandated paid leave for workers, and large subsidies for childcare costs.

"During this pandemic, millions of Americans, through no fault of their own, have lost the dignity and respect that comes with a job and a paycheck," Biden said in a speech to the nation. "There is real pain overwhelming the real economy." The economic rebound had gone into reverse as virus cases surged during the winter and as cities and states imposed new restrictions on economic activity. The nation lost 140,000 jobs in December, and unemployment claims had increased 25 percent from the previous week.[11]

Biden acknowledged the high cost of the program, but he contended that the nation could not afford to do anything less. "The very health of our nation is at stake," he said, adding that such action "does not come cheaply, but failure to do so will cost us dearly."

On January 31, ten Senate Republicans, led by Susan Collins, Lisa Murkowski, and Mitt Romney, put forth an alternative plan for a $618 billion COVID-19 relief package, less than one-third the cost of the president's proposal.[12] They also requested a meeting with the president, which Biden accepted immediately. The senators described the discussion as "excellent," but Biden refused to water down his proposal to bridge the vast gap.[13] He was facing, for the first time, a choice between his preference to work in a bipartisan manner and his commitment to a solution of the size needed for the crisis. If the Republicans thought that the president would blink or split the difference, they were taken by surprise.

On February 4, Vice President Harris cast her first tiebreaking vote to approve the budget blueprint for Biden's $1.9 trillion stimulus package.[14] Several Republican amendments were adopted in the process, including Joni Ernst's proposal to prohibit a minimum wage increase during the pandemic and an amendment from Florida senators Marco Rubio and Rick Scott to prevent tax increases on small businesses during the pandemic. Collins and Manchin, who teamed up with increasing regularity, got unanimous approval of an amendment to restrict high-income individuals from receiving the $1,400 direct payment. Romney's child tax credit also proved popular on both sides of the aisle.[15]

A month later, on March 6, the Senate gave its final approval to President Biden's American Rescue Plan by a vote of 50–49, with no Republicans supporting it. The vote came after a twenty-seven-hour session in which the Democrats denied dozens of Republican amendments but decreased unemployment payments from $400 per week to $300, in order to placate a group of moderate Democrats led by Manchin.[16] The House approved the legislation four days later, and Biden signed it into law on March 11.[17] Remarkably, five days later, the Treasury Department announced that ninety million payments of more than $242 billion had been disbursed.[18]

The Senate Republicans were united in opposition. McConnell, as always, took the lead in excoriating the bill. "Less than 9% of their massive proposal would go to the core healthcare fight against Covid-19. Less than 1% goes to vaccinations. You see, they had to leave room for all the completely unrelated left-wing pet priorities," McConnell said sarcastically on March 2, "like underground rail in Silicon Valley . . . upgrading a bridge from New York to Canada . . . and giving Planned Parenthood access to taxpayer money meant to rescue mom-and-pop Main Street businesses." He closed by saying, "Mostly it's just what the Democrats promised almost a year ago. Taking advantage of the crisis to check off unrelated liberal policies."[19] And at a press conference on March 10, McConnell used language usually reserved for the Affordable Care Act: "I think this is one of the worst pieces of legislation I've seen pass here in the time I've been in the Senate."[20]

More moderate Republicans made similar objections. "Under the guise of providing Covid-19 relief, the Democratic leaders proposed a bloated $1.9 trillion package stuffed full of provisions that have nothing to do with fighting the coronavirus, from either a public health or economic perspective," Susan Collins said.[21] Lisa Murkowski described the budget reconciliation process as "inherently partisan in construct" and expressed regret for the Democrats' "decision to work around the minority." She said, "It's important to remember that last year alone,

Congress directed approximately $4 trillion in Covid relief. The most recent assistance was approved just over two months ago with much of that yet unspent."[22]

But the Republican criticisms did not resonate with the public. An overwhelming majority believed the legislation benefited the middle class, as opposed to the wealthy. According to a poll taken the day after Biden signed the bill, 72 percent of voters supported it, including 95 percent of Democrats, 69 percent of independents, and 44 percent of Republicans.[23] "We got beat on this one," said a Senate Republican aide.[24]

Debating the size and duration of coronavirus relief constituted a return to normal politics, an issue over which serious senators could disagree. From the standpoint of the Biden administration, the American Rescue Plan, like the December coronavirus relief package, was merely a down payment on much larger spending to come. Some of the actions the Democrats envisioned would be relief from the impact of the pandemic, while others would be long-overdue responses to the failings of our system that the pandemic had laid bare. The Democrats were planning to dramatically increase federal spending and make far-reaching new commitments for the federal government, in essence rewriting the social contract by reversing the forty-year increase in inequality that had reached intolerable levels.

The clash of visions between the Democrats and McConnell would play out in a months-long debate over "infrastructure." Neither Republicans nor Democrats had ever understood why for four years President Trump repeatedly promised a trillion-dollar infrastructure bill but never proposed one to Congress. Trump's failure now allowed Biden to seize the banner of infrastructure, which potentially had broad bipartisan support, since every state had roads, bridges, airports, and tunnels that desperately needed modernization. But the Democrats' definition of infrastructure also included a range of social measures, including expanding federal spending on education for pre-kindergarten and community college, family leave, expanded Medicare coverage, childcare allowances, and numerous measures to combat climate change. This truly was McConnell's nightmare, designed by the

Biden administration working with Senator Bernie Sanders, now the chairman of the Budget Committee, who saw a once-in-a-generation opportunity to remake the social contract, at a price of $6 trillion.[25]

The bipartisan group of senators who had spearheaded the December 2020 coronavirus relief legislation was eager to replicate its successful formula on infrastructure. This time, Senators Manchin, Collins, Warner, and Romney found an expanded group of allies; their "Gang of Ten" soon became a "Gang of Twenty-two," with the most prominent new additions being Republican Rob Portman and Democrat Kyrsten Sinema, who assumed leadership of the group. They seemed an unlikely pair; Portman's experience and straitlaced style contrasted with the somewhat unpredictable Sinema, a forty-five-year-old LGBT lawyer and social worker from Arizona whose politics had shifted from working for Ralph Nader to becoming a more conservative Democrat. But they had forged a friendship on a civil rights trip to Alabama a decade earlier, long before Sinema was elected to the Senate.[26]

Now they stayed focused on the goal: the largest investment in infrastructure since the building of the national highway system in the 1950s. Portman stayed committed despite criticism from former President Trump, who derided him as a RINO ("Republican in Name Only") for agreeing to a deal that would give Biden a major legislative victory. Sinema weathered searing personal criticism from progressive Democrats because she opposed the scope of their social infrastructure proposals. The two of them also had to withstand sniping from senior senators who thought they were poaching their turf.

But major legislation is always like a river raft trip on which at any moment the undertaking seems destined to capsize. Through ongoing communication with their Senate gang and the White House, Portman and Sinema navigated the rapids, making needed compromises and holding the bipartisan coalition together. In the end, they fashioned a $1 trillion infrastructure package, which won the support of all fifty Democrats and nineteen Republicans.[27]

McConnell initially condemned Biden's proposal, calling it "the latest liberal wish list" and asserting that "less than 6 percent" of the bill would go to roads and bridges. "This proposal appears to use 'infrastructure' as a Trojan horse for the largest set of tax hikes in a generation," he warned. But as the legislation progressed, McConnell saw the price tag come down from $2.6 trillion to $1 trillion, the tax increases being eliminated, and the bill focusing on "real infrastructure."[28] He also saw that a significant number of Senate Republicans wanted to bring the legislation to a successful finish. On August 10, McConnell cast his vote enthusiastically for the legislation. He described it as a "historic bipartisan infrastructure deal and proof that both sides of the political aisle can still come together around commonsense solutions. By promoting sensible collaborative legislation, we have shown that the Senate still works as an institution."[29]

Former president Trump fumed, calling the bill "a disgrace, and a gift to the Democratic Party, compliments of Mitch McConnell and some RINOs, who have no idea what they are doing." Trump also predicted that the bill "will be used against the Republican Party in the upcoming elections in 2022 and 2024" and warned that "it will be very hard for me to endorse anyone foolish enough to vote in favor of this deal." Trump escalated his criticism of McConnell, saying there was "no evidence to show that he is smart; if he was, he would use the leverage that comes from refusing to raise the debt ceiling to negotiate a good infrastructure package."[30]

To McConnell, Trump remained a divisive and dangerous force, particularly when he raised the specter of contested Senate primaries in which Republican incumbents would have to run again extremist Trump-endorsed candidates. But McConnell had concluded that opposing Biden on everything was not a tenable strategy and that federal spending on physical infrastructure, crucially needed and popular in Republican states as well as Democratic states, was a place where even a "grim reaper" could compromise. Instead, McConnell planned to rally his caucus against the Democrats' "social infrastructure" program, which he saw as completely unaffordable and an effort to "Europeanize" America. The strategy of Biden, Schumer, and Pelosi depended on holding all fifty Senate Democrats together to support a second budget reconciliation package, which could pass the Senate by majority vote. It was difficult to see how the Democrats could remain united, since Manchin and Sinema had signaled early on that they would not support a package that was so expensive and lacked any Republican support.

In a 50–50 Senate, every senator had great influence, and no one seemed to relish that fact more than Joe Manchin. West Virginia, now one of the reddest states in the union, had voted for Trump over Biden by a landslide margin of 69–30, so Manchin had strong political reasons not to be a rubber stamp for Biden's program. Manchin was the most conservative Democrat, particularly on environmental issues, given his commitment to preserving West Virginia's coal industry. But he also showed a strong, philosophical commitment to making the Senate work in a bipartisan way. Eight years earlier, in the aftermath of the horrific mass shooting at Sandy Hook Elementary School, Manchin had teamed with his Republican colleague Pat Toomey on a bill to establish a system of background checks before a handgun could be purchased. That promising legislation could not prevail over opposition from the NRA and Mitch McConnell. But Manchin continued to be a fervent believer in bipartisanship as the only way that the Senate could work.

And to his credit, Manchin was able to demonstrate in the early months of Biden's presidency that the Senate could overcome bipartisanship to enact important legislation, as evidenced by the support for the compromise infrastructure bill. He also repeatedly stated his opposition to the Democratic Party's position that the legislative filibuster should be abolished or at least fundamentally reformed.[31]

To some Senate traditionalists, the filibuster was, literally, "the soul of the Senate";[32] the requirement of a sixty-vote supermajority to cut off debate distinguished the Senate from the majoritarian House and provided a guarantee of extended debate and bipartisan results. However, to most Democrats and students of the Senate, the days when the filibuster—or the threat of the filibuster—produced compromise and bipartisan legislation were hard to remember. They saw the filibuster as an arcane practice and an abused tool that, in the hands of Mitch McConnell, had transformed the Senate into an institution where a determined conservative minority ruled. For progressive Democrats pressing long overdue action in a time of national crisis, Manchin seemed to be either utterly naïve—handing McConnell the keys to the castle—or a closet Republican.

Progressive Democrats were further incensed when Kyrsten Sinema joined Manchin in proclaiming her adamant support for the filibuster.[33] It seemed inexplicable that two Democrats who had come to the Senate in 2013 and 2019 could be so devoted to the filibuster, which had been an instrument of partisan obstruction since 2009, and so oblivious to what it could do to the agenda of President Joe Biden. But it was clearly a principled position from two senators who would still have plenty of power in a 50–50 Senate if the filibuster were abolished or sharply curtailed.

McConnell, demonized by Democrats and taking incoming abuse from Trump, had a rare moment of enjoyment watching the Democrats feud among themselves about the filibuster. He loved to remind them that when Harry Reid had resorted to the "nuclear option" to abolish the filibuster for executive and judicial nominations, the Democrats had lived to regret it.[34] McConnell also frequently noted that he had resisted Trump's demands to get rid of the legislative filibuster.[35] This argument did not move many Democrats, who saw their ambitious agenda uniquely susceptible to being blocked by the Republican minority.

Chuck Schumer had done a masterful job of driving the American Rescue Plan through the Senate and giving Portman, Sinema, and their bipartisan group enough room to work out the infrastructure legislation. In September, however, Schumer, working closely with Speaker Nancy Pelosi, faced two daunting challenges: maintaining unity among the fractious Democrats to pass the massive "social infrastructure" program and then advancing federal voting rights legislation—all at a time when President Biden's standing and reputation for competence were shaken by the Taliban's rapid conquest in Afghanistan and the chaotic evacuation of more than 120,000 Americans and Afghans who had supported the United States in the twenty-year war.

These issues of domestic policy and national security would be the subject of fierce debate in a divided country, falling within the range of normal politics. Other issues, however, distinctly the product of the aberrational Trump presidency, quickly proved to be intractable. In the aftermath of the January 6 insurrection, a broad consensus quickly emerged that an independent commission, modeled after the 9/11 commission, was needed to investigate the attack on the Capitol. On March 17, Serena Liebengood, the widow of Capitol Police officer Howard Liebengood, who had committed suicide following the Capitol insurrection, called for a bipartisan commission to investigate the origins of the insurrection and the security failures that happened that day.[36] Polls showed that two-thirds of the country favored an independent January 6 commission.[37]

On May 16, the House of Representatives, always ferociously divided on partisan lines, passed legislation creating an independent commission that would contain an equal number of Republicans and Democrats. Despite the House Republican leadership urging a "no" vote, thirty-five Republicans joined the united Democrats to pass the legislation, 252–175.[38]

Mitch McConnell was dead set against an independent January 6 commission. On May 19, at a breakfast of the Senate Republicans, McConnell announced that he would not support the House bill. "It is not clear what new facts or additional investigation yet another commission could lay on top of the existing efforts by law enforcement and Congress," he argued.[39] In fact, McConnell knew that an independent investigation could fully explain the insurrection, the events leading up to it, and the security lapses, in a way that other inquiries simply could not. Such an investigation would inevitably shine a spotlight on the role of former president Trump and his closest advisers in inciting the insurrection. It could also probe the involvement of several House Republican members who seemed to have close ties to those who had attacked the Capitol. John Thune, the number-three Senate Republican, was more candid, saying that Republicans were "unsure whether or not this can be, in the end, a fair process . . . that doesn't become a political weapon in the hands of Democrats."[40]

On May 28, in the first filibuster of the Biden era, the Senate Republicans blocked consideration of the House bill. Six Republicans—Susan Collins, Lisa Murkowski, Mitt Romney, Ben Sasse, Bill Cassidy, and Rob Portman—joined the Democrats, but they weren't sufficient to overcome the filibuster. Nine Republicans chose not to vote; McConnell's opposition caused several Republican senators to reverse their earlier support for an independent commission.

It was hard to argue with McConnell's cold-eyed calculus. The report of a high-profile independent commission looking at January 6 could only be embarrassing to Trump and the Republican Party, with potential consequences in the 2022 political cycle. This was the reality that mattered to McConnell, rather than getting a full accounting of the insurrection.

But the January 6 commission was a trivial issue compared to the existential question of voting rights. The Democrats had been agitated about restrictions on voting access ever since the Supreme Court's 2013 decision in *Shelby County v. Holder*, which eliminated Section 5 of the Voting Rights Act, thereby permitting states with a history of voting rights violations to adopt new restrictions on voting, without the requirement that these laws be precleared by the Justice Department. In response, Speaker Pelosi and the House Democrats had drafted an expansive voting rights bill, the For the People Act (H.R. 1), in 2019, but with the Republicans in control of the White House and the Senate, H.R. 1 had no chance of passing. Still, it served as a rallying point for Democrats. The 791-page bill contained numerous transformational features, such as requiring no-excuse mail voting and in-person early voting in every state, establishing automatic and same-day voter registration, giving former felons the right to vote, and neutering voter identification laws.

In 2019, a second voting rights bill, the John Lewis Voting Rights Advancement Act, was also introduced in the House. It was much narrower in scope, simply restoring the preclearance requirement of the Voting Rights Act so that jurisdictions with a history of voting rights violations would have to receive approval from the Justice Department or a federal court before making changes to voting laws. The

Republican Party responded with even more bills at the state level to restrict access to the ballot box. Lindsey Graham spoke bluntly about the need to restrict voting rights. "If we don't do something about voting by mail," he said, "we are going to lose the ability to elect a Republican in this country."[41]

It was not McConnell's style to be as candid as Lindsey Graham about his motives, but he quickly assumed the leadership in attacking the Democrats' proposals as a "power grab." "These same rotten proposals have sometimes been called a massive overhaul for a broken democracy, sometimes just a modest package of tweaks for a democracy that's working perfectly and sometimes a response to state actions, which this bill actually predates by many years," he charged. "The real driving force . . . is the desire to rig the rules of elections permanently—permanently—in Democrats' favor."[42]

The record turnout in the 2020 presidential election, conducted in a time of COVID, could have been seen as a source of national pride, but Trump's "big lie" that the election was stolen intensified the Republicans' drive to restrict voting rights.[43] Republican state legislatures across the country began immediately to consider and then adopt a creative range of legislative proposals to make access to the ballot more difficult.

Although Republicans would assert that each state has the right to supervise its own elections, in fact the Constitution assigns the states and the federal government shared responsibility for federal elections. Article I states, "The Times, Places and Manner of holding Elections for Senators and Representatives, shall be prescribed in each State by the Legislature thereof; but the Congress may at any time by Law make or alter such Regulations."[44] Reasonable people may disagree about the precise provisions of a federal voting rights law, but it represented a far better approach than having wildly differing standards among the fifty states where federal elections were concerned.

Joe Manchin, who remained committed to making the Senate work in a bipartisan way, stepped forward with a scaled-back voting rights bill, focused on expanding early voting, making it easier to vote by mail, and ending partisan gerrymandering. Manchin also included a provision that opened the door to voter identification laws, a high priority for Republicans.[45] It was a serious compromise intended to jump-start bipartisan negotiations. Manchin worked with Republicans Graham, Collins, Romney, and Tim Scott on his bill, and he also reached out to at least five other Republicans to participate.[46]

Any strategy Chuck Schumer had on voting rights depended on getting the votes of all fifty Democrats, so he had little choice but to support Manchin's freelancing. Manchin's efforts also produced significant movement on the part of prominent Democrats. Stacey Abrams, an icon for her leadership in the fight for voting rights, first in Georgia and then nationally, quickly endorsed Manchin's bill, stating that she had no objection to reasonable voter identification requirements.[47] Manchin's initiative also prompted a group of Senate Democrats—led by Amy Klobuchar, Jeff Merkley, and Tim Kaine—to meet with Schumer several times in an effort to fashion a bill that was broader than Manchin's but still scaled down from the original legislation.[48]

McConnell monitored Manchin's efforts closely; he was probably amused that Manchin still thought the game was on the level. Voting rights was not like infrastructure or coronavirus relief; the Republicans would never support any legislation that would be acceptable to the Democrats. McConnell intended to keep all the Republicans in line. Schumer understood this, but he undoubtedly saw some benefit from Manchin finding out that his efforts to forge a bipartisan compromise were futile. Perhaps after making his best effort, Manchin would reluctantly conclude that some carve-out from the filibuster rules was justified in the area of voting rights, although the West Virginia senator was still opposed to that idea.[49] Schumer announced that voting rights would be the first matter to be considered when the Senate reconvened in September.[50]

The debate over the use and abuse of the filibuster underpinned all of the Senate's business in 2021, as it had become clear that unless the filibuster was changed, McConnell would block nearly all of Biden's legislative agenda, just as he had done during Obama's presidency.

Though many senators of both parties vented about the Senate's dysfunction, expressing their dismay and anger in interviews, speeches, articles, and books, they took no meaningful action to reverse the Senate's decline under McConnell. It remains shocking that they worked so hard to get elected but did so little to restore the Senate, one of the rocks of the Republic.

Against this backdrop, the emergence of the bipartisan gangs led by Manchin, Collins, Warner, Romney, Murkowski, Portman, and Sinema is a heartening development. These senators refused to accept inaction when America was in crisis, and they refused to wait for the rare moment when the stars aligned for McConnell to give his blessing to legislation. Their freelancing undoubtedly angered the Republican leader, and sometimes it irritated the chairs and ranking members of committees of jurisdiction, but the Senate—and the American people—derived great benefit.

Reports of their activity conveyed something else, a potentially subversive development: the senators were having fun. They enjoyed working together, building relationships based on trust and open communication. They shared the excitement of highs and lows on the legislative roller-coaster ride. They took pride in the importance of the work they were doing: understanding issues, solving problems that arose, making principled compromises—in short, being real senators in a real Senate. There is no guarantee that this will continue, but the sense of accomplishment that senators feel makes it at least a real possibility. And it undercuts McConnell's efforts to bottle up any legislation of which he disapproves.

Mitch McConnell is already the oldest Senate leader in US history, and in 2023 he will surpass Mike Mansfield's record as the longest-serving leader in the history of the Senate. In his memoir, McConnell described Mansfield as the Senate leader he most admired. But McConnell's tenure bears little resemblance to what Mansfield accomplished in his sixteen years leading the Senate. Working with his Republican counterparts, Mansfield nurtured and built a Senate based on trust, mutual respect, fair dealing, and bipartisanship, a healthy ecosystem in which members and staff shared an understanding of the Senate's responsibility to the nation. The members of Mansfield's Senate had countless major legislative accomplishments that still form the framework for federal law. They worked with Democratic and Republican presidents and held them accountable when necessary. The speeches they gave and the books they wrote convey their pride in being senators and their reverence for the Senate. No greater contrast could be drawn to McConnell's Senate, a bitterly partisan institution that disgusts its members even though they still enjoy being called "Senator." No one person was solely responsible for the changes in the Senate and in American politics. But one person bears disproportionate responsibility: McConnell, who is in every respect the anti-Mansfield.

Even on the metric dearest to McConnell, the judicial conveyor belt, his Senate fell short. President Trump appointed fewer federal district and circuit judges in his four-year term than Jimmy Carter did in his single term as president.[51] McConnell's Senate seemed to be confirming judges endlessly because it was doing almost nothing else. But McConnell is correct in claiming that no other Senate leader matched his impact. He will be principally remembered for remaking the Supreme Court, orchestrating Trump's acquittal in two impeachment trials, and standing by while Trump provided unhinged leadership during the pandemic and trashed our democracy on his way out the door. But McConnell's legacy is far broader and more damaging to our country.

For example, it is fitting that in the same week that the United Nations Intergovernmental Panel on Climate Change (IPCC) report showing the planet's frightening future unless carbon emissions are drastically curtailed,[52] McConnell threatened to oppose raising the debt ceiling because of President Biden's spending plans.[53] Although McConnell is opposed to all of Biden's "radical left" social legislation, he brings a particular animus to Biden's climate change proposals.

Far too intelligent to be a climate change denier, McConnell simply opposes every measure that might respond to this existential crisis while supporting every action that makes the situation worse. The IPCC report emphasizes that the world's nations have very little time to mitigate the worst damage to the planet. McConnell has already used his power for twelve years to delay America's efforts.

After President Barack Obama pledged action on climate change in 2009, "McConnell positioned himself as 'coal's bulwark'—a central element of his across-the-board campaign to thwart the president politically," reported *Bloomberg Businessweek*.[54] If Kentucky's coal interests and defeating Obama were not enough motivation, McConnell, with his unmatched sense of the Republican donor base, knew that nothing mattered more to the Koch brothers and the fossil fuel industry than dismantling environmental regulations.[55]

McConnell waged his war on all fronts, opposing Obama's legislative, regulatory, and global efforts to reduce carbon emissions.[56] After Trump's election, McConnell applauded the new president's decision to appoint Scott Pruitt, the Oklahoma attorney general and a climate change denier, to be administrator of the Environmental Protection Agency.[57] He supported every action taken by the Trump administration to gut environmental regulations, starting with an effort to kill an Obama administration rule requiring the oil and gas industries to limit the emissions of methane, an extremely potent greenhouse gas.[58]

In May 2019, McConnell announced that the Senate would not consider a House bill that would force President Trump to keep the United States in the Paris Agreement on limiting carbon emissions. "This futile gesture to handcuff the U.S. economy through the ill-fated Paris deal will go nowhere here in the Senate," McConnell thundered, unwilling to risk a vote, given the vivid evidence of scorching heat and extreme weather events—hurricanes, floods, and wildfires—that had intensified since 2017.[59]

Two years later, with the frightening impact of climate change increasingly unmistakable, McConnell again stood in opposition to President Biden's climate change agenda, putting down his marker even before Biden was elected. In 2020, he accused the House Democrats of funding climate measures in an infrastructure bill. "This so-called infrastructure bill would siphon billions in funding from actual infrastructure to funnel into climate change policies," McConnell warned. "By putting a huge thumb on the scale for mass transit and

electric vehicles, it revives the old Obama–Biden focus on disproportionately helping major metro areas, leaving less for the rest of the
country. . . . [It] will join the list of absurd House proposals that were
only drawn up to show fealty to the radical left."[60]

McConnell's first political hero was Henry Clay, the Kentuckian
who in the turbulent period from the 1810s through the 1850s served
as speaker of the House, secretary of state, and US senator. Historians
describe Clay as the most gifted American politician who never became
president.[61] He is rightly remembered as a champion of the development of the "American System" to build the nation's economy through
infrastructure and a national bank and as the "Great Compromiser"
who worked tirelessly, even when approaching death, on the Compromise of 1850, dealing with the status of slaves in the new states entering
the union, which probably delayed the Civil War for a decade.

McConnell's contribution to US economic development stands in
stark contrast to Clay. It consists of tax cuts for the wealthy, deregulation for corporations, and line-item appropriations for Kentucky.
The political scientists Jacob Hacker and Paul Pierson, who have studied the rise of inequality in America, identify McConnell as having
"fought campaign finance rules with vigor, taken any step necessary to
get ultra-conservative judges on the federal courts, and worked to pass
policies favorable to corporations and the super-rich. . . . The Senate
he has helped create is a graveyard for policies opposed by conservative
plutocrats, right-wing groups, rural red states—whether these be efforts
to address climate change, to help workers organize, to regulate fire-
arms, or some other measure with majority support among the electorate but not within the Republican coalition."[62]

During the worst period of division in America since the Civil
War, McConnell—despite his two powerful speeches condemning
Trump—has ultimately come down on the side of polarization and
disunion rather than compromise and reconciliation. He has also put
his formidable influence on the side of state voter suppression laws by
opposing any federal voting rights legislation. And when he speaks,
his rhetoric is often sarcastic and inflammatory. It is hard to imagine
any other Senate leader speaking of opponents as "thugs," "the mob,"

"coastal liberals," and "the far left" while railing about "blue state bailouts," "rotten policies," and Democrats "treating religious Americans like strange animals in a menagerie."

McConnell remains a singularly powerful force in American politics and government; no Senate leader has ever combined the length of his tenure and the iron grip of his control on his caucus. From 1955 to 1958, Lyndon Johnson, the legendary "master of the Senate," dragged the Senate into the twentieth century by sheer force of personality and brutal tactics. But after the 1958 midterm election produced a Democratic landslide in the Senate, Johnson lost control of his oversized caucus as Joseph Clark of Pennsylvania, William Proxmire of Wisconsin, and Edmund Muskie of Maine refused to accept his bullying.[63] In 1960, Johnson surprised John F. Kennedy by accepting his invitation to be his running mate, largely because he saw it as the only road to the presidency for a Southerner, but also because he knew his power in the Senate had waned.

Reelected by a landslide to a seventh six-year term in 2020, McConnell is accountable only to the forty-nine other Senate Republicans. His future and the success of the Biden presidency depend on whether a cadre of his loyal colleagues decide that it is time to end his leadership because the Republican Party needs a different face or that the Senate needs to return to being a respected player in American government.

For those who care about the role of the Senate, the best outcome would result from a group of Senate Republicans acting on what they know: that McConnell has been uniquely responsible for the Senate's decline and the key contributor to the viciously partisan nature of our politics. On August 10, the ten senators—five from each party—who spearheaded the bipartisan infrastructure bill issued a statement celebrating "a historic victory for the American people . . . this landmark piece of legislation." The statement went on to note, "Importantly, this achievement is a testament to what we can achieve when we join together and do the hard work it takes to move our country forward. This historic bill is the product of months of good-faith negotiations between Republicans and Democrats unified by their desire to do right by the American people."[64]

Good-faith negotiations between Republicans and Democrats. That says it all, and it defines what has been missing in Mitch McConnell's Senate. The people of America have suffered great damage because a bad-faith player was able to amass and wield extraordinary power over such a long period of time.

Epilogue

$\mathcal{T}$he closing weeks of 2021 concluded a year of significant Senate accomplishments amid continued intense partisanship and dysfunction. On December 18, Senator Joe Manchin of West Virginia declared his opposition to President Joe Biden's $1.7 trillion Build Back Better "social infrastructure" legislation, bringing a months-long drama—"will he or won't he?"—to a crashing end. Manchin's decision, announced on *Fox News Sunday*, ended Biden's first year with a crippling defeat, leaving the president's historic agenda of social legislation and measures to combat climate change unrealized.[1] Manchin's decision also cast doubt on Biden's reputation for political leadership, negotiating skill, and special relations with the Senate. It was likewise a grave blow to Senate Majority Leader Chuck Schumer, who had brought Manchin into the Senate Democratic leadership team and spent countless hours in discussions with the West Virginia senator about what he wanted and needed in the legislation to bestow his support.

This outcome was unexpected. In early November, Biden, Schumer, and Speaker of the House Nancy Pelosi had worked intensively to broker a difficult deal between moderate and progressive Democrats to break the logjam that had prevented the infrastructure bill, which passed the Senate in August, from being considered in the House.[2] The House progressive caucus had refused to advance the infrastructure bill to a floor vote without a guarantee that the Build

Back Better legislation would get through the Senate. After weeks of agonizing deliberation, the progressives changed their position and consented to the infrastructure bill being passed by the House. They put their trust in Biden and Schumer, who had expressed confidence that they could unite all fifty Senate Democrats to pass this bill that covered the progressives' key priorities. A remarkable—and probably unprecedented—situation followed. Manchin, holding the decisive vote, made a series of statements blasting virtually every aspect of the bill, while Biden and Schumer expressed confidence that the Senate would pass the legislation by Christmas.

Biden, Schumer, and the Senate Democrats understood that Manchin (and, to a similar extent, his Arizona colleague Kyrsten Sinema) would use the power of their position to force changes in the legislation, but they also expected that once this was done, Manchin would endorse the package. "He has made some dramatic changes in this bill and its contents and its total," observed Senator Dick Durbin, the Democratic whip. "I've told him 'Joe, you've got your mark on this bill, now close the deal.' I still feel that way."[3] Unfortunately for the Democrats, Manchin was not playing by the rules of politics as usual.

At a critical juncture, the Democrats found the deciding vote in the hands of the most conservative Senate Democrat, from a state that voted for Donald Trump by thirty-nine points in 2020, and who was not only the chairman of the Senate Energy Committee but also a representative of coal and natural gas interests (West Virginia's and his own personal holdings). Manchin demanded, and got, the elimination of the centerpiece of Biden's proposals to meet America's climate objectives: the clean energy standard, which would have required electric power plants to begin converting from fossil fuels to renewables. He then went on to attack three other major climate provisions: the curb on methane emissions, the tax credit for the buyers of electric vehicles, and the ban on offshore drilling.[4] He also objected to the child tax credit and the provision of leave for family medical care.[5] Manchin repeatedly questioned the cost of the package—certainly a reasonable concern given the soaring rate of inflation and the fact that Congress had already committed to spend more than $4 trillion since the onset of the COVID-19 pandemic.[6] But he seemed oblivious to the arguments of prominent economists and policy experts that the legislation would not contribute to inflation and that it would improve the lives of millions of working families, particularly those at or near the poverty line, including many of his constituents in West Virginia, one of the poorest states in the nation.[7]

Although the press often described him as a "moderate Democrat," Manchin's positions and his rhetoric clearly establish him as an extremely conservative Democrat. Months before, he had expressed his opposition to the legislation because he believed it would move America toward becoming "an entitlement society . . . no additional handouts,"[8] terms that evoked memories of Republican attacks on welfare recipients. In a statement issued shortly after the *Fox News Sunday* interview, Manchin said he could not support "this mammoth piece of legislation. . . . I cannot take that risk with a stagging debt of more than \$29 trillion and inflation taxes that are real and harmful to every hard-working American at the gasoline pumps, grocery stores and utility bills with no end in sight."[9]

History shows that the political stars align only very rarely to allow a Democratic president to push through a far-reaching agenda. Both Franklin D. Roosevelt in 1933 and Lyndon B. Johnson in 1965 had overwhelming congressional majorities, which made the New Deal and the Great Society legislation possible. Joe Biden's majority was three seats in the House and Vice President Kamala Harris's deciding vote in the 50–50 Senate. It is fair to ask whether he and Schumer should have recognized this reality and pursued an alternative strategy, breaking the omnibus legislation in separate pieces that would have focused public attention on its popular features, rather than on endless squabbling among Democrats.

In the wake of Manchin's announcement, Biden and Schumer quickly tried to regroup; the president reached out to Manchin in a phone call that was described as "productive and cordial."[10] Schumer promised that Build Back Better would be debated on the Senate floor early in 2022, after federal voting rights legislation, which would be the Senate's first order of business. Both the president and the majority leader tried to project optimism, since the centerpiece of Biden's legislative agenda was at stake; per Schumer's frequently used refrain, "Failure is not an option." Tough decisions would have to be made about whether to rewrite the legislation to focus on a few priority areas—supporting working families, securing affordable health care, combating climate change—and funding them long term.[11] But the president, the majority leader, and the speaker would face the challenge of keeping the progressives on board if many of their priorities were jettisoned.

As 2021 came to an end, there was only one clear winner: Mitch McConnell. During the summer, the minority leader had led his caucus in helping the Democrats pass the infrastructure bill; with his blessing, eighteen other Republicans joined him along with all fifty Democrats in a major bipartisan accomplishment.[12] Later, in an even more challenging situation, McConnell produced fourteen Republicans to adopt a complicated solution negotiated with Schumer by which the Democrats would be allowed to raise the debt ceiling to prevent the government from defaulting, though without any Republican votes.[13] And he also won plaudits for allocating some of his own campaign funds to pay for ads encouraging Kentuckians to get vaccinated against COVID-19.[14]

Former president Donald Trump blasted McConnell for cooperating even in this limited way with Senate Democrats, calling him a weak leader, a RINO ("Republican in name only"), and a "broken old crow" who repeatedly missed chances to block the Democratic agenda.[15] Lindsey Graham continued his own incessant commentary, warning McConnell that Republican leaders had to make peace with Trump.[16] Yet McConnell followed the course he believed would maximize the chances of Republican success. He wanted examples to show voters that the Republicans were not totally obstructionist. He also believed that when Biden, Schumer, and the Democrats were floundering, he should not get in their way. In an angry, divided country, reeling from nearly two years of COVID-19, where dissatisfaction with the government was at record levels, the party out of power had enormous advantages. And passing major legislation is enormously difficult; obstructionists always have a much easier task. As Sam Rayburn of Texas, probably the most powerful House speaker until Nancy Pelosi, once said, "Any jackass can kick down a barn, but it takes a good carpenter to build one."[17]

McConnell had multiple constituencies, but the one that mattered most were the forty-nine other Republican senators, whose loyalty to him seemed unshaken by Trump's blasts or Graham's sniping. He worked successfully to maintain unity on the issues of overriding importance to him. On the Build Back Better legislation, Manchin and Sinema became "the deciders" because the Republicans maintained a stone wall of opposition. The "moderate" Senate Republicans such as Susan Collins, Lisa Murkowski, and Rob Portman evinced no interest in legislation that represented the most ambitious effort to counter child poverty and put in place policies that would respond to the increasingly unmistakable, existential threat of climate change. Those Republicans were clearly not "Trumpists," but they joined McConnell in opposing legislative efforts that would improve conditions in the country, starting with the American Rescue Plan and continuing with Build Back Better, and even Biden's federal mask mandate.

Similarly, Biden and Schumer struggled to advance federal voting rights legislation, because Manchin and Sinema continued to oppose changing the filibuster rule (or even a narrow carve-out for voting rights). Again, the two Democrats assumed such importance because exactly one Republican—Lisa Murkowski—showed any interest in protecting the right to vote or the integrity of the process of counting the vote.[18] Susan Collins, for example, was unmoved by a surge of Republican legislation enacted to restrict access to voting in nineteen states (including efforts to replace nonpartisan election officials with Trump allies) and to allow state legislatures to invalidate election results.[19] In Collins's view, the federal voting rights legislation under consideration by the Senate would constitute a "vast federal takeover of state elections" and was not necessary because Maine conducted clean elections, including early adoption of the innovation of "ranked voting."[20] This was a disappointing response from a senator who had just been comfortably reelected to her fifth term in the United States Senate, with national responsibilities, not the state legislature of Maine.

McConnell found himself on familiar terrain in obstructing a Democratic president with an ambitious agenda during a time of great national need. He was in his element denouncing "the socialist surge that has captured the other side."[21] After Joe Manchin's break with his Democratic colleagues over the Build Back Better legislation in December, McConnell publicly invited the West Virginia senator to join the Republican caucus, observing that "he is clearly not welcome on that side of the aisle."[22] Republicans attacked Biden for the worst inflation since the 1980s and for mismanaging the pandemic, despite the clear evidence that its spread resulted mostly from unvaccinated populations in states that had voted for Trump and had Republican governors. In a tumultuous political environment, nothing was certain, but from McConnell's standpoint Biden's failures would produce Republican victories in the midterm elections, which almost always favored the party out of power.

One wild card was the increasingly focused and intense efforts by the House Select Committee to investigate the January 6 attack on the Capitol. Although McConnell had killed the idea of an independent commission, Speaker Pelosi, undaunted, responded by establishing a select committee, funding it generously, and giving it some bipartisan credibility by including two House Republicans who were unwavering critics of Trump's role in the insurrection: Liz Cheney of Wyoming and Adam Kinzinger of Illinois. By December, it was clear that the Select Committee, chaired by Benny Thompson of Mississippi and co-chaired by the indomitable Cheney, was deadly serious and conducting a far-reaching and carefully considered investigation. Its work focused not only on the events of January 6 but also on the weeks and months leading up to the insurrection, during which Trump and his allies spread the "big lie" that the presidential election results were illegitimate and took actions to undermine public acceptance of Biden's victory. Having interviewed more than 250 witnesses, the Select Committee sought criminal penalties for contempt of Congress against Steve Bannon and Roger Stone, two of Trump's closest outside advisers, and against Mark Meadows, Trump's former chief of staff, for failure to comply with congressional subpoenas.[23]

Meadows appeared to be both pivotal and vulnerable, having turned over nine thousand pages of documents (including texts) and published a book about his time with Trump, before deciding that he would refuse to comply with the Select Committee's subpoena. In riveting hearings on whether to seek charges against Meadows, Cheney read texts that had been sent to Meadows on January 6 by various Republicans, including Donald Trump Jr. and Fox News anchors Sean Hannity and Laura Ingraham, pleading with him to get President Trump to stop the attack. Cheney pointedly read the language of a federal criminal statute, 18 U.S.C. §1512, which makes it a felony to "corruptly obstruct or impede" an official proceeding, such as Congress's certification of the Electoral College vote.[24] Cheney also announced that there would be "weeks of public hearings" in 2022.[25] It seemed increasingly likely that the Select Committee report would detail a wide-ranging conspiracy to keep Donald Trump in the White House, despite Joe Biden's victory in the election. Such findings could well lead the Select Committee to recommend to the Justice Department criminal referrals for numerous people, including Trump's closest allies, Republican members of Congress, or even the former president himself.[26]

"We're watching the investigation that is occurring in the House. Reading about it like everyone else," McConnell said in an interview in mid-December, calling the January 6 attack "a horrendous event" and adding, "I think what they are seeking to find out is something the public needs to know."[27] This was, of course, consistent with the anger he had expressed at Trump's second impeachment trial in February, in which he pointedly noted that impeachment was not the end of the road for the former president. "He didn't get away with anything yet. We have a criminal justice system in this country. We have civil litigation, and former presidents are not immune from being accountable by either one," McConnell had lectured sternly.[28] Nothing would please McConnell more than Trump's removal from national politics, either by being sent to prison or through permanent exile to Mar-a-Lago. But the paramount question for McConnell would always be whether this result could be brought about without taking down the whole Republican Party, including Republicans running for the Senate.

With 2022 already destined to be a combustible political year, the right-wing Supreme Court majority that McConnell had engineered turned up the heat further when oral argument in the case *Dobbs v. Jackson Women's Health Organization* showed that the court was likely to eviscerate *Roe v. Wade*, erasing the nearly fifty-year-old precedent that had established the right for women to choose an abortion during the first two trimesters of pregnancy, or until fetal viability.[29] Despite their professed commitments to *stare decisis*, Justices Neil Gorsuch, Brett Kavanaugh, and Amy Coney Barrett seemed fully prepared to do what they were chosen to do by Trump, McConnell, and the Federalist Society. Other far-reaching rulings, reversing established law concerning the regulation of guns, church-state relations, affirmative action, and environmental protection, seemed likely to follow. As Linda Greenhouse, the former *New York Times* Supreme Court correspondent and the most respected analyst of the court, grimly observed, "Over history, change has tended to come to the Supreme Court incrementally. But in the Trump years, it arrived in a torrent. . . . The resulting path of destruction of settled precedent and long-established norms is breathtaking."[30]

McConnell loved to relive his confirmation triumphs; it served to remind the Republican right of his indispensability and to infuriate the Democrats. In 2019, he stated that "blocking a vote on [Merrick] Garland was the single most consequential thing I've done in my time as Majority Leader," since it saved Justice Antonin Scalia's seat for Neil Gorsuch.[31] In June 2021, he warned the Democrats that Biden could not count on confirmation of a Supreme Court justice in 2024 if the Republicans regained a Senate majority in the 2022 midterm election.[32]

In November, McConnell published an op-ed in the *Washington Post* in which he castigated Democrats for considering radical proposals to expand the Supreme Court or establish term limits for justices. "For decades, Americans across the political spectrum agreed that Franklin D. Roosevelt's attempt in 1937 at Court packing was an embarrassment," McConnell observed accurately.[33] Left unsaid was that this consensus had been broken by McConnell's own court packing: the theft of the seat that should have gone to Merrick Garland and the hurried confirmation of Amy Coney Barrett to deprive Joe Biden of the opportunity to nominate a justice to succeed Ruth Bader Ginsburg.

"Judicial independence is as fragile as it is important," McConnell went on, despite having done unique damage to the court's standing. (Justice Barrett herself felt the need to reassure the country in September 2021 that the Supreme Court is "not comprised of a bunch of partisan hacks," doing so in a speech at the McConnell Center in Louisville, of all places.[34]) McConnell concluded his article with a reminder that "the Senate exists to defeat short-sighted proposals and protect our institutions from structural vandalism"—this coming from the greatest judicial vandal of all.

The Democrats' bitter disappointment as 2021 ended made it hard to recall that the Senate racked up major legislative accomplishments during the year: the American Rescue Plan, the infrastructure legislation, and a sweeping bill to bolster America's ability to compete with China. Learning from past mistakes, the Democrats took a page from the Republican playbook and confirmed forty federal judges, allowing Biden to match the record for a first-year president, set by Ronald Reagan in 1981.[35] But the Senate's paralysis between big accomplishments took a continuing toll. "Welcome to the United States Senate. I've been here 25 years and I've seen the decline of this institution to the point where we no longer function as we once did," Dick Durbin observed. "Until we change the rules of the Senate and get serious about legislating on behalf of the American people, we're going to continue to suffer this frustration."[36]

During the year, intense discussions focused on the filibuster and the changes that could be made to this rule that is so central to the nonfunctioning of the Senate. Yet, as the veteran *Washington Post* congressional correspondent Paul Kane observed, "there's one place the debate hasn't happened: on the Senate floor itself."[37] This situation continues the decades-long unwillingness of the Senate to face up to the fact that its rules and precedents are not working and are not workable. Repeatedly, particularly in the last twelve years, senators have expressed frustration, but the Senate has done nothing. The last serious examination of the Senate rules took place in 1979, when Jimmy Carter was president, and only one of those one hundred senators—Patrick Leahy of Vermont—still serves in the body today.

As far back as 2005, Senator Trent Lott of Mississippi, a former Republican majority leader, wondered how "holds" (which had begun as temporary courtesies to allow interested senators to participate in a debate) had transformed into the power of a single senator to block consideration of a piece of legislation or a presidential nomination. Senator Lott wrote in his memoir, *Herding Cats*, "The Senate in my view had become increasingly dysfunctional. . . . It was time we gave the rules a thorough and fair review. How many of them were simply archaic? And were there new rules that we could adopt in the interest of efficiency and consensus?"[38] No such review occurred, and in 2021, sixteen years after Senator Lott's plaintive observation, we had the spectacle of Ted Cruz blocking, for months, consideration of the nominations of virtually every ambassador nominated by President Biden.[39] Should any single senator have that power? Shouldn't the question at least be asked?

The Senate's rules should be carefully reviewed, perhaps by a group of former senators and outside experts, with necessary changes agreed to take effect in a subsequent Congress, so that is not clear which party would be in the majority or the minority. But as important as the rules are, they pale in significance to the one thing that would transform the Senate and reverse the rising anti-democratic tide in America: breaking Mitch McConnell's long stranglehold on the Senate. The Senate elections of 2022 provide the opportunity for a real debate regarding the direction in which McConnell's leadership has taken the country.

McConnell and his Republican enablers hope to nationalize the midterm elections, to capitalize on widespread unhappiness about inflation and the continuing effects of COVID-19. The Democrats need a powerful counternarrative; they should hammer home Biden's achievements, and they should charge McConnell and his colleagues with prolonging the pandemic, stacking the Supreme Court, opposing needed progressive legislation, and jeopardizing our democracy by failing to put any kind of check on Donald Trump. The map favors the Democrats; of the thirty-four Senate seats up for election, the Republicans must defend twenty, the Democrats only fourteen, and Republican senators have retired in the key states of Pennsylvania, Ohio, and North Carolina, as well as Missouri and Alabama. Nothing would change the direction of our politics more than a Senate with fifty-three or fifty-five Democratic senators, where the majority would not be blocked by one or two of its most conservative members. Joe Manchin was on the mark when he told progressive Democrats that if they didn't like his positions, they should "elect more liberals."[40]

Senate Republicans need to be held accountable for their catastrophic failure during the Trump presidency, the impact of which continues in the resurgent pandemic and the threats to our democracy. As he turns eighty, McConnell has reached an unusual position: enormously powerful, widely known, and intensely disliked. A recent national poll found that McConnell's personal approval raters were 18 percent favorable, with 4 percent very favorable, and 60 percent unfavorable, with 41 percent very unfavorable.[41] The 2022 Senate elections should deliver what America needs: a referendum on whether to extend or end Mitch McConnell's destructive reign.

Acknowledgments

$\mathscr{T}$his is my third book about the Senate in a decade. Countless friends, and occasional adversaries, have contributed to my understanding of American politics and government over more than fifty years. I am profoundly grateful for opportunities that I have been given and the experiences that I have had: to work in the Senate, to serve in the Clinton administration, to run for Congress, and to write these books. It is quite impossible for me to name and thank all the people who have helped me along the way.

Special appreciation goes to Jon Sisk, the senior editor at Rowman & Littlefield for books on American politics, government, policy, and history. Jon encouraged me to write my second book, *Broken*, in 2016; when the catastrophic events of 2020 drove me to write this book, Jon supported it enthusiastically. He also suggested that the book cover should be a caricature, and Sally Rinehart designed a truly memorable cover. I am also grateful to Patricia Stevenson, R&L's experienced, meticulous, and patient production editor, and Sarah Sichina, Jon's talented assistant.

Paul Golob, my editor, has worked on more than three hundred books in his long career. *The Betrayal* and its author benefited enormously from Paul's experience, judgment, candor, and light touch. Every author should have such a fine editor.

Emily Keane, my tireless and gifted research assistant, made an indispensable contribution to this book. I am delighted that Emily, who recently received her master's in foreign service (MSFS) from Georgetown, has started her career at the State Department. I am sure she will be one of many gifted young people who become the new generation of foreign service officers.

I want to recall the men who gave me opportunities to work in the Senate: Jacob Javits, who gave me a summer internship in 1969, which changed my life; Gaylord Nelson, the visionary environmentalist who brought me to Washington in 1975; Tom Eagleton, my best friend in politics; and Jay Rockefeller, who gave me the privilege of serving as first chief of staff. I will always be grateful to Mickey Kantor, the dynamic lawyer and great political operative, who allowed me to realize my hope of serving in a Democratic administration when he asked me to be general counsel when he became US trade representative. Working with Mickey to complete NAFTA, the Uruguay Round, and the auto and auto parts agreement with Japan provided the most exciting and challenging times of my career.

Walter Mondale (or "Fritz"), the great senator and vice president, who passed away earlier this year, was a cherished friend. Our relationship spanned more forty years; when I was negotiating with the Japanese government, Fritz was often the last person I spoke to at night as he started his morning as US ambassador in Tokyo. He would have been a wonderful president.

Finally, I want to acknowledge the enduring impact of Brandeis University, where I came of age during the turbulent years of 1965–1969. I got a superb liberal education there, and I will always appreciate the $600 stipend that helped Nancy and me come to Washington in the summer of 1969. (In those days, $600 covered more than three months of rent!) Brandeis alums have helped me repeatedly when I turned to writing: Peter Osnos, the remarkable publisher who founded PublicAffairs, gave me an advance to write *The Last Great Senate*, along with priceless advice that I still quote; Allan Lichtman, a renowned political historian, introduced me to Jon Sisk and Rowman & Littlefield; and

Sid Blumenthal, the great political journalist and Lincoln biographer, connected me with Paul Golob, my editor. Louis D. Brandeis's commitment to justice and democracy has inspired me. Most important, in this book, and always, I have tried to live by the powerful motto of Brandeis University: "Truth even unto its innermost parts."

A Note on Sources

$\mathscr{I}$ was a Senate insider once, but that period ended thirty-five years ago. I know very few of the current or recent senators, or staff members, and I did not think it would be appropriate to speak to such a small sample. I am not a journalist, so I did not attempt to write a book based on interviews. Consequently, *The Betrayal*—the story of the Senate Republicans' catastrophic and knowing failure to check President Donald Trump—is based on publicly available sources, showing the readers what the senators said and did, and what they failed to say and do, during a dangerous period without precedent in our history. I relied principally on the senators' own statements and the excellent reporting of the *New York Times*, the *Washington Post*, and *Politico*. Although the *Post*'s famous masthead reminds us that "Democracy dies in darkness," we now know that it can have a near-death experience in broad daylight. Whatever else can be said about Trump, Mitch McConnell, and Lindsey Graham, they were, and continue to be, quite transparent. Trump, of course, invented a new form of presidential communication through his use of Twitter; McConnell, at one time tight-lipped, became a constant public presence; and Graham never stopped talking.

In understanding the magnitude of the Senate's failure, it is important for readers to recall some history of the Senate prior to the election of Donald Trump. I have drawn heavily on my prior books—*The Last Great Senate: Courage and Statesmanship in Times of Crisis* (New

York: PublicAffairs, 2012) and *Broken: Can the Senate Save Itself and the Country?* (Lanham, MD: Rowman & Littlefield, 2018)—to provide that background. Chapter 1 describes the Senate at the peak of its power serving the nation in the 1960s and 1970s and traces its long, gradual decline, beginning about thirty years ago. Chapter 2 describes the transformation of the Senate struggling to cope with the centrifugal forces of our politics into the era of Harry Reid and Mitch McConnell, who gave up trying to overcome the partisan divide and became faction leaders rather than Senate leaders.

I have written extensively about Senator McConnell before. In a 2014 article, I described him as "the most destructive Senate leader"; in a 2018 book talk, I called him "the other threat to our democracy." He is, course, the central character in this book. In assessing McConnell, I have particularly benefited from the great reporting and insights of Alec MacGillis, *The Cynic: The Political Education of Mitch McConnell* (New York: Simon & Schuster, 2014); Joshua Green's "Strict Obstructionist," *Atlantic*, January–February 2011; Charles Homans, "Mitch McConnell Got Everything He Wanted: But at What Cost?" *New York Times Magazine*, January 27, 2019; Jane Mayer, "How Mitch McConnell Became Trump's Enabler in Chief," *New Yorker*, April 12, 2020; and Jacob S. Hacker and Paul Pierson, *Let Them Eat Tweets: How the Right Rules in an Age of Extreme Inequality* (New York: Liveright, 2020), as well as Senator McConnell's own memoir, *The Long Game* (2016). I strongly disagreed with the thrust of a very positive biography of McConnell written by John David Dyche, *Republican Leader: A Political Biography of Senator Mitch McConnell* (2009), and was gratified to read that Mr. Dyche had changed his view of McConnell and voted for Amy McGrath, his opponent in the 2020 Senate race.

I also benefited from a rapid-fire series of books in the past decade depicting the increasingly broken Senate. These include David A. Corbin, *The Last Great Senator: Robert C. Byrd's Encounters with Eleven U.S. Presidents* (2012); Neil MacNeil and Richard A. Baker, *The American Senate: An Insider's History* (2013); Robert G. Kaiser, *Act of Congress: How America's Essential Institution Works and How It Doesn't* (New York: Alfred A. Knopf, 2013); Senator Olympia Snowe, *Fighting for Common*

Ground: How We Can Fix the Stalemate in Congress (2013); Sean Theriault, *The Gingrich Senators: The Roots of Partisan Warfare in Congress* (New York: Oxford University Press, 2013); Steven S. Smith, *The Evolution of Procedural Warfare in the Modern U.S. Senate* (2014); Richard A. Arenberg and Robert B. Dove, *Defending the Filibuster: The Soul of the Senate* (Bloomington: Indiana University Press, 2015); Ross K. Baker, *Is Bipartisanship Dead? A Report from the Senate* (2015); Senator Tom Daschle and Senator Trent Lott, *Crisis Point: Why We Must—and How We Can—Overcome Our Broken Politics in Washington and across America* (New York: Bloomsbury Press, 2015); Nick Littlefield and David Nexon, *Lion of the Senate: When Ted Kennedy Rallied the Democrats in a GOP Congress* (2015); Carl Hulse, *Confirmation Bias: Inside Washington's War over the Supreme Court, from Scalia's Death to Justice Kavanaugh* (2019); Ruth Marcus, *Supreme Ambition: Brett Kavanaugh and the Conservative Takeover* (New York: Simon & Schuster, 2019); and Adam Jentleson, *Kill Switch: The Rise of the Modern Senate and the Crippling of American Democracy* (2021). I relied extensively on the excellent, detailed reporting in Marcus's book in describing the Kavanaugh confirmation fight in chapter 4.

While writing my previous book, *Broken*, I spent some time trying to make the case that our political system was in crisis—polarized, paralyzed, dysfunctional—until I realized that it was the only thing that everyone agreed on; it was virtually a "given." Some of the many books that analyze the situation thoughtfully include Amy Gutmann and Dennis Thompson, *The Spirit of Compromise: Why Governing Demands It and Campaigning Undermines It* (2012); Frances E. Lee, *Insecure Majorities: Congress and the Perpetual Campaign* (2016); James E. Campbell, *Making Sense of a Divided America* (2016); and Ezra Klein, *Why We're Polarized* (2020). I often talk about the "thirty-year decline of the Senate," and several important books from the early 1990s remind us just how long our political system—once a source of pride for our country—has been failing: E. J. Dionne Jr., *Why Americans Hate Politics* (1991); Thomas Byrne Edsall and Mary D. Edsall, *Chain Reaction: The Impact of Race, Rights, and Taxes on American Politics* (1991); and Kevin Phillips, *The Politics of Rich and Poor* (1990) and *Boiling Point: Democrats, Republicans and the Decline of Middle-Class Prosperity* (1993).

My thinking owes a special debt to Norm Ornstein, whom I met in 1977 when he was working on reorganizing the Senate committees and I was trying to write an ethics code for the Senate, and his collaborator Tom Mann. *It's Even Worse Than It Looks: How the American Constitutional System Collided with the New Politics of Extremism* (2012), Norm and Tom's superb book, and its subsequent editions—"worse than it was" and "worse than you think"—will be enduring classics because they capture an essential truth about the depressing period of division and dysfunction.

My thinking and writing certainly confirm the views of Ornstein and Mann that years before Donald Trump started his campaign for the presidency, the blame for our current political plight fell asymmetrically, attributable to the seemingly endless movement of the Republican Party to the right, producing extremism, obstruction, and ultimately gridlock on Capitol Hill and in Washington. By now, numerous books have addressed the transformation of the Republican Party into what Mike Lofgren, a twenty-eight-year Republican staffer, in 2011 called "an apocalyptic cult." My favorite is Tim Alberta's *American Carnage: On the Front Lines of the Republican Civil War and the Rise of President Trump* (New York: Harper, 2019).

Since my final assignment in the Senate as Jay Rockefeller's first chief of staff from 1985 to 1987, I have focused on international trade: serving in the Clinton administration as a trade official and then working as a trade lawyer and becoming an international consultant. When Donald Trump shocked the world by winning the presidency, I decided that many other people, in Washington and around the world, could deal with Trump's "America First" trade policy; the threat that Trump and McConnell posed to our democracy seized my urgent attention. It prompted me to write *Broken* in 2017 and now *The Betrayal*. For me, the two most important books of the past few years were *Fascism: A Warning* by Madeleine Albright and *How Democracies Die* by Steven Levitsky and Daniel Ziblatt. I hope that my book can make a small contribution to combating the poisonous antidemocratic tide that threatens America.

Notes

PREFACE

1. Robert C. Byrd, *The Senate, 1789–1989: Addresses on the History of the United States Senate*, Volume 2, Bicentennial Edition (Washington, DC: US Government Printing Office, 1991), 628.

2. David Pultz, "On the Tiger's Back: The George W. Ball Memorandums and the Johnson Administration's March toward Escalation in Vietnam, 1964–1965," Researchgate.net, September 4, 2016.

CHAPTER 1: THE END OF THE LAST GREAT SENATE

1. Tom Daschle and Trent Lott, *Crisis Point: Why We Must—and How We Can Overcome Our Broken Politics in Washington and across America* (New York: Bloomsbury Press, 2016).

2. Daschle and Lott, *Crisis Point*, 1, 4.

3. Jack Doyle, "The Kefauver Hearings, 1950–51," PopHistoryDig.com, April 17, 2008. Quotes in this section from *Life* and *Time* also come from Doyle's article.

4. John F. Kennedy, *Profiles in Courage* (New York: Harper and Brothers, 1957).

5. Thomas Mallon, "'Advise and Consent' at 50," *New York Times Book Review*, June 25, 2009.

6. Scott Simon, "At 50, a D.C. Novel with Legs," *Wall Street Journal*, September 2, 2009.

7. Lewis L. Gould, *The Most Exclusive Club: A History of the Modern United States Senate* (New York: Basic Books, 2005), ix–x.

8. White's famous observation in his Pulitzer Prize–winning book, *Citadel*, was more recently quoted in Michael Tomasky, "The South Shall Not Rise Again," *Daily Beast*, June 29, 2015.

9. Johnson's Senate leadership is most brilliantly described in the magisterial biography by Robert A. Caro, *The Years of Lyndon Johnson: Master of the Senate* (New York: Alfred A. Knopf, 2002).

10. This argument is presented in Ira Shapiro, *The Last Great Senate: Courage and Statesmanship in Times of Crisis* (New York: PublicAffairs, 2012).

11. This summary of Mansfield's leadership first appeared in Shapiro, *Last Great Senate*, 14–17. It drew on two superb books about Mansfield: Don Oberdorfer, *Senator Mansfield: The Extraordinary Life of a Great American Statesman and Diplomat* (Washington, DC: Smithsonian Books, 2003), and Francis R. Valeo, *Mike Mansfield, Majority Leader: A Different Kind of Senate, 1961–1976* (New York: M. E. Sharpe, 1999).

12. I offered this explanation about that Senate's greatness in *The Last Great Senate* and expanded it in *Broken: Can the Senate Save Itself and the Country?* (Lanham, MD: Rowman & Littlefield, 2018), 21–28.

13. Shapiro, *Last Great Senate*, 3–37.

14. Stuart E. Eizenstat, *President Carter: The White House Years* (New York: St. Martin's, 2018); Jonathan Alter, *His Very Best: Jimmy Carter, a Life* (New York: Simon & Schuster, 2020); and Kai Bird, *The Outlier: The Unfinished Presidency of Jimmy Carter* (New York: Penguin Random House, 2021).

15. My analysis of the Senate's decline "from Mansfield to McConnell" is presented more fully in Shapiro, *Broken*, 33–90.

16. David S. Broder, "Southern Powerhouse," *Washington Post*, June 16, 1996.

17. Sean Theriault, *The Gingrich Senators: The Roots of Partisan Warfare in Congress* (New York: Oxford University Press, 2013); and Julian E. Zelizer, *Burning Down the House: Newt Gingrich, the Fall of a Speaker, and the Rise of the New Republican Party* (New York: Penguin Press, 2020).

18. Trent Lott, *Herding Cats: A Life in Politics* (New York: Regan Books, 2005), 112–18.

19. All quotes from the departing senators in 1996 come from Norman J. Ornstein and D. David Eisenhower, *Lessons and Legacies: Farewell Addresses from the Senate* (Reading, MA: Addison-Wesley, 1997).

20. The most comprehensive description of the Clinton impeachment trial is Peter Baker, *The Breach: Inside the Impeachment Trial of William Jefferson Clinton* (New York: Scribner, 2000), which I relied on for the discussion that appears in Shapiro, *Broken*, 58–67.

21. Carl Hulse, "Congressional Memo: A Longtime Courtesy Loses in a Closely-Divided Senate," *New York Times*, April 24, 2004.

22. Gould, *Most Exclusive Club*, xiv.

23. Peter Baker, *Days of Fire: Bush and Cheney in the White House* (New York: Anchor, 2014), 607–8.

24. Mitch McConnell, *The Long Game: A Memoir* (New York: Sentinel, 2016), 170–74.

CHAPTER 2: McCONNELL'S BITTER HARVEST

1. McConnell, *Long Game*, 173.

2. Ibid., 184–86.

3. Joshua Green, "Strict Obstructionist," *The Atlantic*, January–February 2011.

4. Ibid.

5. McConnell, *Long Game*, 184–85.

6. Timothy Geithner, *Stress Test* (New York: Broadway Books, 2015), 256.

7. Ibid., 277.

8. Ibid., 258.

9. Carl Hulse, "Maine Senators Break with Republican Party on Stimulus," *New York Times*, February 10, 2009.

10. McConnell, *Long Game*, 191–93; Charles Homans, "Mitch McConnell Got Everything He Wanted: But at What Cost?" *New York Times Magazine*, January 27, 2019.

11. McConnell, *Long Game*, 191.

12. Ibid.

13. Norman Ornstein, "The Real Story of Obamacare's Birth," *The Atlantic*, July 6, 2015.

14. See, for example, Robert Reich, "Why the Gang of Six Is Deciding Health Care for Three Hundred Million of Us," *The Blog, Huff Post*, September 21, 2009.

15. Olympia Snowe, *Fighting for Common Ground: How We Can Fix the Stalemate in Congress* (New York: Weinstein Books, 2013), 194.

16. McConnell, *Long Game*, 191.

17. Alex Isenstadt, "Town Halls Go Wild," *Politico*, August 3, 2009; and Julie Rovner, "In Health Care Debate, Fear Trumps Logic," NPR, August 28, 2009.

18. Alexander Bolton, "Gang of Six Health Care Negotiations on the Verge of Collapse," *The Hill*, September 4, 2009.

19. Alec MacGillis, *The Cynic: The Political Education of Mitch McConnell* (New York: Simon & Schuster, 2014), 106.

20. Ornstein, "Real Story of Obamacare's Birth."

21. Molly Ball, "Harry Reid Goes Down Fighting," *The Atlantic*, March 27, 2015.

22. Ornstein, "Real Story of Obamacare's Birth."

23. McConnell, *Long Game*, 196–97.

24. Ibid., 197.

25. Ornstein, "Real Story of Obamacare's Birth."

26. Green, "Strict Obstructionist."

27. Senator Carl Levin, interview with author, August 6, 2010.

28. George Packer, "The Empty Chamber," *New Yorker*, August 9, 2010.

29. Shapiro, *Last Great Senate*, xviii, ix.

30. Ira Shapiro, "Senate Holds Key to Fixing Washington," CNN.com, January 15, 2013.

31. McConnell, *Long Game*, 212.

32. Ibid., 202.

33. Ibid., 225–27.

34. McConnell, *Long Game*, 205; Rebekah Metzler, "Tea Party Candidates Hard to Come by in 2014 Races," *U.S. News and World Report*, February 21, 2013.

35. Jonathan Weisman and Ashley Parker, "Riding Wave of Discontent, G.O.P. Takes Senate," *New York Times*, November 4, 2014.

36. The summary of McConnell's rise is based on multiple sources, but particularly McConnell, *Long Game*; MacGillis, *Cynic*; Charles Homans, "Mitch McConnell Got

Everything He Wanted: But at What Cost?" *New York Times Magazine*, January 22, 2019; and Jane Mayer, "How Mitch McConnell Became Trump's Enabler-in-Chief," *New Yorker*, April 12, 2020.

37. Mayer, "How Mitch McConnell Became Trump's Enabler-in-Chief."

38. Ibid.

39. *Citizens United v. Federal Election Commission*, 558 U.S. 210 (2010).

40. Mayer, "How Mitch McConnell Became Trump's Enabler-in-Chief."

41. McConnell, *Long Game*, 136–37.

42. *Citizens United v. Federal Election Commission*.

43. Russell Berman, "Congress' Surprisingly Productive Year," *The Atlantic*, December 23, 2015.

44. Ibid.

45. Michael Bowman, "U.S. Congress Ends 2015 with a Rare Show of Bipartisanship," *VOA News*, December 20, 2015.

46. Sam Levine, "Mitch McConnell Is Apparently Having an 'Almost Out-of-Body Experience' with Obama," *Huffington Post*, May 13, 2015.

47. Green, "Strict Obstructionism."

48. David M. Herszenhorn, "It's a Stretch, but Mitch McConnell Is Reaching across the Aisle," *New York Times*, April 24, 2015.

49. Seung Min Kim, "Mitch McConnell's Historic Judge Blockade," *Politico*, July 14, 2016; and Russell Wheeler, "Senate Obstructionism Handed a Raft of Judicial Vacancies to Trump—What Has He Done with Them?" Brookings Institution *FIXGOV* blog, June 4, 2018.

50. *Hearings before the House Committee on Energy and Commerce, Subcommittee on Energy and Power*, 114th Cong. (March 17, 2015) (testimony of Laurence H. Tribe).

51. Paul Barrett and James M. Rowley, "And Now, I'll Show You Climate Change!" *Bloomberg Business Week*, December 28, 2015.

52. Mitch McConnell, "Obama Takes His Reckless Energy Plan to the United Nations," *Washington Post*, November 17, 2015.

53. McConnell, *Long Game*, 159, 163, 185, 203, 207, 209–10, 215.

54. Ibid., 191.

55. Ibid., 256.

56. Burgess Everett and Glenn Thrush, "McConnell Throws Down the Gauntlet: No Scalia Replacement under Obama," *Politico*, February 13, 2016.

57. Ibid.

58. Ibid.

59. Jonathan Adler, "Again on the Erroneous Argument That the Senate Has a 'Constitutional Duty' to Consider a Supreme Court Nominee," *Washington Post*, March 15, 2016.

60. Pema Levy, "Blocking Scalia's Replacement Could Put GOP Senators in a Bind, Poll Shows," *Mother Jones*, February 22, 2016.

61. Elaine Godfrey, "The Judge Chuck Grassley Can't Ignore," *The Atlantic*, June 8, 2016.

62. Larry Buchanan and Karen Yourish, "The Russia Meeting at Trump Tower Was to Discuss Adoption, Then It Wasn't: How Accounts Have Shifted," *New York*

Times, August 6, 2016; and Philip Bump, "What We Know about the Trump Tower Meeting," *Washington Post*, August 7, 2016.

63. Julian Barnes, "Senate Report Criticizes Response to Russian Meddling," *New York Times*, February 6, 2020; and Michael Isikoff and David Corn, *Russian Roulette: The Inside Story of Putin's War on America and the Election of Donald Trump* (New York: Twelve, 2018), 214–16.

64. David M. Drucker, "McConnell: Vacant Supreme Court Seat Won the Election for Trump," *Washington Examiner*, April 7, 2017.

65. Tim Alberta, *American Carnage: On the Front Lines of the Republican Civil War and the Rise of President Trump* (New York: Harper, 2019), 600.

CHAPTER 3: HANDLING TRUMP

1. Numerous books have documented the chaos in Trump's White House. See, e.g., Bob Woodward, *Fear: Trump in the White House* (New York: Simon & Schuster, 2018); and Philip Rucker and Carol Leonnig, *A Very Stable Genius: Donald J. Trump's Testing of America* (New York: Penguin Press, 2020).

2. John Bresnahan and Burgess Everett, "McConnell and Schumer Hit Rock Bottom," *Politico*, January 19, 2018.

3. Russell Wheeler, "Judicial Nominations in the Bush and Obama Administrations' First Nine Months," Brookings, October 23, 2009; and Jon Greenberg, "Fact-Check: Did Obama Leave Trump with 128 Judges to Appoint?" Politifact.com, reported in the *Austin American-Statesman*, October 5, 2020.

4. Ruth Marcus, *Supreme Ambition: Brett Kavanaugh and the Conservative Takeover* (New York: Simon & Schuster, 2019), 57.

5. Ibid., 26–27.

6. Ibid., 30.

7. Jacob S. Hacker and Paul Pierson, *Let Them Eat Tweets: How the Right Rules in an Age of Extreme Inequality* (New York: Liveright, 2020), 148.

8. Jonathan Cohn, *The Ten Year War: Obamacare and the Unfinished Crusade for Universal Coverage* (New York: St. Martin's Press, 2021), 285–86.

9. Alexander Bolton, "McConnell: We'll Start Obamacare Repeal on Day One," *The Hill*, December 6, 2016.

10. Thomas Kaplan and Robert Pear, "Senate Takes Major Step toward Repealing Health Care Law," *New York Times*, January 12, 2017.

11. Erin Kelly, "Obamacare Takes First Real Step Closer to Repeal after Senate Vote," *USA Today*, January 12, 2017.

12. Michael Kranish and Marc Fisher, *Trump Revealed* (New York: Scribner, 2016), 275.

13. Fred Imbert, "Donald Trump: Mexico Is Going to Pay for the Wall," CNBC, October 28, 2015.

14. Janell Ross, "From Mexican Rapists to Bad Hombres, the Trump Campaign in Two Moments," *Washington Post*, October 20, 2016.

15. Jeremy Diamond, "Donald Trump: Ban All Muslim Travel to the U.S.," CNN Politics, December 28, 2015.

16. Dan Merica, "Trump Signs Executive Order to Keep Out 'Radical Islamic Terrorists,'" CNN Politics, January 30, 2017.

17. Mallory Shelbourne, "McCain, Graham: Trump Order May Become 'Self-Inflicted Wound' in Terrorism Fight," *The Hill*, January 29, 2017.

18. Aaron Blake, "Whip Count: Here's Where Republicans Stand on Trump's Controversial Travel Ban," *Washington Post*, January 31, 2017.

19. Rebecca Savransky, "Portman: Trump's Order 'Not Sufficiently Vetted,'" *The Hill*, January 29, 2017; and Jason Williams and Dan Horn, "Cincinnati Now a 'Sanctuary City.' What's That Mean?" *Cincinnati Enquirer*, January 30, 2017.

20. Sean Sullivan, "Leading Republican Senators Criticize Trump's Travel Ban—48 Hours Later," *Washington Post*, January 29, 2017.

21. Alexander Bolton, "McConnell: Trump's Proposal on Muslims Inconsistent with American Values," *The Hill*, December 8, 2016.

22. Julie Hirschfeld and Mark Landler, "Trump Nominates Neil Gorsuch to the Supreme Court," *New York Times*, January 31, 2017.

23. Alicia Parlapiano and Karen Yourish, "Where Neil Gorsuch Would Fit on the Supreme Court," *New York Times*, February 1, 2017.

24. Peter W. Stevenson, "The Real Reason Senate Democrats Are Going to Oppose Judge Gorsuch for the Supreme Court," *Washington Post*, March 30, 2017.

25. Neal K. Katyal, "Why Liberals Should Back Neil Gorsuch," *New York Times*, January 31, 2017.

26. James D. Zirin, *Supremely Partisan: How Raw Politics Tips the Scales in the United States Supreme Court* (Lanham, MD: Rowman & Littlefield, 2016), 7, 55; and John Dean, *The Rehnquist Choice: The Untold Story of the Nixon Appointment That Redefined the Supreme Court* (New York: Free Press, 2001).

27. Richard J. Ellis, *The Development of the American Presidency* (London: Routledge, 2012), 511–18.

28. Tom Howell Jr., "Justices Roberts, Kennedy Fall from GOP Favor after Recent Supreme Court Decisions," *Washington Times*, July 19, 2015.

29. Adam Liptak, "An 'Ideological Food Fight' (His Words in 2002) Awaits Neil Gorsuch," *New York Times*, March 18, 2017.

30. Burgess Everett and Seung Min Kim, "Gorsuch Battle Brings Senate to the Brink of a New Low," *New York Times*, March 30, 2017.

31. Matt Flegenheimer, "Gorsuch Tries to Put Himself above Politics in Confirmation Hearing," *New York Times*, March 20, 2017.

32. Matt Flegenheimer, "Senate Republicans Deploy 'Nuclear Option' to Clear Path for Gorsuch," *New York Times*, April 6, 2017.

33. Ibid.

34. Zach C. Cohen, "NJ 50: 50 People Changing the Game in Washington," *National Journal*, November 19, 2019.

35. Paul Kane, "Senate Democrats Vastly Outspent by Right in Gorsuch Fight," *Washington Post*, March 18, 2017.

36. Devlin Barrett, Adam Entous, and Philip Rucker, "President Trump Fires FBI Director Comey," *Washington Post*, May 10, 2017.

37. Matthew Rosenberg and Matt Apuzzo, "Days before Firing, Comey Asked for More Resources for Russia Inquiry," *New York Times*, May 10, 2017.

38. Devlin Barrett and Philip Rucker, "Trump Says He Was Thinking of Russia Controversy When He Decided to Fire Comey," *Washington Post*, May 11, 2017.

39. Julie Vitkovskya and Amanda Erickson, "The Strange Oval Office Meeting between Trump, Lavrov and Kislyak," *Washington Post*, May 10, 2017; and Matt Apuzzo, Maggie Haberman, and Matt Rosenberg, "Trump Told Russia That Firing 'Nut Job' Comey Eased Pressure from Investigation," *New York Times*, May 19, 2017.

40. Bridget Bowman, "Bipartisan Senators Call for New Committee on Russia Hacking," *The Hill*, December 18, 2016.

41. Rebecca Savransky, "McConnell Stands Firm: No Select Committee Needed to Investigate Russian Meddling," *The Hill*, December 20, 2016.

42. Paul Kane, "Burr and Warner in the Spotlight, and Arm in Arm, in Russia Probe," *Washington Post*, March 30, 2017.

43. Nicholas Kristof, "'There's a Smell of Treason in the Air,'" *New York Times*, March 23, 2017.

44. Rebecca Ruiz and Mark Landler, "Robert Mueller, Former F.B.I. Director, Is Named Special Counsel for Russia Investigation," *New York Times*, May 17, 2017.

45. Adam Entous and Ellen Nakashima, "Trump Asked Intelligence Chiefs to Push Back against FBI Collusion Probe after Comey Revealed Its Existence," *Washington Post*, May 22, 2017.

46. Matt Flegenheimer and Emmarie Huetteman, "Senate Intelligence Committee Leaders Vow Thorough Russian Investigation," *New York Times*, March 29, 2017; and Seung Min Kim, "Senate Judiciary Committee to Investigate Comey Firing, Clinton E-mail Probe," *Politico*, June 8, 2017.

47. Terri Rupar, "McConnell Also Says He Wants to Hear from Comey," *Washington Post*, May 17, 2017.

48. Paul Kane, "On Capitol Hill, the Race Is On to Get the First Crack at Comey," *Washington Post*, May 18, 2017.

49. Karoun Demirjian, "Senators Strike Comprehensive Deal to Increase Russia Sanctions," *Washington Post*, June 12, 2017.

50. Peter Baker and Sophia Kiskovsky, "Trump Signs Russian Sanctions into Law, with Caveats," *New York Times*, August 2, 2017.

51. David Ignatius, "On Russian Sanctions, Trump Has a Point," *Washington Post*, August 3, 2017.

52. *Face the Nation* transcript, June 12, 2016: Sanders, Lewandowski, Flake.

53. Jeff Flake, "My Party Is in Denial about Donald Trump," *Politico*, July 31, 2017, an excerpt from his book, *Conscience of a Conservative: A Rejection of Destructive Politics and a Return to Principle* (New York: Random House, 2017).

54. Sheryl Gay Stolberg, "Jeff Flake, a Fierce Trump Critic, Will Not Seek Reelection to the Senate," *New York Times*, October 24, 2017.

55. Daniella Diaz, "Donald Trump and Bob Corker: A Timeline," *CNN Politics*, October 24, 2017.

56. Jonathan Martin and Mark Landler, "Bob Corker Says Trump's Recklessness Threatens 'World War III,'" *New York Times*, October 8, 2017.

57. Ibid.

58. Nina Easton, "Bob Corker: Washington's Dealmaker," *Fortune*, December 9, 2010; Robert G. Kaiser, *Act of Congress: How America's Essential Institution Works, and How It Doesn't* (New York: Alfred A. Knopf, 2013), 245–54.

59. David Leonhardt, "The Fight for Obamacare Has Turned," *New York Times*, February 28, 2017.

60. Ibid.

61. Margot Sanger-Katz and Haeyoun Park, "Obamacare Is More Popular Than Ever, Now That It May Be Repealed," *New York Times*, February 1, 2017.

62. Darius Tahir, "Boehner: Republicans Won't Repeal and Replace Obamacare," *Politico*, February 23, 2017.

63. Jeremy Peters, "Patience Gone, Koch-Backed Groups Will Pressure GOP on Health Repeal," *New York Times*, March 5, 2017.

64. Reed Abelson and Katie Thomas, "In Rare Unity, Hospitals, Doctors, and Insurers Criticize Health Bill," *New York Times*, May 4, 2017.

65. Jennifer Haberkorn and Elana Schor, "Bipartisan Health Care Talks Pick Up Steam in the Senate," *Politico*, May 16, 2017.

66. Bolton, "McConnell: We'll Start Obamacare Repeal on Day One."

67. Robert Pear, "13 Men, and No Women, Are Now Writing New G.O.P. Health Bill in the Senate," *New York Times*, May 8, 2017.

68. Adam Cancryn, "Secrecy Boosts GOP's Obamacare Repeal Push," *Politico*, June 20, 2017.

69. Sean Sullivan, Juliet Eilperin, and Kelsey Snell, "Senate GOP Leaders Will Present Health Bill This Week, Even as Divisions Flare," *Washington Post*, June 20, 2017.

70. Lauren Fox, "Conservatives on Capitol Hill Anxiously Await Health Care Bill," CNN, June 20, 2017.

71. Jennifer Steinhauer, "Old Truth Trips Up G.O.P. on Health Law: A Benefit Is Hard to Retract," *New York Times*, July 17, 2017.

72. Thomas Kaplan and Robert Pear, "Senate Health Bill in Peril as C.B.O. Predicts 22 Million More Uninsured," *New York Times*, June 26, 2017.

73. Marc Fisher and Sean Sullivan, "Mitch McConnell, America's No. 1 Obstructionist, Is Trying to Make Big Things Happen," *Washington Post*, June 30, 2017.

74. Clare Foran, "GOP Senator Dean Heller Won't Support Senate Health Care Bill," *The Atlantic*, June 23, 2017.

75. Robert Pear and Jennifer Steinhauer, "G.O.P. Rift over Medicaid and Opioids Imperils Senate Health Bill," *New York Times*, June 20, 2017.

76. Brooke Singman, "Senate Health Care Bill: 4 Key Republicans Come Out against GOP Plan," June 22, 2017.

77. Paul Kane, "If These Two Republicans Can't Agree, the Senate Can't Pass a Health-Care Bill," *Washington Post*, June 29, 2017.

78. Juliet Eilperin, Sean Sullivan, and Ed O'Keefe, "Senate Republicans' Effort to 'Repeal and Replace' Obamacare All but Collapses," *Washington Post*, July 18, 2017.

79. Elise Viebeck, Paul Kane, and Ed O'Keefe, "McCain Returns to Senate for Health-Care Vote to Emotional Applause from Colleagues," *Washington Post*, July 25, 2017.

80. Juliegrace Brufke, "Johnson, McCain, Graham Seek Assurance That the 'Skinny Repeal' Isn't the Final Bill," *Daily Caller*, July 27, 2017.

81. Ed O'Keefe and Paul Kane, "The Week John McCain Shook the Senate," *Washington Post*, July 28, 2017.

82. Matt Flegenheimer and Maggie Haberman, "Mitch McConnell's 'Excessive Expectations' Comment Draws Trump's Ire," *New York Times*, August 9, 2017.

83. Jeff Mason and Kevin Drawbaugh, "Obama Targets Foreign Profits with Tax Proposal, Republicans Skeptical," *Reuters*, February 1, 2015.

84. Binyamin Appelbaum, "Trump Tax Plan Will Not Bolster Growth, Economists Say," *New York Times*, May 12, 2017.

85. Binyamin Appelbaum, "Trump Tax Plan Benefits Wealthy, Including Trump," *New York Times*, December 27, 2017.

86. Jim Tankersley and Matt Phillips, "Trump's Tax Cut Was Supposed to Change Corporate Behavior: Here's What Happened," *New York Times*, November 12, 2018.

87. Alan Rappeport and Thomas Kaplan, "Senate Republicans Embrace Plan for $1.5 Trillion Tax Cut," *New York Times*, September 19, 2017.

88. Ibid.

89. Thomas Kaplan and Jim Tankersley, "Senate Plans to End Obamacare Mandate in Revised Tax Proposal," *New York Times*, November 14, 2017.

CHAPTER 4: SAVING BRETT KAVANAUGH

1. Michael D. Shear, "Trump Lines Up Establishment Republicans to Vouch for Rex Tillerson," *New York Times*, December 13, 2016; and Peter Nicholas, Michael C. Bender, and Carol E. Lee, "How Rex Tillerson, a Late Entry to Be Secretary of State, Got Donald Trump's Nod," *Wall Street Journal*, December 14, 2016.

2. Jason Zengerle, "Rex Tillerson and the Unraveling of the State Department," *New York Times*, October 17, 2017; and Shamila N. Chaudhary, "Tillerson Was a Disaster for the State Department: Can Pompeo Do Better?" *Politico*, March 17, 2018.

3. Ashley Parker, Philip Rucker, John Hudson, and Carol D. Leonnig, "Trump Ousts Tillerson, Will Replace Him as Secretary of State with CIA Chief Pompeo," *Washington Post*, March 13, 2018.

4. Jeremy Diamond, "Trump Hits China with Tariffs, Heightening Concerns of Global Trade War," CNN, March 23, 2018.

5. Department of Justice, Office of Public Affairs, "Attorney General Announces Zero-Tolerance Policy for Criminal Illegal Entry," April 6, 2018; and Joshua Barajas, "How Trump's Family Separation Policy Became What It Is Today," *PBS News Hour*, June 14, 2018.

6. Mark Landler, "Trump Abandons Nuclear Deal He Long Scorned," *New York Times*, May 8, 2018.

7. David J. Lynch, Josh Dawsey, and Damian Paletta, "Trump Imposes Steel and Aluminum Tariffs on the E.U., Canada, and Mexico," *Washington Post*, May 31, 2018.

8. Tom McTague, David M. Herszenhorn, and Andrew Restuccia, "Trump Blows Up G7 Agenda," *Politico*, May 30, 2018.

9. Marcus, *Supreme Ambition*, 4.

10. Ibid., 48.

11. Ibid., 3.

12. Grace Panetta, "Trump's Business Career Is More Connected to Supreme Court Justice Anthony Kennedy Than We Ever Knew," *Business Insider*, June 29, 2018.

13. Andrew Weissmann, *Where Law Ends: Inside the Mueller Investigation* (New York: Random House, 2020), 221–22.

14. Mark Landler and Maggie Haberman, "A Besieged Trump Says He Misspoke on Russian Election Meddling," *New York Times*, July 17, 2018.

15. Aris Folley, "Wall Street Journal Editorial Board Rips Trump on Helsinki: It Was a 'National Embarrassment,'" *The Hill*, July 17, 2018.

16. Sarah D. Wire, "'Disgraceful': Republicans Sharply Criticize Trump's Behavior at News Conference with Putin," *Los Angeles Times*, July 16, 2018.

17. Peter Baker, "For Republicans, 'The Dam Has Broken': But for How Long?" *New York Times*, July 17, 2018.

18. Kevin Liptak and Jeff Zeleny, "Trump, Facing Fury, Says He Misspoke with Putin," CNN Politics, July 18, 2018.

19. Baker, "For Republicans, 'The Dam Has Broken.'"

20. Weissman, *Where Law Ends*, 221–23.

21. Wire, "'Disgraceful.'"

22. Marcus, *Supreme Ambition*, 94–119. The description of the battle over Judge Kavanaugh's nomination is drawn predominantly from Marcus's excellent book.

23. Ibid., 19–20, 30–34.

24. James Hohmann, "The Daily 202: Why U.S. v. Nixon Matters—Now More Than Ever," *Washington Post*, July 24, 2018.

25. The summary discussion of Kavanaugh's judicial record comes from Ira Shapiro, "The Kavanaugh Nomination: A Defining Moment for the Senate, the Court and the Country," *The Hill*, September 8, 2018.

26. Marcus, *Supreme Ambition*, 35.

27. Adam Liptak, "Brett Kavanaugh, a Conservative Stalwart in Political Fights and on the Bench," *New York Times*, July 9, 2018.

28. Marcus, *Supreme Ambition*, 87.

29. Ibid., 41.

30. Ibid., 171.

31. Mark Gitenstein, *Matters of Principle: An Insider's Account of America's Rejection of Robert Bork's Nomination to the Supreme Court* (New York: Simon & Schuster, 1992), is a superb account of the confirmation fight.

32. Marcus, *Supreme Ambition*, 201.

33. Ibid., 172.

34. Peter Suderman, "Mitch McConnell Says Caring about Legislative Process Is for Losers: He's Wrong," *Reason*, December 6, 2017; and Marcus, *Supreme Ambition*, 182.

35. Marcus, *Supreme Ambition*, 180–86, 195–97.

36. Floor statement of Senator Grassley on the passage of the First Step Act, December 19, 2018.

37. Niels Lesniewski, "Grassley Pitches Trump on Whistleblowers," *Roll Call*, February 6, 2017.

38. Marcus, *Supreme Ambition*, 178–79.

39. Ibid., 198.

40. Ibid., 199.

41. Ibid., 198–99.

42. Ibid., 200.

43. Ibid.

44. Elizabeth Williamson, Rebecca Ruiz, and Emily Steel, "For Christine Blasey Ford, a Drastic Turn from a Quiet Life in Academia," *New York Times*, September 19, 2018. This section also draws on the chapter "Paddling In," in Marcus, *Supreme Ambition*, 219–41.

45. Marcus, *Supreme Ambition*, 226.

46. Ibid., 240–46.

47. Ibid., 245–47.

48. Ibid., 253, 255.

49. Ibid., 255–56.

50. Tara Culp-Ressler, "23 Years Later, Senator Who Interrogated Anita Hill Still Doesn't Understand Sexual Harassment," ThinkProgress, May 7, 2014.

51. Ibid., 265.

52. Ibid., 254.

53. Chris White, "McConnell Reassured Trump: 'I'm Stronger Than Mule Piss' on Kavanaugh," *Daily Caller*, October 7, 2018.

54. Marcus, *Supreme Ambition*, 298.

55. Ibid., 298–302.

56. Ibid., 303.

57. Ibid., 304.

58. Ibid., 305–7.

59. Ibid., 307–9.

60. Ibid., 335–39.

61. The Editors, "It Is Time for the Kavanaugh Nomination to Be Withdrawn," *America, the Jesuit Review*, September 27, 2018.

62. Susan Svrluga, "'Unfathomable': More Than 2,400 Law Professors Sign Letter Opposing Kavanaugh's Confirmation," *Washington Post*, October 4, 2018.

63. Julie Zauzmer Weil, "The National Council of Churches Makes a Rare Statement to Oppose Kavanaugh," *Washington Post*, October 4, 2018.

64. Marcus, *Supreme Ambition*, 317.

65. The Editors, "Anyone Who Recognizes the Humanity of the Unborn Should Support the Nomination of Judge Kavanaugh," *America, the Jesuit Review*, July 9, 2018.

66. Marcus, *Supreme Ambition*, 341–47, 356–59.

67. Ibid., 364.

68. Ibid., 357.

69. Seung Min Kim, "McConnell Calls Opposition to Kavanaugh 'A Great Political Gift' to Republicans," *Washington Post*, October 6, 2018.

70. Sabrina Siddiqui, "Democrats Got Millions More Votes—So How Did Republicans Win the Senate?" *The Guardian*, November 8, 2018.

71. Carl Hulse, "Why the Senate Couldn't Pass a Crime Bill Both Parties Backed," *New York Times*, September 16, 2016.

72. Nicholas Fandos and Maggie Haberman, "Trump Embraces a Path to Revise U.S. Sentencing and Prison Laws," *New York Times*, November 14, 2018.

73. Colby Itkowitz, "Why Isn't Mitch McConnell Bringing Up Criminal Justice Reform?" *Washington Post*, November 30, 2018.

74. Nicholas Fandos, "McConnell Feels the Heat from the Right to Bring Criminal Justice Bill to a Vote," *New York Times*, November 20, 2018.

75. Ibid.

76. Nicholas Fandos, "Criminal Justice Bill Will Go Up for a Vote," *New York Times*, December 11, 2018.

77. Annie Karni, "The Senate Passed the Criminal Justice Reform Bill. For Jared Kushner, It's a Personal Issue and a Rare Victory," *New York Times*, December 14, 2018.

78. Nicholas Fandos, "Senate Passes Bipartisan Criminal Justice Bill," *New York Times*, December 18, 2018.

79. Mikhaila Fogel and Benjamin Wittes, "Bill Barr's Very Strange Memo on Obstruction of Justice," *Lawfare*, December 20, 2018.

80. "Graham on Syria: This Is a High-Risk Strategy," *CNN Video*, December 19, 2018.

81. Mark Landler, Helene Cooper, and Eric Schmitt, "Trump to Withdraw U.S. Forces from Syria, Declaring 'We Have Won Against ISIS,'" *New York Times*, December 19, 2018.

82. Deirdre Shesgreen, "McConnell: Senate Will Stop Any Immigration Bill Trump Opposes and Won't Shut Down Government," *USA Today*, May 25, 2018; and Erik Wasson, "McConnell Puts Low Odds on December Shutdown over Border Wall," *Bloomberg News*, October 16, 2018.

83. Julie Hirschfeld Davis and Emily Cochrane, "A Shutdown Looms: Can G.O.P Get Lawmakers to Show Up to Vote?" *New York Times*, December 16, 2018.

CHAPTER 5: TO IMPEACH OR NOT TO IMPEACH

1. McConnell, *Long Game*, 215.

2. Susan Page, *Madam Speaker: Nancy Pelosi and the Lessons of Power* (New York: Twelve, 2021), 284–85.

3. Jordain Carney, "McConnell Pledges to Be 'Grim Reaper' for Progressive Policies," *The Hill*, April 22, 2019.

4. John Gramlich, "How Trump Compares with Other Recent Presidents in Appointing Federal Judges," Pew Research Center, January 13, 2021.

5. Katie Benner and Nicholas Fandos, "Senate Confirms Barr as Attorney General," *New York Times*, February 14, 2019.

6. Barack Obama, *A Promised Land* (New York: Crown, 2020), 505.

7. Glenn Thrush, Jo Becker, and Danny Hakim, "Tap Dancing with Trump: Lindsey Graham's Quest for Relevance," *New York Times*, August 14, 2021.

8. Mark Leibovich, "How Lindsey Graham Went from Trump Skeptic to Trump Sidekick," *New York Times*, February 25, 2019.

9. Nicholas Fandos, Sheryl Gay Stolberg, and Peter Baker, "Trump Signs Bill Reopening Government for 3 Weeks in Surprise Retreat from Wall," *New York Times*, January 25, 2019.

10. Weissmann, *Where Law Ends*, xiv, xvi.

11. Mark Mazzetti and Michael S. Schmidt, "Mueller Objected to Barr's Description of Russia's Investigation Findings on Trump," *New York Times*, April 30, 2019.

12. David A. Graham, "Barr Misled the Public—and It Worked," *The Atlantic*, May 1, 2019.

13. Mark Mazzetti and Katie Benner, "Mueller Finds No Trump-Russia Conspiracy, but Stops Short of Exonerating President on Obstruction," *New York Times*, March 24, 2019.

14. Laura McGann, "Robert Mueller's Report Shows William Barr's Statements Were Incomplete at Best," Vox, April 18, 2019.

15. Phillip Bailey, "McConnell: Full Mueller Report Should Make President Trump 'Feel Good,'" *Louisville Courier-Journal*, May 7, 2019.

16. Seung Min Kim and Mike DeBonis, "McConnell Calls for End to Investigations of Trump, Says 'Case Closed,'" *Washington Post*, May 7, 2019.

17. Catie Edmondson, "'Case Closed': McConnell Urges Congress to Move on from Mueller Report," *New York Times*, May 7, 2019.

18. Emma Dumain, "Lindsey Graham 'Not Interested' in Calling Mueller to Testify before the Judiciary Committee," McClatchy, April 18, 2019.

19. Li Zhou, "Senate Republican Inaction in the Wake of the Mueller Report, Explained," Vox, May 1, 2019.

20. Page, *Madam Speaker*, 260–64, 267–68.

21. Gary Langer, "31% Believe Trump Exonerated after Mueller Report; 56% Oppose Impeachment: Poll," ABC News, April 26, 2019.

22. Page, *Madam Speaker*, 204–6.

23. "Nancy Pelosi on Impeaching Trump: 'He's Just Not Worth It,'" *Washington Post Magazine*, March 11, 2019.

24. Ben Berwick and Kristy Parker, "President Trump Argues He Is above the Law: A Thousand Prosecutors Say He Is Wrong," *Los Angeles Times*, May 30, 2019.

25. Julie Hirschfeld Davis and Mark Mazzetti, "Highlights of Robert Mueller's Testimony to Congress," *New York Times*, July 24, 2019.

26. Chris Cillizza, "What Robert Mueller Failed to Do," CNN Politics, July 25, 2019.

27. Jen Kirby, "The Last Minutes of Mueller's Testimony Made the Best Case for the Russia Investigation," Vox, July 24, 2019.

28. Maggie Haberman, Julian E. Barnes, and Peter Baker, "Dan Coats to Step Down as Intelligence Chief; Trump Picks Loyalist for Job," *New York Times*, July 28, 2019.

29. Paul Kane, "Burr and Warner: In the Spotlight, and Arm in Arm, on Russia Probe," *Washington Post*, March 30, 2017.

30. Scott Shane, "Political Divide about C.I.A. Torture Remains after Senate Report's Release," *New York Times*, December 9, 2014.

31. Caitlin Emma and Connor O'Brien, "Trump Holds Up Ukraine Military Aid Meant to Confront Russia," *Politico*, August 28, 2019.

32. "Shaheen, Portman Lead Bipartisan Ukraine Caucus Leadership Letter Urging Trump Administration to Release Obligated Military Security Assistance of Ukraine," Jeanne Shaheen, US Senator for New Hampshire, September 3, 2019.

33. Alan Cullison, Rebecca Ballhaus, and Dustin Volz, "Trump Reportedly Pressed Ukraine President to Investigate Biden's Son," *Wall Street Journal*, September 21, 2019 (updated).

34. Nicholas Fandos, "Nancy Pelosi Announces Formal Impeachment Inquiry of Trump," *New York Times*, September 24, 2019.

35. "Seven Freshman Democrats: These Allegations Are a Threat to All We Have Sworn to Protect," *Washington Post*, September 23, 2019.

36. Veronica Stracqualursi, "McConnell Urged Trump to Release Ukraine Call Summary, Source Says," CNN Politics, September 28, 2019.

37. Rachel Bade, Mike DeBonis, and Karoun Demirjian, "Pelosi Announces Impeachment Inquiry, Says Trump's Courting of Foreign Policy Help Is 'a Betrayal' of National Security," *Washington Post*, September 24, 2019.

38. Graham Statements on Impeachment and the Release of Transcripts, Lindsey Graham, US Senator for South Carolina, September 25, 2019.

39. Robert Costa, "Cracks Emerge among Senate Republicans over Trump Urging Ukrainian Leader to Investigate Biden," *Washington Post*, September 25, 2019.

40. Kenneth P. Vogel, "Rudy Giuliani Plans Ukraine Trip to Push for Inquiries That Could Help Trump," *New York Times*, May 9, 2019.

41. Ryan Lucas, "Rudy Giuliani Subpoenaed by House Intel Committee in Impeachment Inquiry," NPR, September 30, 2019.

42. Jessica Taylor, "Trump Administration Says It Won't Comply with Impeachment Inquiry," NPR, October 8, 2019.

43. Michael S. Schmidt, "Sondland Updates Impeachment Testimony, Describing Ukraine Quid Pro Quo," *New York Times*, November 5, 2019; and Rachel Bade, Aaron C. Davis, and Matt Zapotosky, "Sondland Acknowledges Ukraine Quid Pro Quo, Implicates Trump, Pence, Pompeo and Others," *Washington Post*, November 20, 2019.

44. Adam Liptak, "Key Excerpts from Legal Scholars' Arguments on Impeachment," *New York Times*, December 4, 2019.

45. Ibid.

46. Ibid.

47. Ibid.

48. Noah Weiland, "Trump Was Impeached. Here's a Recap of the Day," *New York Times*, December 18, 2019.

49. Sylvan Lane, "House Approves USMCA Trade Deal Amid Shadow of Impeachment," *The Hill*, December 19, 2019.

50. Eugene Kiely, "Pelosi's Bipartisanship Boast," FactCheck.org, December 17, 2019; and James Crowley, "'Grim Reaper' Mitch McConnell Admits There Are 395 House Bills Sitting in the Senate: 'We're Not Going to Pass Those,'" *Newsweek*, February 14, 2020.

51. Catie Edmondson, "Senate Approves $738 Billion Defense Bill, Sending It to Trump," *New York Times*, December 17, 2019.

CHAPTER 6: THE SHAM TRIAL

1. "McConnell: Potential Trial Should Follow Unanimous Bipartisan Precedent from 1999," Senate Republican Leader Mitch McConnell, US Senator for Kentucky, December 19, 2019.

2. Ibid.

3. Jeffrey Toobin, *True Crimes and Misdemeanors: The Investigation of Donald Trump* (New York: Doubleday, 2020), 411–12.

4. "McConnell Speaks on Senate Role in Impeachment Trial," Senate Republican Leader Mitch McConnell, US Senator for Kentucky, January 3, 2020.

5. "McConnell: The Senate Will Not Cede Our Authority on Impeachment," Senate Republican Leader Mitch McConnell, US Senator for Kentucky, January 8, 2020.

6. "McConnell: Democrats' Impeachment Has Been 'Purely Political' from the Beginning," Senate Republican Leader Mitch McConnell, US Senator for Kentucky, January 15, 2020.

7. Darren Samuelson, "Trump's Impeachment, Starring Bill Clinton," *Politico*, January 18, 2020; and Laurence Tribe and Joshua Matz, *To End a Presidency: The Power of Impeachment* (New York: Basic Books, 2018), xii–xiii, 214–20.

8. Ambassador Michael McFaul, Twitter thread, November 21, 2019.

9. "Graham on Impeachment: Democrats Are on a Crusade to Destroy Trump," Lindsey Graham, US Senator for South Carolina, January 22, 2020.

10. Eric Lipton and Maggie Haberman, "Schumer Demands Witnesses Be Called at Senate Impeachment Trial," *New York Times*, December 30, 2019, updated January 29, 2020; and Doug Jones, "Every Trial Is a Pursuit of the Truth: Will My Senate Colleagues Uphold That?" *Washington Post*, December 30, 2019.

11. Sheryl Gay Stolberg, "Emotional Schiff Speech Goes Viral, Delighting the Left and Enraging the Right," *New York Times*, January 24, 2020.

12. Aris Folley, "McConnell Chokes Up Saying Goodbye to 'Friend' Lamar Alexander in Floor Speech," *The Hill*, December 2, 2020.

13. "Schumer Statement after Senate GOP Blocked Witnesses & Documents in Senate Impeachment Trial," January 31, 2020.

14. Carl Hulse, "Once Skeptical, Senate Republicans Are All in for Trump," *New York Times*, January 31, 2020.

15. Ibid.

16. Nicholas Fandos, Emily Cochrane, and Patricia Mazzei, "Lamar Alexander, Key G.O.P. Senator, Plans to Oppose Move for New Evidence," *New York Times*, January 30, 2020.

17. Dareh Gregorian, "Murkowski Says Trump's Actions 'Shameful' but She'll Vote to Acquit," NBC News, February 3, 2020.

18. Sheryl Gay Stolberg, "Emotional Schiff Speech Goes Viral, Delighting the Left and Enraging the Right," *New York Times*, January 24, 2020.

19. Zack Budryk, "Alexander: Trump Will 'Think Twice' Before Engaging in Conduct That He Was Impeached for Again," *The Hill*, February 2, 2020.

20. Peter Baker, "Will Acquittal Empower Trump?" *New York Times*, February 1, 2020.

21. Mark Leibovich, "Romney, Defying the Party He Once Personified, Votes to Convict Trump," *New York Times*, February 5, 2020.

22. McConnell's Final Reflections on Impeachment: "Should Never Have Come to the Senate Like This," Senate Republican Leader Mitch McConnell, US Senator for Kentucky, February 13, 2020.

23. Burgess Everett, "Manchin Proposes Lesser Punishment of Censure for Trump," *Politico*, February 3, 2020.

24. Baker, *The Breach*, 380–88.

25. Peter Baker, Maggie Haberman, Danny Hakim, and Michael S. Schmidt, "Trump Fires Impeachment Witnesses Gordon Sondland and Alexander Vindman in Post-Acquittal Purge," *New York Times*, February 7, 2020.

26. Caitlin Oprysko, "Trump Attacks Manchin for Impeachment Vote, Accusing Him of Being a Democratic 'Puppet,'" *Politico*, February 7, 2020.

27. Brooke Singman, "Trump Says 'Hoax' Impeachment Should Be Expunged," Fox News, February 7, 2020.

CHAPTER 7: A POLITICIZED PANDEMIC

1. Natasha Bertrand and Maggie Severns, "From Distraction to Disaster: How Coronavirus Crept Up on Washington," *Politico*, March 30, 2020.

2. Michael Greiner, "America's Five Worst Senators," Medium, July 5, 2020.

3. Bertrand and Severns, "From Distraction to Disaster."

4. Sarah Owermohle, "Trump: Chinese Coronavirus 'Totally Under Control,'" *Politico*, January 22, 2020.

5. Eric Lipton, David E. Sanger, Maggie Haberman, Michael D. Shear, Mark Mazzetti, and Julian E. Barnes, "He Could Have Seen What Was Coming: Behind Trump's Failure on the Virus," *New York Times*, April 11, 2020.

6. Bruce Lee, "Bill Gates Warns of Epidemic That Could Kill Over 30 Million People," *Forbes*, February 19, 2017.

7. Matthew Mosk, "George W. Bush in 2005: 'If We Wait for a Pandemic to Appear, It Will Be Too Late to Prepare,'" ABC News, April 5, 2020.

8. Jason Karlawish, "A Pandemic Plan Was in Place. Trump Abandoned It—and Science—in the Face of Covid-19," *Stat*, May 17, 2020.

9. Ronald Klain, "Confronting the Pandemic Threat," *Foreign Policy*, no. 40 (Spring 2016).

10. Dan Diamond and Nahal Toosi, "Trump Team Failed to Follow NSC's Pandemic Playbook," *Politico*, March 25, 2020.

11. Karlawish, "A Pandemic Plan Was in Place."

12. Bertrand and Severns, "From Distraction to Disaster."

13. Ibid.

14. Ibid.

15. Eric Lipton and Nicholas Fandos, "Senator Richard Burr Sold a Fortune in Stocks as G.O.P. Played Down Coronavirus Threat," *New York Times*, March 19, 2020.

16. Katelyn Burns, "Sen. Kelly Loeffler Sold at Least $1.8 Million More in Stocks before the Coronavirus Crash Than Previously Reported," Vox, April 2, 2020.

17. Morgan Watkins, "Mitch McConnell on Woodward Book: 'We All Knew' Covid-19 Was Dangerous in February," *Louisville Courier-Journal*, September 10, 2020.

18. Jim Tankersley and Emily Cochrane, "House Passes Coronavirus Relief after Striking Deal with White House," *New York Times*, March 13, 2020.

19. Colby Itkowitz, "McConnell Absent as Pelosi, White House Reach Deal on Coronavirus Economic Relief Program," *Washington Post*, March 13, 2020.

20. Elizabeth Williamson and Rebecca R. Ruiz, "McConnell Protégé Takes Center Stage in Fight to Remake Judiciary," *New York Times*, May 5, 2020.

21. Jordain Carney, "Pelosi, Schumer Clash over Next Coronavirus Bill," *The Hill*, April 5, 2020.

22. Carl Hulse and Emily Cochrane, "As Coronavirus Spread, Largest Stimulus in History United a Polarized Senate," *New York Times*, March 26, 2020.

23. Tobias Hoonhout, "Dem Rep. Told Colleagues Coronavirus Bill Is a 'Tremendous Opportunity to Restructure Things to Fit Our Vision,'" *National Review*, March 23, 2020.

24. Hulse and Cochrane, "As Coronavirus Spread, Largest Stimulus in History United a Polarized Senate."

25. Jim Tankersley and Emily Cochrane, "Congress Shovels Trillions at Virus, with No Endgame in Sight," *New York Times*, April 24, 2020.

26. Lipton et al., "He Could Have Seen What Was Coming."

27. Carl Hulse, "McConnell Says States Should Consider Bankruptcy, Rebuffing Calls for Aid," *New York Times*, April 22, 2020.

28. Caitlin Oprysko, "'There's No Stigma Attached to Wearing a Face Mask': McConnell Makes Plea in Favor of Masks," *Politico*, May 27, 2020.

29. Ibid.

30. David Rubin and Elaine Nsoesie, "Is the US Heading for a Second Wave of Coronavirus Infections?" *The Guardian*, June 11, 2020.

31. Burgess Everett and Marianne LeVine, "Coronavirus Spike Rattles Senate Republicans," *Politico*, June 25, 2020.

32. Michael D. Shear, Maggie Haberman, Noah Weiland, Sharon LaFraniere, and Mark Mazzetti, "Trump's Focus as the Pandemic Raged: What Would It Mean for Him?" *New York Times*, December 31, 2020.

33. Josh Dawsey, Michael Scherer, and Annie Linskey, "Campaign of Contrasts: Trump's Raucous Crowds vs. Biden's Distanced Gatherings," *Washington Post*, September 9, 2020.

34. Noah Weiland, "Tulsa Officials Plead for Trump to Cancel Rally as Virus Spikes in Oklahoma," *New York Times*, June 16, 2020.

35. Ibid.

36. Michael D. Shear, Maggie Haberman, and Astead W. Herndon, "Trump Rally Fizzles as Attendance Falls Short of Campaign's Expectations," *New York Times*, June 20, 2020.

37. Ira Shapiro, "As COVID Cases Top 3 Million, It's Past Time to End the Catastrophic Trump Presidency," *USA Today*, July 9, 2020.

38. Bob Woodward, *Rage* (New York: Simon & Schuster, 2020), 308–10, 317–18.

39. Joe Pinsker, "The Pandemic Recession Is Approaching a Dire Turning Point," *The Atlantic*, August 23, 2020; Everett and LeVine, "Coronavirus Spike Rattles Senate Republicans"; and Ben Casselman, "Millions Relying on Pandemic Aid Can See Its End, and They're Scared," *New York Times*, May 28, 2020.

40. Judy Woodruff and Daniel Bush, "McConnell: Some Republicans Think 'We Have Already Done Enough' Pandemic Aid," PBS, July 29, 2020.

41. Jason DeParle, "A Year of Hardship, Helped and Hindered by Washington," *New York Times*, February 14, 2021.

42. Stacy Cowley, "Relief Deal Would Give Small Business a Shot at Second Loan," *New York Times*, December 21, 2020.

43. Policy Responses to Covid-19, International Monetary Fund, May 7, 2021.

44. Aishvarya Kavi, "5 Takeaways from 'Rage,' Bob Woodward's New Book about Trump," *New York Times*, September 9, 2020.

45. Alexander Bolton, "McConnell Has 17-Point Lead over Democratic Challenger McGrath, Poll Says," *The Hill*, August 4, 2020.

CHAPTER 8: THE BANANA REPUBLIC CONFIRMATION

1. Nina Totenberg, "Justice Ruth Bader Ginsburg, Champion of Gender Equality, Dies at 87," NPR, September 18, 2020.

2. Kevin Roose, "Trump Jump-Starts Misinformation on Ginsburg 'Dying Wish,'" *New York Times*, September 21, 2020.

3. Carl Hulse, "How Mitch McConnell Delivered Justice Amy Coney Barrett's Rapid Confirmation," *New York Times*, October 27, 2020.

4. Patrice Taddonio, "On Night of Ginsburg's Death, McConnell Pushed Trump to Nominate Amy Coney Barrett," PBS, November 24, 2020.

5. Marcus, *Supreme Ambition*, 342.

6. Jonathan Swan and Sam Baker, "Scoop: Trump 'Saving' Judge Amy Coney Barrett for Ruth Bader Ginsburg Seat," Axios, March 31, 2019.

7. Vicky Baker, "Amy Coney Barrett: Who Is Trump's Supreme Court Pick?" BBC, October 27, 2020.

8. Adam Liptak, "Barrett's Views: A Conservative Who Would Push the Supreme Court to the Right," *New York Times*, November 2, 2020.

9. Mary Clare Jalonick and Elana Schor, "No 'Dogma': Democrats Walk Tightrope on Barrett's Faith," AP, October 10, 2020.

10. Tal Axelrod, "Graham on Potential Supreme Court Vacancy: 'This Would Be a Different Circumstance Than Merrick Garland,'" *The Hill*, May 16, 2020.

11. Aaron Blake, "The GOP's Josh Hawley Problem on Amy Coney Barrett and Roe v. Wade," *Washington Post*, October 13, 2020; and Senator Josh Hawley, "Justice Barrett Is Pro-Life and Pro-Faith—Good News for Religious Conservatives," Fox News, October 30, 2020.

12. Ronn Blitzer, "McConnell: Attacks on Barrett's Faith by Dems, Media 'Are a Disgrace,'" Fox News, October 7, 2020.

13. Andrew Solender, "Murkowski Joins Collins in Opposing Supreme Court Vote before Election—Here's Who Matters Now," Forbes, September 20, 2020.

14. Kevin Liptak, "Inside One Celebration That Helped Spread the Virus across the US Government," CNN Politics, October 7, 2020.

15. David Morgan, "McConnell Avoids White House, Citing Laxity on Masks, COVID-19 Precautions," Reuters, October 8, 2020.

16. Alex Rogers and Manu Raju, "Two GOP Senators Test Positive for Covid-19, Potentially Jeopardizing Barrett Confirmation Vote," CNN Politics, October 3, 2020.

17. Ruth Graham and Sharon LaFraniere, "Inside the People of Praise, the Tight-Knit Faith Community of Amy Coney Barrett," *New York Times*, October 8, 2020.

18. Mark Sherman, "Barrett Cites 'Ginsburg Rule' That Ginsburg Didn't Follow," AP, October 13, 2020.

19. Charlie Savage, "Barrett Says She Would Not Be 'Used as a Pawn' to Decide Potential Election Case," *New York Times*, October 13, 2020.

20. Noah Feldman, "Amy Coney Barrett Deserves to Be on the Supreme Court," *Bloomberg Law*, September 26, 2020.

21. "Klobuchar Highlights How Rushed Supreme Court Nomination Will Jeopardize Health Care Coverage for Millions of Americans," Amy Klobuchar, Senator for Minnesota, October 12, 2020.

22. Andrew Naughtie, "Video of Lindsey Graham Insisting Supreme Court Vacancies Should Never Be Filled in Election Years Goes Viral," *The Independent*, September 19, 2020.

23. @realDonaldTrump, Twitter, September 19, 2020.

24. @LindseyGrahamSC, Twitter, September 19, 2020.

25. Jacob Pramuk, "Mitt Romney Supports Holding a Vote on Trump's Supreme Court Pick This Year," CNBC, September 22, 2020; and "Romney Announces Support for Judge Amy Coney Barrett," Mitt Romney, Senator for Utah, October 15, 2020.

26. Ted Barrett and Manu Raju, "Republican Leaders Vow to Fill a Potential Supreme Court Vacancy This Year, Despite Some Apprehension," CNN, July 21, 2020.

27. Brianne Pfannenstiel, "Sen. Chuck Grassley Won't Oppose Holding Supreme Court Nomination Hearings This Year," *Des Moines Register*, September 21, 2020.

28. Lyndsey Layton, "To Get Support for Education Bill, Senators Conjure Lost Art: Compromise," *Washington Post*, July 28, 2015; Danielle Douglas-Gabriel, "Can Alexander and Murray Recapture the Bipartisan Magic to Pass Higher Education Legislation?" *Washington Post*, February 9, 2016; and Juliet Eilperin and Carolyn Y. Johnson, "Obama, Paying Tribute to Biden and Bipartisanship, Signs 21st Century Cares Act," *Washington Post*, December 13, 2016.

29. "Alexander Votes to Confirm Judge Amy Coney Barrett to the Supreme Court," Lamar Alexander, Senator for Tennessee; and Rich Lowry and John McCormack, "How Republicans Quickly Lined Up to Confirm a Supreme Court Nominee," *National Review*, September 26, 2020.

30. Eleanor Clift, "Susan Collins' 'Hall Pass' on Amy Coney Barrett Vote Won't Save Her from Maine Voters," *Daily Beast*, October 17, 2020.

31. John Bresnahan and Burgess Everett, "No Apologies: McConnell Says Barrett a 'Huge Success for the Country,'" *Politico*, October 27, 2020; and Nicholas Fandos, "Senate Confirms Barrett, Delivering for Trump and Reshaping the Court," *New York Times*, October 26, 2020.

32. Vivian Ho, "'She Represents the Past': A Senate Hug Symbolizes California's Dianne Feinstein Fatigue," *The Guardian*, October 17, 2020.

33. Lindsay Wise, "Senate Advances Supreme Court Nomination Confirmation of Amy Coney Barrett," *Wall Street Journal*, October 25, 2020; and Allison Pecorin and Trish Turner, "Senate Republicans Move Barrett Supreme Court Nomination Toward Final Vote," ABC News, October 22, 2020.

34. Tim Hains, "McConnell Praises Deal on Coronavirus Relief: 'The Senate Stepped Up,'" Real Clear Politics, March 25, 2020.

35. Carl Hulse, "How Mitch McConnell Delivered Justice: Amy Coney Barrett's Rapid Confirmation," *New York Times*, October 27, 2020.

36. "These Confirmation Hearings Are Not Really about Amy Coney Barrett," Editorial, *Washington Post*, October 14, 2020.

37. Steven Levitsky and Daniel Ziblatt, *How Democracies Die* (New York: Crown, 2018), 125–43.

38. Mike Lillis, "Pelosi: 'Rogue' McConnell Must Decide Next Steps on Impeachment Articles," *The Hill*, December 19, 2019; and Justine Coleman, "Pelosi Rips McConnell as 'Rogue Leader' after Trump Acquittal," *The Hill*, February 13, 2020.

39. McConnell, *Long Game*, 209–10, 216.

CHAPTER 9: THE BIG LIE

1. Terrance Smith, "Trump Has Longstanding History of Calling Elections 'Rigged' If He Doesn't Like the Results," ABC News, November 11, 2020.

2. Amy Tennery, "Trump Accuses Cruz of Stealing Iowa Caucuses through 'Fraud,'" Reuters, February 3, 2016.

3. "U.S. Election 2016: Trump Says Election 'Rigged' at Polling Places," BBC News, October 17, 2016.

4. Arnie Seipel, "Trump Makes Unfounded Claim That 'Millions' Voted Illegally for Clinton," NPR, November 27, 2016.

5. Jim Rutenberg, "How President Trump's False Claim of Voter Fraud Is Being Used to Disenfranchise Americans," *New York Times*, September 30, 2016.

6. Steve Inskeep, "Timeline: What Trump Told Supporters for Months before They Attacked," NPR, February 8, 2021.

7. Ronn Blitzer, "Trump Pushes Back against Critics on Coronavirus, Addresses Whether He Will Accept Election Results in Exclusive Interview," Fox News, July 19, 2020.

8. "President Trump Remarks in Oshkosh, Wisconsin," *C-SPAN*, August 17, 2020.

9. "President Trump Speaks at 2020 Republican National Convention," *C-SPAN*, August 24, 2020.

10. Sam Levine and Alvin Chang, "Revealed: Evidence Shows Huge Mail Slowdowns after Trump Ally Took Over," *The Guardian*, September 21, 2020.

11. Elliott Davis, "Election Turnout Estimated to Break Record," *US News & World Report*, November 4, 2020.

12. Soo Rin Kim and Will Steakin, "How Trump, RNC Raised Hundreds of Millions Pushing Baseless Election Fraud Claims," ABC News, February 2, 2021.

13. McConnell on Elections: "We Respect the Rule of Law and Trust Our Institutions," Senate Republican Leader Mitch McConnell, US Senator for Kentucky, November 9, 2020.

14. Peter Baker and Maggie Haberman, "In Torrent of Falsehoods, Trump Claims Election Is Being Stolen," *New York Times*, November 5, 2020.

15. Dominick Mastrangelo, "Lindsey Graham Says 'Enough Is Enough' on Trump Bid To Overturn the Election: 'Count Me Out,'" *The Hill*, January 6, 2021.

16. Matthew Daly, "Some in GOP Break with Trump over Baseless Vote-Fraud Claims," AP, November 5, 2020.

17. Michael Crowley, "Trump's False Election Fraud Claims Split Republicans," *New York Times*, November 6, 2020.

18. Mitt Romney, Twitter, November 7, 2020.

19. Brittany Bernstein, "Sen. Sasse Calls on Trump to Present 'Real Evidence' of Voter Fraud," Yahoo, November 6, 2020.

20. Joseph Morton, "Sen. Ben Sasse Congratulates President-Elect Joe Biden on His Win," *Omaha World-Herald*, November 8, 2020.

21. Kim and Steakin, "How Trump, RNC Raised Hundreds of Millions."

22. Amy Gardner, Tom Hamburger, and Josh Dawsey, "Graham's Post-Election Call with Raffensperger Will Be Scrutinized in Georgia Probe, Person Familiar with Inquiry Says," *Washington Post*, February 12, 2021.

23. David E. Sanger and Nicole Perlroth, "Trump Fires Christopher Krebs, Official Who Disputed Election Fraud Claims," *New York Times*, November 17, 2020.

24. Tessa Berenson, "Donald Trump and His Lawyers Are Making Sweeping Allegations of Voter Fraud in Public: In Court, They Say No Such Thing," *Time*, November 20, 2020.

25. Annie Grayer, Caroline Kelly, and Maegan Vazquez, "Michigan Lawmakers Who Met with Trump Say They See Nothing to Change Election Outcome," CNN, November 21, 2020.

26. Amy Gardner, Colby Itkowitz, and Josh Dawsey, "Trump Calls Georgia Governor to Pressure Him for Help Overturning Biden's Win in the State," *Washington Post*, December 5, 2020.

27. William Cummings, Joey Garrison, and Jim Sergent, "By the Numbers, President Donald Trump's Failed Efforts to Overturn the Election," *USA Today*, January 6, 2021.

28. Trip Gabriel, "Trump Asks Pennsylvania House Speaker about Overturning His Loss," *New York Times*, December 8, 2020.

29. Greg Sargent, "Raging Trump Wants the Supreme Court to Save Him: Here's Why It Probably Won't," *Washington Post*, October 27, 2020; and James D. Zirin, "Will the Supreme Court Protect the Rule of Law, or Donald Trump?" *The Hill*, December 16, 2019.

30. Emma Platoff, "U.S. Supreme Court Throws Out Texas Lawsuit Contesting 2020 Election Results in Four Battleground States," *Texas Tribune*, December 11, 2020.

31. David Brooks, "The Winter Mitch McConnell Created," *New York Times*, December 3, 2020.

32. Luke Broadwater, "For Manchin, a Divided Senate Is a 'Golden Opportunity' for Action," *New York Times*, November 30, 2020.

33. Nicholas Fandos, Luke Broadwater, and Emily Cochrane, "A Dinner, a Deal and Moonshine: How the Stimulus Came Together," *New York Times*, December 21, 2020.

34. Ibid.

35. Emily Cochrane, "Congress Strikes Long-Sought Stimulus Deal to Provide $900 Billion in Aid," *New York Times*, December 20, 2020.

36. Paul Blumenthal, "Trump Calls Them 'My Judges': Will They Side with Him in Separation of Powers Fight?" *HuffPost*, October 24, 2020.

37. Richard Cowan, "U.S. Senate Leader McConnell Acknowledges Biden Victory; Laments Trump Defeat," Reuters, December 15, 2020.

38. Marianne LeVine and Melanie Zanona, "McConnell Warns Senate Republicans against Challenging Election Results," *Politico*, December 15, 2020.

39. Billy House and Laura Litvan, "Thune Sees Challenge to Biden Going Down Like 'Shot Dog,'" *Bloomberg*, December 21, 2020.

40. Manu Raju, Ali Zaslav, and Daniella Diaz, "GOP Senators Still Won't Acknowledge Biden's Win as Some Begin to Recognize Reality," CNN, December 14, 2020.

41. Katie Benner, "Trump Pressed Official to Wield Justice Dept. to Back Election Claims," *New York Times*, June 15, 2021.

42. Ryan Goodman, Mari Dugas, and Nicholas Tonckens, "Incitement Timeline: Year of Trump's Actions Leading to the Attack on the Capitol," *Just Security*, January 11, 2021.

43. Emma Green, "The Knives Come Out for Josh Hawley," *The Atlantic*, February 4, 2021.

44. Catie Edmondson and Michael Crowley, "Hawley Answers Trump's Call for Election Challenge," *New York Times*, December 30, 2020.

45. Kyle Cheney, "'Institutional Arsonist Members of Congress': Sasse Rips GOP Lawmakers Challenging 2020 Results," *Politico*, December 31, 2020.

46. Burgess Everett, "At Least 12 GOP Senators to Challenge Biden's Win," *Politico*, January 2, 2021.

47. Ben Riley-Smith, "Georgia Run-Offs: Democratic Odd Couple Carry Joe Biden's Hopes of Senate Control on Their Shoulders," *Telegraph*, January 5, 2021.

48. Ella Nilsen, "Georgia's Two Super-Competitive Senate Races, Explained," Vox, October 29, 2020.

49. Jaclyn Peiser, "Democrats Pressure McConnell to Give In to Trump's Demand for $2,000 Stimulus Checks: 'Let's Do It!'" *Washington Post*, December 23, 2020.

50. Tia Mitchell and Greg Bluestein, "Georgia Senate Republicans Back $2,000 Stimulus Checks under Pressure from Trump, Democrats," *Atlanta Journal-Constitution*, December 29, 2020.

51. Burgess Everett, "McConnell and GOP Reject House's $2,000 Stimulus Checks," *Politico*, December 30, 2020.

52. Carol D. Leonnig, Aaron C. Davis, Peter Hermann, and Karoun Demirjian, "Outgoing Capitol Police Chief: House, Senate Security Officials Hamstrung Efforts to Call in National Guard," *Washington Post*, January 10, 2021.

53. David Jackson and Matthew Brown, "'Wild' Protests: Police Brace for Pro-Trump Rallies When Congress Meets Jan. 6 to Certify Biden's Win," *USA Today*, December 31, 2020.

54. Laurel Wamsley, "What We Know So Far: A Timeline of Security Response at the Capitol on Jan. 6," NPR, January 15, 2021.

55. "Planning and Execution for the National Guard's Involvement in the January 6, 2021, Violent Attack at the U.S. Capitol," U.S. Department of Defense, January 8, 2021.

56. "Mayor Bowser Continues Preparation for Upcoming First Amendment Demonstrations," Government of the District of Columbia, January 3, 2021.

57. Carol D. Leonnig, "Capitol Police Intelligence Report Warned Three Days before Attack That 'Congress Itself' Could Be Targeted," *Washington Post*, January 15, 2021.

58. Leonnig, Davis, Hermann, and Demirjian, "Outgoing Capitol Hill Police Chief."

59. Devlin Barrett and Matt Zapotosky, "FBI Report Warned of 'War' at Capitol, Contradicting Claims There Was No Indication of Looming Violence," *Washington Post*, January 12, 2021.

60. Amber Phillips, "Mitch McConnell's Forceful Rejection of Trump's Election 'Conspiracy Theories,'" *Washington Post*, January 6, 2021.

61. Chris Cillizza, "Three-Quarters of Republicans Believe a Lie about the 2020 Election," CNN Politics, February 4, 2021.

62. Adam Goldman and Shaila Dewan, "Inside the Deadly Capitol Shooting," *New York Times*, January 23, 2021.

63. Jamie Gangel, Kevin Liptak, Michael Warren, and Marshall Cohen, "New Details about Trump-McCarthy Shouting Match Show Trump Refused to Call Off the Rioters," CNN Politics, February 12, 2021.

64. "We Will Discharge Our Duty under the Constitution for Our Nation," Senate Republican Leader Mitch McConnell, US Senator for Kentucky, January 6, 2021.

CHAPTER 10: ACQUITTING THE INSURRECTIONIST

1. Representative Liz Cheney, press release, January 12, 2021.

2. Marianna Sotomayor and Jacqueline Alemany, "House Republicans Oust Cheney for Calling Out Trump's False Election Claims, Minimize Jan. 6 Attack on Capitol," *Washington Post*, May 12, 2021.

3. Jeremy Diamond, "Trump: I Could 'Shoot Somebody and I Wouldn't Lose Voters,'" CNN Politics, January 14, 2016.

4. Jonathan Martin and Maggie Haberman, "McConnell Is Said to Be Pleased about Impeachment, Believing It Will Be Easier to Purge Trump from the G.O.P.," *New York Times*, January 12, 2021.

5. Alexander Bolton, "How McConnell Derailed Trump's Impeachment Trial Before It Started," *The Hill*, January 29, 2021.

6. "McConnell's Statement on Proposed Pre-Trial Schedule," Senate Republican Leader Mitch McConnell, US Senator for Kentucky, January 21, 2021.

7. "Senate Republicans Strongly Believe We Need a Full and Fair Process," Senate Republican Leader Mitch McConnell, US Senator for Kentucky, January 22, 2021.

8. "Schumer Gives Impeachment Timeline for Trump's Second Trial," AP, January 22, 2021.

9. Lindsey Graham, Twitter, January 8, 2021.

10. Lindsey Graham, Twitter, January 13, 2021.

11. "Senator Marco Rubio: Trump Impeachment Trial Is 'Stupid, Counterproductive,'" Fox News, January 24, 2021.

12. Marco Rubio, Twitter, January 26, 2021.

13. James Brooks, "Alaska Sen. Lisa Murkowski Calls on President Trump to Resign, Questions Her Future as a Republican," *Anchorage Daily News*, January 9, 2021.

14. Maria Arias, "Romney on Impeachment: 'It's Pretty Clear That the Effort Is Constitutional,'" Axios, January 24, 2021.

15. Alexander Bolton, "McConnell Circulates Procedures for Second Senate Impeachment Trial of Trump," *The Hill*, January 8, 2021.

16. Jared P. Cole and Todd Garvey, "The Impeachment and Trial of a Former President," Congressional Research Service, January 15, 2021.

17. "Constitutional Law Scholars on Impeaching Former Officers," *Politico*, January 21, 2021.

18. "U.S. Senate Kills Republican Move to Upend Trump Impeachment Trial," Reuters, January 26, 2021.

19. Josh Dawsey, Tom Hamburger, and Amy Gardner, "Trump's Legal Team Exited after He Insisted Impeachment Defense Focus on False Claims of Election Fraud," *Washington Post*, January 31, 2021.

20. Tom McCarthy and Joanna Walters, "Donald Trump Hires New Impeachment Team after Lead Lawyers Quit," *The Guardian*, January 31, 2021.

21. Burgess Everett, Marianne LeVine, and Meredith McGraw, "Trump Sends a Message to Senate Republicans Ahead of His Trial," *Politico*, January 25, 2021.

22. *Trial Memorandum of the United States House of Representatives in the Impeachment Trial of President Donald J. Trump*, US House of Representatives, 117th Congress, January 28, 2021.

23. Nicholas Fandos and Maggie Haberman, "Impeachment Case Argues Trump Was 'Singularly Responsible' for Capitol Riot," *New York Times*, February 2, 2021.

24. Alana Wise, "Trump Will Not Testify in Impeachment Trial, Adviser Says," NPR, February 4, 2021.

25. Michael S. Schmidt and Maggie Haberman, "Trump Answers Mueller's Questions on Russian Interference," *New York Times*, November 20, 2018.

26. Nicholas Fandos, Michael S. Schmidt, and Maggie Haberman, "144 Constitutional Lawyers Call Trump's First Amendment Defense 'Legally Frivolous,'" *New York Times*, February 5, 2021.

27. Linda So, "Georgia Secretary of State's Office Launches Probe into Trump's Election Phone Call," Reuters, February 8, 2021.

28. Nicholas Fandos, "House Lays Out Case against Trump, Branding Him the 'Inciter in Chief,'" *New York Times*, February 10, 2021. I have quoted extensively from this brilliant article, finding that I could neither shorten it nor improve upon it.

29. Barbara Sprunt and Lucas Ryan, "With New Video Footage, Managers Show How Close Rioters Got to Pence and Lawmakers," NPR, February 10, 2021.

30. Eileen Sullivan, "Takeaways from Day 4 of Trump's Impeachment Trial," *New York Times*, February 12, 2021.

31. Melissa Quinn, "Graham Says Outcome of Trump Impeachment Trial 'Is Really Not in Doubt,'" CBS News, February 8, 2021.

32. Mike DeBonis and Tom Hamburger, "Late-Night Talks and a Moment of Chaos: Inside the Democrats' Eleventh-Hour Decision to Forgo Impeachment Witnesses," *Washington Post*, February 13, 2021.

33. "McConnell on Impeachment: 'Disgraceful Dereliction' Cannot Lead Senate to 'Defy Our Own Constitutional Guardrails,'" Senate Republican Leader Mitch McConnell, US Senator for Kentucky, February 13, 2021.

34. Justine Coleman, "Pelosi Rips McConnell as 'Rogue Leader' after Trump Acquittal," *The Hill*, February 5, 2020.

35. "Senator Burr Statement on Vote to Convict Former President Trump on Article of Impeachment," Richard Burr, US Senator for North Carolina, February 13, 2021.

36. "Murkowski Votes to Convict President Donald J. Trump," Lisa Murkowski, US Senator for Alaska, February 14, 2021.

37. Senator Bill Cassidy, Twitter, February 13, 2021.

38. "Senator Collins Delivers Remarks on Impeachment Article," Susan Collins, US Senator for Maine, February 13, 2021.

39. "Sasse Statement on Impeachment Trial," Ben Sasse, US Senator for Nebraska, February 13, 2021.

40. "NCGOP Chairman Michael Whatley's Statement on Senator Burr's Contradictory Impeachment Vote," NCGOP, February 13, 2021; "OFFICIAL: The LAGOP Executive Committee Unanimously Votes to Censure Senator Bill Cassidy," LAGOP, February 13, 2021; Aaron Sanderford, "Nebraska GOP Rebukes Sen. Ben Sasse, Stops Short of Censure," *Omaha World-Herald*, May 19, 2021 (updated); and Jonathan Tamari, "Pa. Republicans Rebuke Pat Toomey over Trump Impeachment Vote—but Don't Censure Him," *Philadelphia Inquirer*, March 2, 2021.

41. Ronn Blitzer, "Graham: McConnell 'Put a Load on Republicans' Back' with Anti-Trump Speech," Fox News, February 14, 2021.

42. David Catanese, "'Dour, Sullen and Unsmiling Political Hack': Trump Attacks Mitch McConnell," Associated Press, February 16, 2021.

43. "Trump Welcomes Impeachment Acquittal, Says His Movement 'Has Only Just Begun,'" Fox8, February 13, 2021.

CHAPTER 11: GOOD FAITH, BAD FAITH

1. McConnell, *Long Game*, 209–10.

2. Mark Hensch, "Beau Biden Funeral Draws Political Heavyweights," *The Hill*, June 6, 2015.

3. Joe Biden, "We Are Living Through a Battle for the Soul of This Nation," *The Atlantic*, August 27, 2017.

4. Ashley Parker, "As a Candidate, Biden Promised 'Results, Not a Revolution': Then Covid Changed Everything," *Washington Post*, April 27, 2021.

5. Lindsay Wise, "McConnell Says '100% of His Focus is on Blocking Biden's Agenda,'" *Wall Street Journal*, May 5, 2021.

6. Mike DeBonis, "Trump Attacks McConnell as 'Political Hack,' Says He Will Back Pro-Trump Candidates," *Washington Post*, February 16, 2021; and Mike DeBonis, "Trump-Inspired Republican Candidates Create Early Tensions over Direction of the Party," *Washington Post*, March 25, 2021.

7. Having worked with Senator Portman when he was US trade representative, I had frequent conversations with friends who were mystified and disappointed by his silence about Trump and allegiance to McConnell.

8. Pema Levy, "Rob Portman Is Retiring Because of Senate Dysfunction He Spent Years Supporting," *Mother Jones*, January 25, 2021.

9. Burgess Everett and Elana Schor, "Senate Democrats Settle on Leadership Team, Sanders Elevated," *Politico*, November 16, 2016.

10. Alexander Bolton, "Senate Democrats Reelect Schumer as Leader by Acclamation," *The Hill*, November 10, 2020.

11. Jim Tankersley and Michael Crowley, "Biden Outlines $1.9 Trillion Spending Package to Combat Virus and Downturn," *New York Times*, January 14, 2021.

12. Dana Bash, Lauren Fox, Devan Cole and Daniella Diaz, "GOP Senators Offer Covid-19 Relief Counterproposal to Force Talks with White House Back to the Middle," CNN, January 31, 2021.

13. Barbara Sprunt, "Meeting with Republicans on COVID-19 Relief, White House Says Biden 'Will Not Settle,'" NPR, January 31, 2021.

14. Jim Tankersley and Luke Broadwater, "With Economy in 'Crisis,' Biden Is Ready to Bypass G.O.P. on Stimulus," *New York Times*, February 5, 2021.

15. Luke Broadwater, Hailey Fuchs, and Jim Tankersley, "Senate Backs Biden's Stimulus, but Rejects Quick Minimum Wage Increase," *New York Times*, February 4, 2021.

16. Emily Cochrane, "Divided Senate Passes Biden's Pandemic Aid Plan," *New York Times*, March 6, 2021.

17. Quint Forgey, "Biden Signs $1.9 trillion Covid Relief Bill," *Politico*, March 11, 2021.

18. Tara Siegel Bernard and Ron Lieber, "90 Million Stimulus Payments Have Gone Out, the Treasury Says," *New York Times*, March 16, 2021.

19. "Democrats Using Crisis to Check Off Unrelated Liberal Priorities," Senate Republican Leader Mitch McConnell, US Senator for Kentucky, March 2, 2021.

20. "A Classic Example of Big Government Overreach," Senate Republican Leader Mitch McConnell, US Senator for Kentucky, March 11, 2021.

21. "Senator Collins Opposes Partisan $1.9 Trillion Spending Bill," Susan Collins, US Senator for Maine, March 6, 2021.

22. "Murkowski Statement on Reconciliation Vote," Lisa Murkowski, US Senator for Alaska, March 7, 2021.

23. Steven Shepard, "Poll: 72 Percent Approve of Covid Relief Law," *Politico*, March 17, 2021.

24. Gabby Orr, Christopher Cadelago, Meredith McGraw, and Natasha Korecki, "Republicans on Biden's Covid Bill: We Bungled This One," *Politico*, March 17, 2021.

25. Jim Tankersley and Jeanna Smialek, "Biden Plan Spurs Fight over What 'Infrastructure' Really Means," *New York Times*, April 5, 2021; and Joshua Zeitz, "What the "Infrastructure' Fight Is Really About," *Politico*, May 1, 2021.

26. Emily Cochrane, "An Unlikely Pair, Portman and Sinema Steer Infrastructure Deal," *New York Times*, July 30, 2021 (updated August 3, 2021).

27. Ibid.

28. "Democrats' Spending Proposal Is Neither an 'Infrastructure' Plan nor a 'Jobs Plan,'" Senate Republican Leader Mitch McConnell, US Senator for Kentucky, April 26, 2021.

29. "Senator McConnell Supports Bipartisan Infrastructure Investment and Jobs Act; Delivers for Kentucky," Senate Republican Leader Mitch McConnell, US Senator for Kentucky, August 10, 2021.

30. Statement by Donald J. Trump, 45th President of the United States of America, Save America JFC, August 7, 2021.

31. Mychael Schnell, "Manchin 'Can't Imagine' Supporting Change to Filibuster for Voting Rights," *The Hill*, August 1, 2021.

32. Richard A. Arenberg and Robert B. Dove, *Defending the Filibuster: The Soul of the Senate* (Bloomington: Indiana University Press, 2015).

33. Kyrsten Sinema, "We Have More to Lose Than Gain by Ending the Filibuster," *Washington Post*, June 21, 2021.

34. Mitch McConnell, "The Filibuster Plays a Crucial Role in Our Constitutional Order," *New York Times*, August 22, 2019.

35. "Top Senate Republican Rejects Trump's Filibuster Idea," Reuters, May 2, 2017.

36. Kyle Cheney, "Capitol Police Officer's Widow Presses Congress for 1/6 Commission," *Politico*, March 17, 2021.

37. Ron Elving, "Why a '9/11 Commission' Is Popular but May Not Happen for the Jan. 6 Capitol Attack," NPR, May 26, 2021.

38. Mike DeBonis, Colby Itkowitz, and Jacqueline Alemany, "House Passes Bill to Investigate Jan. 6 Attack on Capitol, but Its Chances in the Senate Are Dim," *Washington Post*, May 19, 2021.

39. Burgess Everett and Marianne LeVine, "McConnell Turns Senate Republicans against Jan. 6 Commission," *Politico*, May 19, 2021.

40. Carl Hulse, "Election Considerations Drive G.O.P. Opposition to Jan. 6 Panel," *New York Times*, May 20, 2021.

41. Adam Payne, "Lindsey Graham Says the Republicans Will Never Win Another Election If They Don't 'Do Something' about Mail-In Voting," *Business Insider*, November 10, 2020.

42. Nicholas Fandos, "Republicans Block Voting Rights Bill, Dealing a Blow to Biden and Democrats," *New York Times*, June 22, 2021; and Marianne LeVine and Burgess Everett, "Sinema to Senate Dems: What's the Plan on Voting Rights?" *Politico*, May 13, 2021.

43. Michael Wines, "In Statehouses, Stolen-Election Myth Fuels a G.O.P. Drive to Rewrite Rules," *New York Times*, February 27, 2021.

44. US Const., art. I, § 4, cl. 1.

45. Nicholas Fandos, "Democrats Unite Behind Voting Rights Bill as It Faces a Senate Roadblock," *New York Times*, June 21, 2021.

46. Laura Barron-Lopez, Marianne LeVine, and Burgess Everett, "Manchin Moves Shake Up Dem Strategy for Massive Elections Bill," *Politico*, June 16, 2021.

47. Dominick Mastrangelo, "Stacey Abrams Says She 'Absolutely' Supports Manchin Voting Rights Compromise," *The Hill*, June 17, 2021.

48. Mike DeBonis, "Democrats Craft Revised Voting Rights Bill, Seeking to Keep Hopes Alive in the Senate," *Washington Post*, July 28, 2021.

49. Mike DeBonis, "Senate Adjourns Until September without Advancing Voting Rights Legislation," *Washington Post*, August 11, 2021.

50. Ibid.

51. John Gramlich, "How Trump Compares with Other Recent Presidents in Appointing Federal Judges," Pew Research Center, January 13, 2021.

52. Brad Plumer and Henry Fountain, "A Hotter Future Is Certain, Climate Panel Warns: But How Hot Is Up to Us," *New York Times*, August 9, 2021.

53. Caitlin Emma, "McConnell Vows No GOP Help on Debt Limit Hike," *Politico*, August 6, 2021.

54. Paul M. Barrett and James Rowley, "And Now I'll Show You Climate Change," *Bloomberg Businessweek*, December 28, 2015.

55. Jane Mayer, *Dark Money: The Hidden History of the Billionaires Behind the Rise of the Radical Right* (New York: Anchor Books, 2016), 246–78.

56. Shapiro, *Broken*, 222–28.

57. Coral Davenport, "Senate Confirms Scott Pruitt as E.P.A Head," *New York Times*, February 17, 2017.

58. Darius Dixon and Nick Juliano, "GOP Assault on Obama Regs Is Just Beginning," *Politico*, February 3, 2017.

59. Jordain Carney, "McConnell: Senate Won't Take Up Bill Preventing US Withdrawal from Paris Deal," *The Hill*, May 2, 2019.

60. "McConnnell: House Democrats' 'Cousin of the Green New Deal' Is 'Not Going Anywhere in the Senate,'" Senate Republican Leader Mitch McConnell, US Senator for Kentucky, July 1, 2020.

61. Bob Ewegen, "Henry Clay Was Never President, but He Saved the Union," *Denver Post*, July 11, 2008.

62. Jacob Hacker and Paul Pierson, *Let Them Eat Tweets: How the Right Rules in an Age of Extreme Inequality* (New York: Liveright, 2020), 190.

63. Robert A. Caro, *Master of the Senate* (New York: Alfred A. Knopf, 2002), 1015–17.

64. "Senators' Statement on Passage of Landmark Bipartisan Infrastructure and Investment and Jobs Act," Lisa Murkowski, US Senator for Alaska, August 10, 2021.

EPILOGUE

1. Emily Cochrane and Catie Edmondson, "Manchin Says No, Deserting Biden over Prized Bill," *New York Times*, December 20, 2021.

2. Jonathan Weisman, Emily Cochrane, and Catie Edmondson, "House Passes $1 Trillion Infrastructure Bill," *New York Times*, November 15, 2021.

3. Emily Cochrane and Jim Tankersley, "Democrats Ready to Put Social Policy Bill to 2022 as Manchin Balks," *New York Times*, December 15, 2021.

4. Jonathan Weisman and Lisa Friedman, "Behind Manchin's Opposition, a Long History of Fighting Climate Measures," *New York Times*, December 21, 2021.

5. Farnoush Amiri and Lisa Mascaro, "What Manchin Wanted, Rejected, and Got in Biden's $2T Bill," Associated Press, December 18, 2021.

6. Ibid.

7. See, for example, Paul Krugman, "The Bogus Bashing of Build Back Better," *New York Times*, December 13, 2021; Catherine Rampell, "Yes, Inflation Is Worrisome. But It Has Little Relevance to the Debate over Build Back Better," *Washington Post*, December 16, 2021.

8. Amiri and Mascaro, "What Manchin Wanted."

9. Jim Tankersley, "Biden Agenda Sinks under Its Own Ambitions," *New York Times*, December 19, 2021.

10. Emily Cochrane and Michael D. Shear, "Biden Tries to Salvage Domestic Policy Bill After Rift with Manchin," *New York Times*, December 20, 2021.

11. Ben Ritz, "Joe Manchin Has Given Democrats a Chance to Save Their Agenda," *New York Times*, December 21, 2021.

12. Emily Cochrane, "Senate Passes Sweeping $1 Trillion Infrastructure Bill," *New York Times*, August 10, 2021.

13. Burgess Everett and Marianne LeVine, "How McConnell and Schumer Got the Debt Deal Done," *Politico*, December 8, 2021.

14. Christina Wilkie, "McConnell Will Use Campaign Funds to Promote Covid Vaccinations in Kentucky," CNBC, July 28, 2021.

15. Thomas Kika, "Trump Attacks McConnell, House 'RINOs' over Passage of the Non-Infrastructure Bill," *Newsweek*, November 7, 2021; Felicia Sonmez and Mike DeBonis, "Trump and Allies Target McConnell over Deal to Avoid Default," *Washington Post*, October 7, 2021.

16. Katie Balevic, "Republican Leaders Must Have a 'Working Relationship with Donald Trump' to Succeed, Lindsey Graham Says," *Business Insider*, December 12, 2021.

17. *Forbes Quotes: Thoughts on the Business of Life* (January 2022) is one of many sources that reports Speaker Rayburn's famous wisdom.

18. Grace Panetta, "Lisa Murkowski Was the Sole GOP Senator to Vote to Advance a Major Democratic Voting Rights Bill," *Business Insider*, November 3, 2021.

19. Fredreka Schouten, "19 States Passed This Year Laws to Restrict Voting, New Tally Finds," CNN Politics, October 4, 2021.

20. Colin Woodard, "Sens. Collins, King Sharply Divided as Republicans Block Democratic Voting Rights Bill," *Portland Press Herald*, October 21, 2021.

21. Carl Hulse, "McConnell to Manchin: We'd Love to Have You, Joe," *New York Times*, December 22, 2021.

22. Ibid.

23. Luke Broadwater and Alan Feuer, "Jan. 6 Committee Recommends Contempt Charge for Meadows," *New York Times*, December 13, 2021.

24. Aaron Blake, "What Crime Might Trump Have Committed on Jan. 6? Liz Cheney Points to One," *Washington Post*, December 14, 2021.

25. Mark Sumner, "Cheney Promises That 2022 Will Bring 'Weeks of Public Hearings' on Events Leading up to January 6," *Daily Kos*, December 3, 2021.

26. Michael S. Schmidt and Luke Broadwater, "Jan. 6 Committee Weighs Possibilities of Criminal Referrals," *New York Times*, December 20, 2021.

27. Mariana Alfaro, "McConnell Says What the Jan. 6 Committee Uncovers Is 'Something the Public Needs to Know,'" *Washington Post*, December 17, 2021.

28. Christina Zhao, "Mitch McConnell Warns Trump 'Didn't Get Away with Anything,' Can Still be Criminally Prosecuted," *Newsweek*, February 13, 2021.

29. Adam Liptak, "With Roe at Risk, Justices Explore a New Way to Question Precedents," *New York Times*, December 13, 2021.

30. Linda Greenhouse, "The Supreme Court, Weaponized," *New York Times*, December 16, 2021.

31. Charles Homans, "Mitch McConnell Got Everything He Wanted: But at What Cost?" *New York Times Magazine*, January 27, 2019.

32. Carl Hulse, "McConnell Suggests He Would Block a Biden Nominee for the Supreme Court in 2024," *New York Times*, June 14, 2021.

33. "Opinion: Mitch McConnell: Democrats, Leave the Court Alone," *Washington Post*, November 11, 2021.

34. Dominick Mastrangelo, "Barrett: Supreme Court 'Not Comprised of a Bunch of Partisan Hacks,'" *The Hill*, September 13, 2021.

35. Catie Edmondson, "Senate Confirms Biden's 40th Judge, Tying a Reagan-Era Record," *New York Times*, December 18, 2021.

36. Jonathan Weisman, "Congress Ends 'Horrible Year' with Divisions as Bitter as Ever," *New York Times*, December 18, 2021.

37. Paul Kane, "The Filibuster Debate Still Hasn't Happened in the Only Place It Matters," *Washington Post*, December 19, 2021.

38. Trent Lott, *Herding Cats: A Life in Politics* (New York: Harper Paperbacks, 2006), 284.

39. Michael Crowley, "Empty Desks at the State Department, Courtesy of Ted Cruz," *New York Times*, October 2, 2021.

40. Kaelan Deese, "Manchin Says 'Elect More Liberals' to Democrats Who Want a Pricier Reconciliation Bill," *Washington Examiner*, September 30, 2021.

41. Erin Duffin, "Favorability of Mitch McConnell among U.S. Adults, as of November 2021," *Statista*, December 1, 2021.

Index

About the Author

Ira Shapiro's forty-five-year Washington career has focused on American politics and international trade. Mr. Shapiro served twelve years in senior staff positions in the US Senate, working for a series of distinguished senators: Jacob Javits, Gaylord Nelson, Abraham Ribicoff, Thomas Eagleton, Robert Byrd, and Jay Rockefeller. He served in the Office of the US Trade Representative during the Clinton administration, first as general counsel and then chief negotiator with Japan and Canada, with the rank of ambassador. From 2012 to 2017, he was the chairman of the National Association of Japan-America Societies (NAJAS) and received a commendation from the foreign minister of Japan. He is the author of two previous critically acclaimed books about the Senate: *The Last Great Senate: Courage and Statesmanship in Times of Crisis* (2012) and *Broken: Can the Senate Save Itself and the Country?* (2018). His articles have appeared in the New York Times, USA Today, cnn.com, *The Hill, Bloomberg, Daily Caller, Newsmax,* and several local newspapers around the country.